M000315495

Problems of institutional design and turing, acquired particular poignancy ~~through research ranging~~ from eastern Europe to southern Africa. At the same time, scholars in each of several disciplines – political science, economics, sociology, history, and philosophy – have increasingly come to appreciate the important independent role that is, and should be, played by institutional factors in social life.

In this volume, disparate theories of institutional design given by specialists in each of those several disciplines are synthesized and their peculiar power illustrated. Drawing upon traditions from Kantian ethics to public choice economics, from organizational sociology to discourse analytics, the contributors emphasize the important interpenetration of normative and empirical analysis in examples ranging from changes in the British welfare state through the reward structure of the modern university to the transition of eastern European societies.

THE THEORY OF
INSTITUTIONAL DESIGN

Series Editor
Robert E. Goodin
Research School of Social Sciences
Australian National University

Advisory Editors
Brian Barry, Russell Hardin, Carole Pateman, Barry Weingast,
Stephen Elkin, Claus Offe, Susan Rose-Ackerman

Social scientists have rediscovered institutions. They have been increasingly concerned with the myriad ways in which social and political institutions shape the patterns of individual interactions that produce social phenomena. They are equally concerned with the ways in which institutions emerge from such interactions.

This series is devoted to the exploration of the more normative aspects of these issues. What makes one set of institutions better than another? How, if at all, might we move from a less desirable set of institutions to a more desirable set? Alongside the questions of what institutions we would design, if we were designing them afresh, are pragmatic questions of how we can best get from here to there: from our present institutions to new revitalized ones.

Theories of Institutional Design is insistently multidisciplinary and interdisciplinary, both in the institutions on which it focuses, and in the methodologies used to study them. There are interesting sociological questions to be asked about legal institutions, interesting legal questions to be asked about economic institutions, and interesting social, economic, and legal questions to be asked about political institutions. By juxtaposing these approaches in print, this series aims to enrich normative discourse surrounding important issues of designing and redesigning, shaping and reshaping the social, political, and economic institutions of contemporary society.

Other book in the series
Brent Fisse and John Braithwaite, *Corporations, Crime, and Accountability*
Itai Sened, *The Political Institution of Private Property*
Bo Rothstein, *Just Institutions Matter*
Jon Elster, Claus Offe and Ulrich Preuss, *Institutional Design in Post-Communist Societies: Rebuilding the Ship at Sea*
Mark Bovens, *The Quest of Responsibility*

The Theory of Institutional Design

Edited by
ROBERT E. GOODIN
Research School of Social Sciences
Australian National University

Published by the Press Syndicate of the University of Cambridge
The Pitt Building, Trumpington Street, Cambridge CB2 1RP
40 West 20th Street, New York, NY 10011–4211, USA
10 Stamford Road, Oakleigh, Melbourne 3166, Australia

First published 1996
First paperback edition published 1998

Printed in the United Kingdom at the University Press, Cambridge

Library of Congress Cataloging-in-Publication Data
The theory of institutional design / edited by Robert E. Goodin.

     p.   cm. – (Theories of institutional design)

    Includes index.

    ISBN 0-521-47119-2 (hc)

    1. Social institutions.   2. Institution building.   I. Series.
HM101.T476   1996
306 – dc20   95-11380
                                            CIP

A catalog record for this book is available from the British Library.

ISBN 0 521 47119 2 hardback
ISBN 0 521 63643 4 paperback

Contents

Notes on Contributors

GEOFFREY BRENNAN is Professor of Economics at the Research School of Social Sciences at the Australian National University. His books include *The Reason of Rules*, with James Buchanan, and *Democracy and Decision*, with Loren Lomasky.

BRUCE TALBOT CORAM is an Associate Professor in Political Science at the University of Western Australia. He has published on philosophy, sociology, and political economy, with recent articles in the *British Journal of Political Science, Political Studies,* and *Comparative Politics.* He is currently completing a book entitled *State and Political Economy: A Game Theoretical Approach.*

JOHN S. DRYZEK is Professor of Political Science at the University of Melbourne. His books include *The Politics of the Earth, Democracy in Capitalist Times* and *Discursive Democracy: Politics, Policy, and Political Science.* He writes and teaches on democratic theory, environmental politics, history and philosophy of social science, public policy analysis, critical theory, and the scientific study of subjectivity.

ROBERT E. GOODIN is Professor of Philosophy in the Research School of Social Sciences at the Australian National University, specializing in political theory and applied moral philosophy. Editor of *The Journal of Political Philosophy* and the Cambridge University Press series Theories of Institutional Design, he has recently published *Utilitarianism as a Public Philosophy* and, with David Schmidtz, *Social Welfare and Individual Responsibility*, both with Cambridge University Press.

RUSSELL HARDIN is Professor of Politics at New York University and author of *Morality within the Limits of Reason* and *One for All.*

RUDOLF KLEIN is Professor of Social Policy and head of the Centre for the Analysis of Social Policy at the University of Bath. He is coeditor of the *Political Quarterly* and author of many path-breaking books on British social Policy, public expenditure, and the National Health Service.

DAVID LUBAN is Professor of Law at the University of Maryland and author of *Lawyers and Justice*.

CLAUS OFFE is Professor of Sociology and Political Science at Humboldt University, Berlin. He is author of *Contradictions of the Welfare State* and *Beyond Employment* and has written, with Jon Elster and Ulrich Preuss, a major study, *Institutional Design in Post-Communist Societies: Rebuilding the Ship at Sea*, for publication by Cambridge University Press in the same series.

PHILIP PETTIT is Professor of Social and Political Theory at the Research School of Social Sciences at the Australian National University and author of, most recently, *The Common Mind and Republicanism*.

KENNETH A. SHEPSLE is Professor of Government at Harvard University. His research focuses on formal models of institutions with special emphasis on legislatures. He current is working on a positive theory of parliamentary government.

Preface

This collection faces two directions at once. Looking inward, it serves to showcase work done under the auspices of the Institutional Design Project, sponsored by and conducted within the Research School of Social Sciences at the Australian National University. All of these chapters grow out of work originally presented at seminars and conferences of that Project, the bulk of them at a pair of conferences in July and December 1992. We are grateful to the many other participants in those conferences, and to the many other visitors to the Project over the years, for exchanges that have enlivened and enriched the intellectual life of the School. Such close collaboration among economists, political scientists, lawyers, sociologists, and philosophers is precisely the sort of thing that a research school of social science should stand for and hope to foster.

Looking outward, this collection serves as both flagship and sampler for the new Cambridge University Press series on Theories of Institutional Design. That series, like this book, will be insistently cross-disciplinary – looking to law as much as to political science, to history as much as to sociology, to philosophy as much as to economics. The thematic core underlying all this interdisciplinary effervescence is a concern with the role of institutions in social life, and the way in which societies shape and reshape those institutions in turn. Behind all that is a continuing quest for theories, normative as well as empirical, to guide as well as explain those important institutional transformations.

In its own formative period, the Institutional Design Project was well served by a highly talented administrative assistant, Annette Ritchie. We are grateful for her help in getting the Project off the ground, in organizing the conferences and seminars, the final fruits of which appear herein, and generally in keeping us all on track. We should also record various other debts: to John Braithwaite, as head of the larger Reshaping Australian Institutions Project within the School, which came to subsume our own more modest venture; to him and Barry Weingast, for excellent advice on the overall shape of the book; and to Robin Derricourt, who eased this book's way into print.

1

Institutions and Their Design

THE PRINCIPAL AIM of this introduction is to sketch the contours
of the existing literature as it touches upon theories of institutional design. It will situate the contributions of the present collection as well as
map the domain of the larger series within which this collection is set.

The chapter starts by tracing continuities and discontinuities in the
study of institutions, in the first instance, on a discipline-by-discipline
basis. I avoid prematurely and preemptorily defining the term "institution," preferring instead to let each discipline speak with its own
voice. Inevitably, each discipline (and indeed subdiscipline) focuses on
different institutions as paradigmatic and picks out different characteristics as their defining features. I propose to harness rather than straight-
jacket this diversity. Once I have let all these disparate disciplines have
their say in their own ways, all of them will then be consolidated into
a few broader reflections upon the form and function of social institutions. As part of that, I identify a minimalist definition of "institutions"
upon which most institutionalists, old and new and across a range of
disciplines, can broadly agree.

That analysis provides a platform from which to address, in the final
two sections, questions about the perfectability of social institutions.
Key questions there concern the extent to which institutions acciden-

An earlier, very different paper served as background for the ANU conferences from
which most other chapters of this book are drawn. I am grateful to Geoff Brennan
for helping to develop, and to conference participants for helping us to clarify, those
issues. I am also grateful to Paul Bourke for the opportunity to try out these ideas on
the Australian Historical Association and for other comments and criticisms from
David Austen-Smith, John Braithwaite, John Dryzek, Patrick Dunleavy, Patricia Har-
ris, Barry Hindess, Claus Offe, Philip Pettit, Peter Self, Barry Weingast and, most particularly, from John Ferejohn and Diane Gibson.

1

tally emerge or automatically evolve, and the extent to which they are subject to intentional design and redesign. Insofar as intentional (re)design of some sort or another is a feasible aspiration in any sense at all, further questions arise about what sorts of principles, both normative and empirical, might properly be employed in those endeavors.

1.1 Institutionalisms, Old and New

Each of the several disciplines that collectively constitute the social sciences contained an older institutionalist tradition. In each case that tradition has recently been resurrected with some new twist. Just as the older institutionalism within each discipline had focused on some slightly different aspects of the phenomenon, seeing social institutions as solutions to the problems which each respective discipline deemed central, so too does the new institutionalism mean something rather different in each of these alternative disciplinary settings. Each of these perspectives has something to contribute to a more rounded view of the ways in which institutions shape social life. But the advantages that come from building toward the larger truth in this way can come only through the realization that the "new institutionalism" is not one thing but many.[1]

1.1.1 New Institutionalism in History

Not so long ago, history was principally political history, the study of wars and kings and courtly intrigues. Of course it is also true that history is, and has always been, essentially a matter of storytelling; and a good story requires a good *dramatis personae*. Thus traditional political history has always been highly personalized and in it institutions are always inevitably personified: states by their princes, estates of the realm by their friends at court, and so on.

Although told through stories of striking personalities and individual daring, traditional histories were essentially stories of political institutions, their shaping and reshaping. Kings and courts, states constituted around them, and wars between them are institutional artifacts – the products of political organization. In that sense, history as a discipline has traditionally been highly institutional in its fundamental orientation.

Traditionally, though, it was the specifically political subset of social institutions that attracted most of the historian's attention. The work-

---

[1]In ways well captured in, e.g., Smith's 1988 account.

ings of social and economic institutions were certainly also considered, of course, but basically just as they touched upon the political. That focus upon several institutions, but essentially just political institutions, constitutes what I shall here characterize as history's "old institutionalism."

Over the course of this century, the understanding of history as the study of kings and wars has fallen out of fashion. Political history has gradually given way to social history. In that shift – symbolized as much as precipitated by the *Annales* movement – history has increasingly come to be seen as the history of everyday life. And if what counts as central in history is the lived experience of the past, court history is largely irrelevant. Historically, courtly doings have impinged only on the margins of everyday existence – even, historically, when they resulted in war.

In recent years, the focus of history as a discipline has shifted once again. The everyday life of the ordinary person, we have come to appreciate, does not stand alone and utterly apart from the rest of the larger society. There has, accordingly, been a shift back to the study of larger social institutions. The focus of these new histories is not necessarily upon kings and courtly doings (or their contemporary equivalents: presidents and cabinets, legislatures and judges, financiers and media magnates). Certainly newer forms of historical inquiry do not focus on that to the exclusion of all else, in a way that older forms of historical inquiry might once have done.

The newer focus is, at one and the same time, both broader and narrower. The focus is both upon social institutions more broadly (like churches, the family, and the labor market) and upon organs of the state more narrowly (like the workings of social relief agencies, the Children's Bureau, or public works or public health agencies).[2] As a result of this reorientation, history is once again largely a story about the workings of social structures, albeit now with a new focus upon the actual impact of those structures on real people's ordinary lives.

The peculiarly historical contribution to institutionalism, old or new, lies in history's fixation upon the past. If in social scientific terms each discipline "owns" one particular variable, time is history's. Insofar as it has social scientific aspirations, history is just the study of the way in which the past shapes the present and the future. Or, in less Whiggish mode, we might say that history just amounts to the telling of stories

[2]For good samplers, see Evans et al. (1979) and Steinmo et al. (1992). For exemplary studies, see Theda Skocpol's *Protecting Soldiers and Mothers* (1992) or Karen Orren's *Belated Feudalism* (1991).

about the past which we internalize as our own and which, in the telling and retelling, shape us and our future actions.[3]

That the past exerts this sort of influence over us is the central claim of history as a discipline, and that is the peculiar emphasis it imparts to its various forms of institutionalism. Questions of why and how the past exerts that sort of sway are essentially left to other disciplines to resolve. Good historians naturally speculate upon the psychological or sociological or political dynamics at work. They will gesture toward the satisfaction that comes from fitting one's life into some large narrative structure, or to the historical construction of the *conscience collective*, or to organization as both the mobilization and ossification of bias. But gestures these typically remain.

Even when historians' attention is caught by the workings of social institutions, their interest is in the particular tale surrounding the particular institutions at the particular historical juncture. The peculiarly historical interest tends not to lie in what broader theory can be constructed around those and other cognate cases. Indeed, those of a peculiarly historical cast of mind often shy away from such larger generalizations, thinking that they necessarily do violence to the historical particularity surrounding each of the specific cases that together, in very stripped-down form, constitute the more scientistic social scientist's "data."[4]

1.1.2 New Institutionalism in Sociology

From its beginnings, sociology too was essentially concerned with the study of social institutions. At the outset, this concern took the form of fixating rather unimaginatively upon a standard catalogue of institutions. Herbert Spencer's 1879 *Principles of Sociology*, for example, progresses through a tedious array of ceremonial institutions, political institutions, professional institutions, industrial institutions, and so on.

The ensuing classics of modern sociology imposed far richer theoretical overlays upon such pedestrian partitionings of the sociological problematique. But it is fair to say that all the masters of modern sociology – Pareto, Mosca, and Michels; Tönnies and Durkheim; Simmel

---

[3]That alternative formulation crucially differs in that it acknowledges the ways in which we read the past in light of the present. But centrality of "the past" remains: what gives these largely fictitious reconstructions the power of "history" is precisely the fact that they are fictions about the past.

[4]Contrast, for example, Tilton's (1990) study of the peculiar circumstances surrounding the foundation of the Swedish welfare state with Jackman's (1972) sixty-nation study of the emergence of welfare states in general; for a nice compromise between the two, see Esping-Anderson 1990.

and Weber; and, most especially, Marx – were all centrally concerned with the ways in which collective institutions subsume and subordinate the individual. All those classic studies – of "organic solidarity" as much as studies of "mechanical solidarity," of identification theory as much as of organization theory, of "base" as much as of "superstructure" – essentially amount to stories about mechanisms for effecting social control over individual volition.[5]

Nowhere is this blending of concerns clearer than in the work of Talcott Parsons, on some accounts the greatest contemporary sociologist. His early work on *The Structure of Social Action* was officially concerned with the sources of voluntaristic individual action. But his collaborative *General Theory of Social Action* then formalized what in that earlier work were merely inchoate notions of "the social system" as a control mechanism, notions which achieved their fullest (and most rococo) elaboration in his later book of that same name.[6]

Inevitably there then came a reaction against what was seen as an overemphasis upon the way individuals' volitions were shaped by collective social structures. Critics complained of "the oversocialized conception of man" in the dominant structural-functionalist sociology, entering pleas instead for "bringing man back in."[7] The ways in which these midcentury critics proposed doing that varied, from essentially phenomenological stories about the "social construction of reality" to social-psychologically inspired behavioralism and "action theory."[8]

Whatever precise form the countervailing theories took, their basic thrust was to downgrade (but without ever totally denying) the importance of collective social structures and institutions in determining the actions and choices of individuals and groups within any given society. The emphasis within this midcentury sociological reaction against old institutionalism was upon the role of individual and collective choice as against social-structural determinism of all outcomes of social (or anyway sociological) consequence.

The "new institutionalism" within contemporary sociology is a reaction against that reaction, in turn. In part it amounts to little more than picking up older institutionalist-cum-structuralist themes and giving them a different normative spin. Old structuralist-institutionalists tended to be conservatives: observing structures, they tended simply to assume that they made some functional contribution to social stability;

---

[5]One of the best early renderings of that increasingly submerged theme in sociology is E. A. Ross's (1901) little book on *Social Control*, originally published as a series of articles spread across the first three volumes of the *American Journal of Sociology*.

[6]Parsons 1937. Parsons and Shils 1951. Parsons 1952.

[7]Wrong 1961; Homans 1964.

[8]Berger and Luckman 1966. Manis and Meltzer 1967. Goffman 1970.

and they were inclined to celebrate that fact, thoroughly approving of
the various ways in which the collective conscience got a grip on individuals.[9] One group of new sociological institutionalists are basically
radicals who, observing the same phenomenon ("structuration," and
domination of individual and group agency by structural determinants
more generally), bemoan the ways in which such institutions exercise
hidden power over helpless social agents, be they individuals or marginalized groups.[10]

Other new institutionalists within sociology, often no less radical in
their politics, confine themselves to more narrowly analytic points. Individual action, they observe, is "embedded" within the context of collective organizations and institutions. Those actions are shaped, and
their effects affected and deflected, by the institutional contexts in
which they are set.[11] New sociological institutionalists of this stripe
point, in particular, to the important role that intermediate organizations can and do play in shaping and reshaping both individual actions
and collective outcomes emanating from them. The family is one obvious example very much at the center of many current controversies.[12]
But theories of civil society, the density of institutional networks and
mediating structures quite generally also figure largely in such accounts.[13]

Feminist accounts of the family and cognate social institutions combine these two approaches. Such mediating structures, they say, do so
much mediating that certain institutionalized patterns of dominance
and subordination disappear altogether from view. Feminists focus in
particular upon the "public/private dichotomy," which is so central to
the self-conception of liberal societies; and they proceed to show the
various ways in which collective, institutional relations of power and
dominance reach into what were supposed to be purely privately ordered spheres. Thus, feminists say, opponents of social oppression need
to examine the power relations embodied in the mediating structures
of the putatively "private" sphere just as much as they do those embodied in more straightforwardly public institutions.[14]

[9]Contested though this familiar charge may be, as against American structural-
functionists, it is frankly and forthrightly true of the most influential postwar German
institutionalist, Arnold Gehlen (Berger and Kellner 1965).
[10]Giddens 1984. Lukes 1974. Dahrendorf's classic 1958 essay "Out of Utopia" is a
calmer precursor in broadly the same spirit.
[11]Granovetter 1985; 1992.
[12]Berger and Berger 1983.
[13]Theoretical speculations (Hirst 1994; Cohen and Arato 1992) are powerfully confirmed by Putnam's (1993) painstaking empirical analysis of the causes and consequences of civic traditions in modern Italy.
[14]Macintosh and Barrett 1982. See also Elshtain 1981, Pateman 1983/1989, and
Okin 1989.

Were we assigning "key variables" to disciplines, the one owned by sociology might be said to be "the collective."[15] The old institutionalism within sociology focused upon ways in which collective entities – the family, the profession, the church, the school, the state – create and constitute institutions which shape individuals, in turn. The new institutionalism focuses, more modestly perhaps, upon ways in which being embedded in such collectivities alters individuals' preferences and possibilities. But it is the hallmark of sociological institutionalism, whether old or new, to emphasize how individual behavior is shaped by (as well, perhaps, as shaping) the larger group setting.

1.1.3 New Institutionalism in Economics

Within economics, the dominant tradition has long centered around a neoclassical paradigm involving idealized free agents interacting in an idealized free market. Within that model, order and patterns emerge out of those interactions: they do not prefigure it. But there has long been, both within European public finance and American economics more generally, an "institutionalist" tradition predating and (especially in America) crystalizing explicitly into an opposition movement against that neoclassical orthodoxy.

The original notion of American institutional economics, as promulgated by John R. Commons and his followers, was to examine ways in which collective action can be institutionally embodied and in that form shape and constrain subsequent individual choice.[16] The more positive and constructive side of the project was to study institutions and mechanisms – property law and the rules of the courts enforcing them, particular exchanges and the practices governing them, credit institutions and merchant banks, trade unions and trade associations, and so on – which create and control economic life. The more negative aim was to undermine the neoclassical orthodoxy by showing the many ways in which its idealized notions of "free markets" misrepresent the institutional reality of any actual economy, which is in fact dominated by actors (corporations, classes, central banks, or whatever) with precisely the sort of power to shape market outcomes (especially but not exclusively by altering relative prices of commodities and resources) that is assumed away in fictitiously idealized free markets.[17]

Still, the neoclassical paradigm remained much the dominant orthodoxy within twentieth-century economics. As that paradigm consoli-

---

[15]"Class" is, of course, just a special case of that more general formulation.

[16]Commons 1931, 1934.

[17]The papers collected in Samuels 1988, and especially the editor's introduction, provide a good overview of these themes.

dated its hold on the profession, its ambitions ranged ever more widely. From the outside, it seemed to be a clear case of microeconomics run amok, staging a takeover bid not only for macroeconomics but also (in its "public choice" guise) exercising imperial ambitions over large areas of explicitly "nonmarket" (especially political) decision-making as well.[18]

The highest aspiration and continual quest, within this neoclassical program, was to provide "microfoundations" for macro-level phenomena in economics and elsewhere.[19] The aim was to reduce all economic behavior – and, ultimately, all social behavior more generally[20] – to the interaction of individual preferences under conditions of scarcity (meaning just that not all of everyone's preferences can simultaneously be completely satisfied). Smooth and more-or-less instantaneous response functions were simply assumed; "stickiness," deriving from institutions or otherwise, was essentially just assumed away. Constrained maximization was the basic analytical device, equilibrium the preferred solution concept.

The attempted reduction never quite came off. But along the way the essentially anti-institutional program of neoclassical economics was powerfully sustained, both positively and negatively. Among the most crucial positive breakthroughs was Arrow and Hahn's *General Competitive Analysis,* providing a proper microeconomic proof of the fundamental theorems of welfare economics (roughly speaking, that Adam Smith was right: the invisible hand really will, under idealized assumptions, work precisely the magic claimed for it).[21] Negatively, too, Arrow contributed powerfully to the loss of faith in power of collective decisions to decide anything (that is the way his General Impossibility Theorem, showing that majority voting can lead us around in circles, was standardly – if not altogether correctly – interpreted[22]) and to the loss

[18]To borrow a phrase from the title of the first issues of what later became *Public Choice,* the flagship journal of this movement.
[19]Weintraub 1979.
[20]The work of Gary Becker (1976, 1981) best epitomizes this vaunting ambition.
[21]Arrow and Hahn 1971.
[22]Arrow (1951), as interpreted particularly by, e.g., Riker (1980, 1983). That interpretation is variously flawed, however. All that Arrow's proof actually shows is that cycling can happen, not that it necessarily will. Furthermore, that is true only on certain further assumptions which may not actually obtain (e.g., on the assumption that voters' preferences are not substantially "single-peaked" across the community). Cycling is not in any case inevitable, because giving up on transitivity is only one among many possible responses (accepting someone's preferences as "dictatorial" is another). Finally, note that the Arrow theorem applies as much to markets as to politics: the same results should apply equally in aggregating preferences there, too; and the main way we get equilibria in market economies is, in practice, precisely

of faith in the power of collectivities to organize to implement anything (which is the explicit thrust of his influential lectures on *The Limits of Organization*[23]).

Latterly, however, there has been a resurgence of interest in institutional economics, reacting against the hyperindividualism of this microeconomic putsch. This resurgence is represented most notably, perhaps, in the work of Nobel laureate Douglass North. But because his work is in economic history, the power of the general points he makes – about the importance of institutional frameworks as background conditions for the emergence and operation of markets as we know them – might be blunted.[24] Perhaps a better representative for this purpose might be Oliver Williamson, whose transaction-cost economics generalizes Coase's observations about the nature of the firm into a larger theory, *The Economic Institutions of Capitalism*.[25]

Whomever we choose as our representative, the basic point of this new institutionalism in economics is to show the various ways in which the actual functioning of the free markets of neoclassical economics requires and presupposes a fair bit of prior institutional structure. Most especially, institutions reduce transaction costs and in that way facilitate exchange. They promote trades, and hence trade.[26]

Neoclassical economists value unfettered trade because it helps people to realize their desires and give effect to their choices, to the maximal extent possible within the limits imposed by scarce resources. Institutions facilitate trade. The way they do so, though, is precisely by constraining choice. If we could not sign a binding contract (or its social equivalent: stake our reputation on a binding promise) then we could never enter into any deferred-performance exchanges, in which one party has to act first, trusting the other to act later. Putting ourselves in a position to be sued, should we fail to keep our contract, is putting ourselves under a constraint – but it is one that we welcome, for absent

through imperfect (monopolistic or oligopolistic) competition creating concentrations of power that make some actors' preferences to a greater or lesser extent "dictatorial" in just this way. I am grateful to David Austen-Smith for forcefully impressing all these points upon me.

[23]Arrow 1974. See similarly Wolf 1990.

[24]North 1990. For a splendid case study – but also an example of the sort of thing that leads people to dismiss such work as consisting of purely historical curiosities – see his marvelous coauthored paper on the origins of the Law Merchant in the medieval trade fairs (Milgrom, North, and Weingast 1990).

[25]Coase 1937. Williamson 1985. For a sociological perspective on the same themes, see Granovetter (1985, 1992).

[26]Coleman (1990, esp. chap. 3) offers a compelling example of this, building up to a central clearing house and money economy from the increasing efficiency of mediated exchanges over barter ones.

such a system of constraints a raft of mutually beneficial exchanges could never take place.[27]

In saying that institutions facilitate trade, it must also be recognized that institutions facilitate some trades more than (and in a world driven by relative prices, at the expense of) others. Institutions similarly facilitate certain trading channels and partnerships at the expense of other possible ones. In that way, institutions do indeed introduce and reinforce biases in favor of some interactions and interacting agents and against others. None of that should come as a surprise. After all, institutions are in essence just ossified past practices and the power imbalances and bargaining asymmetries embodied in them.[28]

Emphasizing the importance of economic institutions thus amounts to emphasizing the importance of things past as determinants of present economic choices. That is something that the neoclassical paradigm, in its purest form, would have hoped to wash away.[29] Borrowing a phrase from Hume's precepts about causation more generally, the neoclassical paradigm in economics would have liked to be able to insist that there can be "no action at a distance" – here, at a temporal distance. It would have liked to be able to insist that complete descriptions of the present state of affairs, together with suitable covering-law style generalizations, are all we need to make reliable predictions about future states of affairs.

In a way, that is certainly true. Unless the past leaves a residue in the present, it is incapable of influencing either the present or the future through it.[30] But the past does leave such residues. Among those traces are the institutions created by past behavior and choices. Also among them is the impact of past choices and experiences in shaping our present preferences.[31] In these and many other respects, what matters in our economic (and other) choices is not just where we sit at the moment but also how we got there. Most phenomena in social life manifest "path dependence" of just this sort. That influence of the past on the

---

[27]The contract example is offered by Schelling (1960, p. 43) and elaborated by Hardin (1982b, pp. 260–62); the point is further generalized by Streeck (1992).

[28]Knight 1992.

[29]Except, perhaps, by reference to sunk costs in existing plant and lock-in to particular technologies at particular historical junctures (Arthur 1989). But for neoclassicists, while differential costs of technological retooling might help to explain the relatively greater competitiveness of some economies than others at any given moment, sunk costs are of course to be ignored in deciding what to do next. Their advice is always to look to the present and future, not to the past, in framing choices. Bygones are bygone forever.

[30]Elster 1983, chap. 1.

[31]von Weiszäcker 1973; Stigler and Becker 1977.

present, although scorned by neoclassicists, is precisely what is central to institutionalism, both old and new, within economics.

Were we assigning key variables to particular social sciences, "choice" would have to be the one allocated to economics. Precisely because notions of individual choice are so central to economics, discussions of collective institutional constraints on those choices have always remained as a somewhat peripheral subtheme within the larger disciplinary discourse. Still, it is an important subtheme. Choices are always made in a context – and the context is not set by material scarcities and production technologies (or, to shift to another analytical frame that nonetheless shares the same myopia, by the modes and forces of production) alone.

Not only does economics need to appeal to some institutionalist story to set the context for individual choices. Through its emphasis upon individual choice and the ways in which those individual choices concatenate into collective ones, economics is also capable of providing a distinct (albeit, perhaps, distinctly partial) perspective upon the genesis and evolution of those institutions through the past choices of individuals and groups.

1.1.4 New Institutionalism in Political Science

Much of the new institutionalism in political science derives directly from cross-fertilization from this new institutionalism in economics through the subdiscipline of "public choice" which so successfully straddles that larger disciplinary divide.

Within public choice, the particular problem to which the new institutionalism is a solution is principally this. In both neoclassical economics and public choice models of politics built around them, the name of the game is to find an equilibrium. In that context, the Arrow-Condorcet problem – the specter of a perpetual disequilbrium, resulting from the intransitivity of majority voting – seems to be a (indeed, perhaps the) central problem in political life.[32] Political institutions that constrain the possible range over which such voting might cycle provide one nifty solution to that central problem. Institutional devices such as committee structures in legislatures, or bicameral legislatures, or judicial norms or constitutional constraints on the majoritarian de-

---

[32]Arrow (1951), especially as elaborated by Schofield (1976) and McKelvey (1979). Mathematically, these results are highly robust (Sen 1982, 1993). But, as I have noted in my discussion of economics above, their political and economic consequences are often greatly exaggerated.

cision-making can sometimes ensure a "structure-induced equilibrium" in a situation where none would otherwise exist.[33]

Another crossover to political science from new institutionalism in economics takes the form of a public choice theory of the state bureaucracy, modeled upon the economic theory of the firm. The central problem in both cases is, within this tradition, conceived to be one of ensuring that the wishes of "principals" are actually carried out by those who are supposed to serve as their "agents." How best to do this depends upon complex calculations of the comparative costs of monitoring in both directions, internally (keeping an eye on behavior of subordinates) as well as externally (keeping an eye on the quality of the goods and services delivered by outside providers). But in the public agency just as in the private firm, it sometimes makes most sense to minimize transaction costs by "institutionalizing" certain activities, internalizing some activities within a single organization rather than contracting privately with outside suppliers.[34]

Focusing too tightly upon these important new institutionalist crossovers from economics, however, would lead us to overlook the distinctive perspectives on institutions that are to be gleened from political science. After all, the new institutionalism in political science explicitly harks back to an honored old tradition within "Government" (as the discipline was then called) of studying the state in its institutional form: organization charts, agencies and bureaux, public administration quite broadly conceived, and what has subsequently come to be called "the state apparatus." An exemplary text here might be Bryce's masterly 1888 work on the *American Commonwealth*, which surveys the branches of national, state, and local governments, together with political parties and "social institutions" ranging from the bar and bench through Wall Street and the railroads.[35]

The thrust of the "behavioral revolution" within political science – indeed, the revolution that gave birth to that more modern name for the discipline – was to deny that form mapped function, to deny that organization charts and institutional myths were accurate representa-

[33]Shepsle 1979. Shepsle and Weingast 1981. Brennan and Hamlin 1992.

[34]On the private sector, see Williamson (1975, 1981), building on Coase (1937). These calculations come out particularly clearly in Hitch and McKean's (1960, chap. 12) discussion of internal markets and contracting in defense procurement. On public sector applications more generally, see Moe 1984, 1990, 1991; Niskanen 1971; Dunleavy 1991; McCubbins 1985; Calvert, McCubbins, and Weingast 1989, and, most especially, Weingast and Marshall 1988. For economic theories of rent-seeking, as applied to politics more generally, see Buchanan, Tollison, and Tullock 1980.

[35]Bryce 1888.

tions of actual practice.[36] What matters is not what people are supposed to do, but what they actually do. Insofar as people internalize those role expectations, then form is a good guide to function and myth to practice; but insofar as they diverge (and this is often very far indeed), then it is function and practice, actual behavior rather than ruling myth, that students of real-world politics must study.

The truth of these central precepts of the behavioral revolution is undeniable. But the perfect generality of their applicability has been greatly exaggerated. For there are important respects in which institutions matter to behavior, and it is those to which the "new institutionalist" resurrection of that older institutionalist tradition within public administration points. The behavioralist focus usefully serves to fix attention upon agency, upon individuals and groupings of individuals whose behavior it is. But those individuals are shaped by, and in their collective enterprises act through, structures and organizations and institutions. What people want to do, and what they can do, depends importantly upon what organizational technology is available or can be made readily available to them for giving effect to their individual and collective volitions.[37]

This presents itself to individual citizens as a constraint, to managers of the state apparatus as an opportunity. Governance – to use the new institutionalist catchphrase within public administration – is nothing less than the steering of society by officials in control of what are organizationally the "commanding heights" of society.[38]

There are of course limits to the sorts of commands that might effectively be issued from those commanding heights. Managers of the state apparatus themselves face various constraints, both in what others will let them do and in what others will help them do. They are constrained both in their "relative autonomy" and in their "power to command" (i.e., to implement their decisions).[39] Old institutionalists might have been insufficiently sensitive to those constraints. But by the same token, behavioralist revolutionaries were insufficiently sensitive to those possibilities. For a moderately full account of political outcomes, we need

[36]Within public administration, the most telling landmark was Nobel laureate Herbert Simon's *Administrative Behavior* (1957); on the behavioral revolution more generally, see Ranny 1962.

[37]This history is effectively traced, and these connections drawn, by March and Olsen (1984, 1989).

[38]Indeed, *Governance* is the name of the unofficial journal of this movement in its Anglo-American form; in discussions on Continent, the phrase "steering" figures more prominently (Bovens 1990; Kaufmann, Majone, and Ostrom 1985).

[39]Nordlinger 1981. Weaver and Rockman 1993.

to "bring the state back in" to supplement behavioralists' essentially individual-level accounts of political dynamics.[40]

The behavioralist account of individual action is essentially social-psychological in its inspiration. The other dominant account, within political science, builds more economistic models of human action: upon notions of instrumentally rational, goal-seeking behavior. Within that tradition, too, the same belated recognition of the importance of institutionalized social conventions has recently emerged.

The principal analytic tool within rational-actor analysis of politics is game theory. In more popular representations of those techniques, the principal game serving as a template for all of social life is the infamous Prisoner's Dilemma.[41] The peculiarity of that game – what makes it such a good template for so many aspects of social life – is that it arguably captures the core of logic underlying the problem of collective (in)action.[42] Within that game payoffs are structured in such a way that it is true, at one and the same time, that: (a) each player would be better off if all players pursued some cooperative course of action; (b) each player would be yet better off, whatever others did, defecting from that cooperative course; (c) the concatenation of such strictly dominant strategies for individual players in a one-shot playing of Prisoner's Dilemma yields an outcome in which everyone defects, leaving all worse off than they would have been had everyone (including themselves) cooperated.

That turns out to be true, however, only in one-off playings of the game. When the game is iterated (played over and over again among the same players) the strategic structure of the situation changes dramatically. More cooperative forms of play are then rationally preferred, since each player will have a strategic interest in acquiring a reputation as someone who is prepared to cooperate with cooperative others.[43] Thus, cooperative norms evolve in this fashion over time even among the hyperrational egoists of the most individualistic game theory.

[40]By the same token, we have to "bring the state back in" to supplement excessively society-centered accounts that try to trace all outcomes to structural-functional imperatives and system dynamics, of one sort or another (see Evans et al. 1979, esp. Skocpol 1979; Krasner 1984).

[41]In any more refined applications, cooperative/coordination games loom equally large. See, e.g., Luce and Raiffa 1957; Snidal 1985; Ordeshook 1986.

[42]Hardin 1982a.

[43]See, e.g., Taylor 1987; Axelrod 1984, 1986; and Hardin 1982a,b; for an interesting application to cattle-trespass disputes and boundary fencing in the American West, see Ellickson 1991. Among "pure" strategies, tit-for-tat (doing whatever the other did last time) is the only exemplar, and it is the most famous such strategy in consequence. But there is in principle any number of "mixed strategies" which could yield better results for all players than endless mutual defection.

Through them conventions emerge and institutions arise, on even this most individualistic model of human behavior.[44]

Thus there is convergence, within political science, from several directions upon the importance of institutions. Individualistic models – whether grounded in psychological models of individual behavioral propensities or in rational choice models of strategic calculation – cannot really explain individual choices, much less social outcomes, without some reference to the larger social institutional context of those individuals' actions. Behavioralists find they need to bring the state back in, game theorists find it emerging from within their models. Either way, institutions (political and otherwise) have once again come to the fore in political studies.

In addition to these intellectual currents within the discipline, there have of course also been developments within the external world which have served to remind students of politics of the importance of institutions. The breakdown of American hegemony toward the end of the post–World War II world led to an increased focus, among international relations scholars, on the various international regimes and institutions through which coordination was nonetheless achieved.[45] The breakdown of state socialism across central and eastern Europe with the end of the Cold War led to a flurry of political scientific interest in the sort of constitutions one might write, and the institutions one might try to impose, in a world in which the mediating institutions of civil society and the internal checks of civic virtue have so systematically been destroyed.[46] Finally, the breakdown of state sovereignty in western Europe, and the emergence of the European Community as an autonomous agent with serious power over its constituent members, has created renewed interest among political scientists there in questions concerning the proper design of federal institutions.[47]

Were we assigning key variables among the social sciences, the key variable within political science would be "power."[48] The capacity for one person or group to control the actions and choices of others – or, better yet, to secure its desired outcomes without regard to anyone else's

---

[44]Hardin 1982a,b. Elster 1989. For skeptical reflections on this account, see Bates 1988

[45]Keohane 1984; 1986. Keohane and Nye 1977. Ruggie 1982.

[46]Offe 1991; Offe and Preuss 1991; Elster, Offe and Preuss forthcoming. Similar issues arise, of course, with respect to the consolidation of "democratic transitions" elsewhere across the world, from Southern Europe and South Africa to Latin America and Asia (O'Donnell et al. 1986; Stepan and Skach 1993).

[47]Sandholtz and Zysman 1989. Moravcsik 1991. Garrett 1992.

[48]The nicest short statement of this position is still Dahl's 1963 *Modern Political Analysis*.

actions or choices – is what politics is all about. This larger disciplinary focus upon the causes and consequences of political power struggles imparts a peculiar cast to political science's institutionalism, both old and new. "Organization," in Schattschneider's famous phrase, "is the mobilization of bias."[49] The existence of institutions make certain things easier to do and other things harder to do. Holding positions within or control over those institutions gives some people greater capacity to work their will upon the world, at the expense of others lacking access to such institutionalized power resources. This was the focus of old-institutionalist analysts of *Politics, Parties, and Pressure Groups*, to borrow the title of V. O. Key's great book.[50] It remains central to the concerns of new-institutional analysts within political science quite generally.

1.1.5 New Institutionalism in Social Theory

All of this new institutionalism within each of the constituent social sciences speaks to larger themes within social theory more generally, ranging from the philosophy of social science to normative political philosophy. The issues raised by new institutionalists across the several disciplines have appeared and reappeared in those higher-order discourses in various guises over recent years. Inevitably, I will provide here only a stylized sketch of debates which often purport (occasionally rightly so) to query the very deepest truths of metaphysics or epistemology or ontology.

There has undeniably been a "return to grand theory in the human sciences."[51] In part, that is just to say that large-scale, comprehensive explanatory projects are back on the agenda. The many such projects afoot basically bifurcate into two strands. One offers "structure" as the key explanatory variable, and supposes that a sufficient rich, elaborate explication of the ways in which structures shape social outcomes could in principle provide a completely comprehensive account. The other

---

[49]Schattschneider 1960.

[50]Key 1942.

[51]Skinner 1985. There is also of course now a retreat from "grand theory," under the poststructuralist, postmodernist banner. The emphasis there is upon contingency and uncertainty, of institutions as much as of anything else; in that version, however, poststructuralism lines up with the new institutionalism in history, which admits and indeed celebrates the historical contingency of the particular institutions we have but proceeds to use the fact of those institutions to explain what subsequently occurs. Others, sensitive to problems of contingency and uncertainty, see institutionalization as a solution to precisely that problem: that is the focus of, for example, the "new institutionalists" (although they do not themselves embrace the term) in the recent French social science debates (Wagner 1994).

strand sees "agency" as central, and supposes that a sufficiently rich, elaborate explication of the ways in which agents act and interact would in principle provide a completely comprehensive account of social outcomes.

This basic argument plays itself out in a myriad of ways, and a myriad of places. Sometimes it is portrayed as a dispute between disciplines, with sociologists cast as advocates of structural explanations and economists as advocates of individualistic, agency-based ones.[52] Other times it takes the form of an intramural argument within some particular discipline or even within some particular theoretical tradition – most notably in recent years within Marxism, where we have seen the "rise and fall of structural Marxism" of an Althusserian bent, the emergence of a school of "rational choice" Marxism, and the attempt within that school to square essentially individualistic action premises with a broadly functionalist macrosociological framework of some recognizably Marxian form.[53]

In the realm of social theory more generally, new institutionalism might be seen as nothing more (and nothing less) than the recognition of the need to blend both agency and structure in any plausibly comprehensive explanation of social outcomes.[54] Even the staunchest advocate of rational choice models as explanatory tools must concede that people's preferences (which are the driving force in that model) have to come from somewhere outside the model; and one need not excavate very deeply to see that they come, ultimately, from structures of past experiences, prior socialization or social location.[55] And even the staunchest advocate of structural explanations cannot escape the fact that there have to be agents – albeit "socially constructed" ones – to serve as the carriers and enforcers of those structural imperatives, which those agents inevitably reshape in the process of reapplying and reinforcing them.[56]

Proceeding in parallel to those discussions in empirical political and social theory is an allied dispute within normative political philosophy.

---

[52]Barry 1970.

[53]On the Althusserian moment, see Benton (1984). Rational choice Marxism reaches its fullest fruit in the work of Elster (1985a) and Roemer (1986). G. A. Cohen (1978) lays functionalist foundations he intends to be broadly consistent with that account, although the success of that particular aspect of his project is powerfully queried by Joshua Cohen (1982). Giddens's 1984 work on "structuration," previously mentioned, is perhaps the best of many attempts by Marx-inspired scholars unaffiliated with either camp to trace the interpenetration of agency and structure in a loosely Marxian framework, more generally.

[54]Lukes 1973. Wendt 1987.

[55]Satz and Ferejohn 1994. Gintis 1972.

[56]Hindess 1988.

That is ordinarily posed as an argument between liberalism and communitarianism. In this highly stylized dispute, liberals are represented as championing Enlightenment models of human agency: individuals are rational, free-thinking, cosmopolitan, universalist, unencumbered. Communitarians point, in contrast, toward the ways in which individuals are inevitably embedded in social relations: when young, we all have to be taught something by somebody; and along the way we have all come to acquire various attachments to people and principles and projects growing out of our various social experiences. These, on the communitarian view, are the true "sources of the self."[57] In the real world, there simply is no completely independent, free-thinking, unencumbered self capable of performing the sorts of heroically universalistic calculations that figure so centrally in liberal Enlightenment just-so stories.

Here, too, there seems to be some prospect of a rapprochement between the two camps.[58] Enlightenment liberals can, and should, acknowledge the undeniable fact that everyone has been, and probably has to have been, raised in some particular culture or another, with its own distinctive values and concerns. Everyone has to start somewhere, and where you start and what baggage you bring with you makes it easier to move in some directions than in others. All those things can, and should, be readily conceded all round.[59] Even the staunchest liberal can easily agree to the importance of commitments (to other people, to principles, to causes) in people's lives: in Sen's wonderful phrase, rational maximization that fails to take due account of those sorts of values model the behavior not of "rational agents" as such but merely of "rational fools."[60]

That we are all socially embedded in such ways does not necessarily imply that we can never transcend our original upbringing. That we start somewhere, and that we experience greater or lesser difficulties in overcoming the prejudices of that upbringing, does not privilege those prejudices. It does not mean that we cannot or should not try to achieve (or anyway approximate) the Archimedian point idealized by Enlightenment universalism. Liberals would staunchly insist that we can and

---

[57]Sandel 1982; Taylor 1989.

[58]By which I mean to say simply that liberal Enlightenment theorists have agreed that they should, and argued that they can, take on board much of what communitarians say as a matter of empirical sociology – without its having the devastating consequences for their larger theories that communitarians claim. Whether communitarian critics of liberalism will be satisfied with that concession is, of course, another matter.

[59]Kymlicka 1989. Hardin 1995.

[60]Sen 1977; see also Mansbridge 1990.

should try to overcome our particular prejudices and interests in judging what is right and good, both for our own societies and indeed for the world at large.[61]

Whether that residual liberal Enlightenment aspiration is in the end feasible, and if so how best to accomplish it, remain hotly debated questions in contemporary political philosophy.[62] This is not the place to enter into that dispute. The important thing to note, in the context of the present discussion, is what can be agreed rather than what remains in dispute. The point is just that, in normative as well as empirical social theory, there has been a recent recognition of the importance of somehow blending accounts of social structure and human agency into some larger composite model of the human condition.

1.1.6 New Institutionalism: One from Many

New institutional themes thus emerge in a variety of forms in a variety of disciplinary contexts. Despite their differences, all those variations on new institutionalist themes are essentially, and importantly, complementary.

The new institutionalism is at root a reminder of the various contextual settings within which social action is set. Drawing together all those diverse disciplinary strands, a consolidated new institutionalism would serve to remind us, inter alia, of the following propositions.

1. Individual agents and groups pursue their respective projects in a context that is collectively constrained.

Among the many forms those constraints take, to some significant extent,

2. Those constraints take the form of institutions – organized patterns of socially constructed norms and roles, and socially prescribed behaviors expected of occupants of those roles, which are created and re-created over time.[63]

Furthermore,

---

[61]Thereby achieving what Nagel (1986) regards as almost impossible: the "view from nowhere."

[62]The most notable recent contributions have been made by, and in response to, second-wave Rawlsian theorizing (Rawls 1993a,b).

[63]Eisenstadt (1968, p. 409), notice, would distinguish between roles and institutions; in deference to his arguments there, I include non-role-specific normative expectations as well.

3. Constraining though they are, those constraints nonetheless are in various other respects advantageous to individuals and groups in the pursuit of their own more particular projects.[64]

That is true in many ways, but in part it is because

4. The same contextual factors that constrain individual and group actions also shape the desires, preferences, and motives of those individual and group agents.

Elaborating on the nature of those constraints, we can say at least this much with confidence:

5. Those constraints characteristically have historical roots, as artifactual residuals of past actions and choices;

and

6. Those constraints embody, preserve, and impart differential power resources with respect to different individuals and groups.

At the end of the day, however,

7. Individual and group action, contextually constrained and socially shaped though it may be, is the engine that drives social life.

Different new institutionalists from different disciplines would vary the emphasis across these various propositions. Indeed, some new institutionalists (some whole disciplines) may demur when it comes to any particular one of those propositions. Still, some such synthesis seems to capture the moving spirit of the new institutionalism as a whole. Indeed, it is the very breadth of that larger vision that makes the movement so compelling for so many from such diverse disciplinary backgrounds.

1.2 The Forms and Functions of Social Institutions

There is wide diversity within and across disciplines in what they construe as "institutions" and why. That diversity derives, in large measure, from the inclination within each tradition to look for definitions that are somehow "internal" to the practices they describe. The

[64]Strikingly, this theme is central among institutionalists in economics, where the neoclassical paradigm would lead us least to expect it. John Commons (1931, p. 649) literally builds this into his definition of "an institution" as "collective action in control, liberation, and expansion of individual action."

theoretical thrust is for an explanatory account that is at least in part hermeneutic: the aim is to provide an account of what institutions are, and why they arise, that would in some sense or another be recognized by participants themselves as describing their own behavior. When we are looking at contract law or congressional committees or whatever, what "the" institution is (and hence, to some extent, what "an" institution is in that setting) is traditionally tied up with what it does and why it is there. And since explanandums vary across disciplines, so do explanations – and hence so too do definitions of the very notion of an "institution" itself.

That definitional diversity derives, however, almost entirely from the inclination to opt for a discipline-based, theory-impregnated internalist-style definition of the term. Let us now shift our focus away from these internal accounts, and not worry so much about the role that particular institutions play in the lives of people in particular contexts. Let us instead adopt an "external" account of what institutions are and what they do. This is not a story that those engaged in the practice will necessary recognize as their own: it will not describe their motives or goals or perceptions. Rather, it is a story told from the outside, by an observer not internal to the practice, about the effects of institutions. It is a story about "what they do," not about "why they do it."

Shifting to that externalist stance, it is much easier to come to an agreed definition of what an institution is. From this external point of view a social institution is, in its most general characterization, nothing more than a "stable, valued, recurring pattern of behavior."[65] That characterization might be a little too general to be terribly helpful. We may, for example, want to further stipulate that an institution is necessarily a social phenomenon. Individuals are not themselves institutions, however "stable, valued and recurring" their patterns of behavior.[66] Neither do idiosyncratic habits of private individuals count as "institutions" for our purposes, however "stable, valued and recurring" the behaviors issuing from them.[67]

Still, a relatively general characterization is precisely what is needed

---

[65]Huntington 1968, p. 12. See similarly Eisenstadt 1968, p. 409.

[66]Even if personal identity is inconstant over time (as Parfit [1984] suggests) or unstable at any moment in time (as the "multiple self" literature [Elster 1985] suggests), we would still be reluctant to describe the "negotiated settlement" that constitutes any given individual's ongoing identity as being "institutionalized," except in some highly metaphorical sense.

[67]This is to recall Hart's (1961, p. 54) distinction between habit and rule: the difference between our (valued) habit of going to the cinema every Saturday night and our collective rule of men taking off their hats in church.

to capture the diverse range of social activities that we would want to deem to be institutions and to theorize alongside one another as such. At a minimum, we would want to include institutions in:

- "the sphere of institutions of *family and kinship*, which focuses on the regulation of the procreative and biological relations between individuals in a society and on the initial socialization of new members of each generation";
- "the sphere of *education*," which extending the former "deals with the socialization of the young into adults and the differential transmission of the cultural heritage of a society from generation to generation";
- "the sphere of *economics*," which "regulates the production, distribution and consumption of goods and services within any society";
- "the sphere of *politics*," which "deals with the control of the use of force within a society and the maintenance of internal and external peace of the boundaries of the society, as well as control of the mobilization of resources for the implementation of various goals and the articulation and setting up of certain goals for the collectivity";
- "the sphere of *cultural institutions*," which "deals with the provision of conditions which facilitate the creation and conservation of cultural (religious, scientific, artistic) artifacts and with their differential distribution among the various groups of a society"; and
- "the sphere of *stratification*, which regulates the differential distribution of positions, rewards, and resources and the access to them by the various individuals and groups within a society."[68]

A central defining feature of "institutionalization" across all these spheres is the stable, recurring, repetitive, patterned nature of the behavior that occurs within institutions, and because of them. "Institutionalism" has been characterized as "the process by which organizations and procedures acquire value and stability."[69] In an institutionalized setting, behavior is more stable and predictable. Furthermore, that is not an incidental by-product of institutionalization – not merely the consequence of "coming to value a certain organization or procedure" for some independent reasons. Instead, that very stability and predictability is, to a very large extent, precisely why we value institutionalized patterns and what it is we value in them.[70]

---

[68]Eisenstadt 1968, p. 410.
[69]Huntington 1968, p. 12. See similarly Eisenstadt (1964; 1968, p. 410, 414–18).
[70]Soskice, Bates, and Epstein 1992.

This fact is absolutely central to new-institutionalist analyses within both political science and economics, in particular. The role of institutions, economically, is seen as reducing costs associated with uncertainty across time. The crucial mechanism by which that is done is through a system of "nested rules," with rules at each successive level in the hierarchy being increasingly costly to change.[71] An only slightly exaggerated way of putting that point is to say that there can be a market in anything only if there is not a market in everything. Property rights and contracts for exchanges of property would be worthless if it were cheaper to buy and sell policemen and judges than it is to buy and sell parcels of property. It is precisely the stability and reliability of the more deeply nested rules governing the judicial system that makes feasible the flux of the market. Similarly, much of ordinary political bargaining and exchange is possible only against the backdrop of the stability provided by more deeply nested, institutionalized rules, ranging from informal norms of congressional behavior and committee structures to the Constitution itself.[72]

Think for a moment about the nature of constitutions. They are supposed by their nature to be enduring, stable, hard to change; and for that very reason, they typically contain within them requirements for very large majorities and extraordinary procedures to be followed for their amendment and change. But, upon reflection, surely it should be something of a mystery why successive generations ever feel bound by those rules. The Founders were not superhuman demigods. What they did was simply scrap one set of institutional arrangements and start afresh. Why should successive generations feel bound to live by their rules for amending the Constitution, rather than feeling free to do as the Founders did in their day and start afresh themselves?[73]

The answer lies, of course, in the value that we all derive from having our activities constrained in precisely the ways that enduring constitutions do. Being able to embody certain fundamental agreements in presumptively unchangeable rules allows us to make commitments to one another that are credible, in a way that they would not be were they embodied merely in ordinary legislation that was subject to amendment or repeal by any successive annual assembly. Just as in individual affairs contract law (the right to put ourselves in a position to be sued) allows us to make commitments for deferred delivery to people that might not otherwise be credible, so too in collective affairs does constitutional law (the right to put ourselves in a position to be judi-

[71]North 1990.
[72]Buchanan and Brennan 1985. Hardin 1989. Ordeshook 1992.
[73]Ackerman 1991.

cially overruled) allow us to make commitments to minority groups and sectoral interests that might not otherwise be trusted.

1.3 The Emergence and Change of Institutions

Institutions, though relatively stable, are not however eternal and immutable. In this section I shall consider, briefly, larger issues concerning the emergence and change of institutions. In the first instance, the issues are primarily empirical: where do institutions come from, and according to what forces do they change? The appropriate scope, or lack thereof, for theories of institutional design is often thought to turn upon a peculiarly intentionalist answer to those questions: in Section 1.3.2 I argue against any such easy presumption, having first (in Section 1.3.1) surveyed different generic styles of explanation of social and institutional change. I proceed, in Section 1.3.3, to survey design theories to try to adduce what "good design" might mean in these contexts. These design theories uncomfortably straddle both empirical and normative realms in ways that I try to sort out in Section 1.3.4.

1.3.1 Models of Social Change: Accident, Evolution, and Intention

There are, roughly speaking, three basic ways in which social institutions (or human societies more generally) might arise and change over time.[74] First, social change might occur by accident. There are, on this account, no forces of natural or social necessity at work, no larger causal mechanisms driving things. What happens just happens. It is – in a characteristically postmodernist turn of phrase that is also effectively captures the highly contextualized spirit of many microhistorical explanations – purely a matter of contingency.[75]

Second, social change might be a matter of evolution. As in biological analogues from which these models borrow, the initial variation might have occurred utterly at random, as a matter of pure accident and happenstance. But there are, on these accounts, some selection mechanisms at work, usually competitive in nature, which pick out some variants

---

[74]Though different in detail, this partitioning owes its inspiration and in crucial places its elaboration to Elster (1983); Knight (1992) usefully elaborates upon the evolutionary and intentional themes in rather different ways than those developed here.

[75]Rorty 1989. There is in comparative politics a parallel, if less insistent, emphasis upon particular historical conjunctions as essential facilitating conditions for social change.

for survival.[76] Those variants which do survive over a protracted period might therefore be said to be somehow "better fitted" to their environment than those that did not.[77]

Third, social change might be a product of intentional intervention. That is to say, the change might be the product of the deliberate interventions of purposive, goal-seeking agents. Those agents might be either isolated individuals or organized groups.[78] The changes that ensue from their intentional interventions may or may not be exactly what was intended by any one (or by any subset) of them. The changes may benefit some or all or none of the intentional agents.[79] Even where the outcome was intended by no one, however, the basic explanatory logic is still basically intentional in form, insofar as the story is still to be told essentially in terms of intentions and interactions among those intentions.

Any actual instance of social or institutional change is almost certain to involve a combination of all three of these elements. The problems that groups face, the solutions they concoct, and the way that they implement those solutions are all subject to accident and error. But the accidents and errors are rarely purely stochastic; and even when they are, they nonetheless typically arise in the backwash of intentionality, through the oversights and miscalculations of purposive agents engaged in projects of their own. Thus, what intentional agents intentionally do (or, more typically, fail to do) is important even in modeling social and institutional change as essentially accidental.

Intentionality has an even more central role to play in evolutionary stories about social and institutional change, for the "selection" mechanism that winnows out some variations in favor of others is in the social setting often essentially intentional in form. Agents, individually

[76]This sort of analysis underlies everything from the Whig theory of history to neoclassical models of capitalist competition and one of the most recent theories of the development of the firm (Nelson and Winter 1982; Winter and Williamson 1991). Recent work on the emergence of cooperation in other social settings builds explicitly upon evolutionary models (see, e.g., Axelrod 1984, 1986; Ellickson 1991).

[77]That may be faint praise, depending upon what you think of the competitive environment as a selection mechanism; just as bad art and music might coarsen people's aesthetic sensitivities and thereby drive out good art and music, so too might some competitive environments select for the worst or the most common rather than the finest social forms.

[78]The very fact that they have some internal decision mechanisms for settling upon joint action plans qualifying them as "intentional agents" for these purposes (French 1979).

[79]"Benefiting all" recalls models which (after the fashion of Hume or Smith) analyze institutions in terms of conventions. "Benefiting some" recalls models which are more sensitive to power asymmetries and bargaining relations (Knight 1992).

or more often collectively, sometimes find themselves literally asked to decide which sort of social arrangements they would prefer to retain and reproduce. More often, they find themselves "voting with their feet," deciding which among several alternative arrangements they would themselves prefer to participate in, with the institutions with relatively more participants being at a comparative advantage (economically, militarily, or whatever) vis-à-vis ones with fewer. In both these cases, the "selection mechanism" central to evolutionary models involves the intentional actions of purposive agents, either directly or indirectly.

Alternatively, that selection mechanism may take a more Hegelian form. This would ordinarily be described in terms of a "central animating idea" underlying any particular institution, with institutional change over time being analyzed in terms of that institution "working itself pure" in respect of that central idea.[80] One common example is the obvious tension, present at the founding of the American republic, between the "inalienable rights" ascribed to all men and the institution of slavery; on a Hegelian reading, which of course many would resist, the next half century of American history just amounted to this tension working itself out. For a possibly less contentious example, consider the history of the expansion of suffrage: once universal manhood suffrage was granted, it was very hard to provide any good, principled grounds for denying the suffrage to women or blacks as well. Many would tell a similar tale about expanding notions of citizenship rights more generally: once fundamental civil rights have been granted to all, there is an inexorable slide toward granting people basic political rights; and once those have been granted, there is another inexorable slide toward granting everyone certain basic welfare rights.[81] Or, again, there might be a similar story to tell about the expansion of the European Union: the narrow initial idea of a free market in goods and labor necessarily entails a breakdown of barriers to free movement of labor across borders, which necessarily entails that pensions be made portable and social security entitlements uniform or transferable, so in the end much more than a common market for goods and services "naturally" evolves.

Whether or not any of those particular stories is compelling, the broader style of analysis that they represent certainly merits inclusion in this larger explanatory menu. What is going on, in each case, is most naturally described in terms of the "animating idea" of the system

---

[80]I am grateful to John Ferejohn for impressing upon me the significance of this alternative in the present connection.

[81]Goodin 1992, chaps. 1,5. Marshall 1949. Another example might be the breakdown of master–servant law in the United States, as traced in Orren (1991).

somehow "working itself out." It is still, in basic form, an evolutionary explanation, perhaps. But what is distinctive about this form of evolution is that the "selection" involved is done in terms of the "animating idea": that, rather than in terms of pressures from a harshly competitive environment, explains the greater survival prospects of some institutional variants over others.

Thus this Hegelian story might be seen as basically evolutionary in form. But it is also at least in part intentional, as well. The selection may be being done *in terms of* the animating idea of the institution in question, but the selection is done *by* intentional agents working within and internalizing the animating ideas of that institution. In the case of slavery, it is the difficulty that the likes of Washington and Jefferson had reconciling their public and private lives – in good conscience denying their own slaves the treatment that their professed principles said was due to all men – that created the tension in question. In the case of expanding rights of suffrage or of citizenship, it is the difficulty of those resisting such expansions in finding any principled grounds for stopping anywhere along the slippery slope that creates the tension. And so on.

Animating principles are themselves inanimate. They are incapable of "working themselves out," in any literal sense at all. What animating principles "animate" is intentional agents who internalize them, and what "working themselves out" amounts to is those intentional agents implementing them consistently across the whole range of their appropriate application. Thus, even in this Hegelian version of the evolutionary story of social and institutional change, intentional agents are still central players. In that, as apparently in all other cases, we will need an explanatory account that draws on notions of intentionality and perhaps accident as well as pure evolutionary pressures.

1.3.2 Intentionality and Design

Much more can and should be said under each of these headings, of course. Much more can and should be said about the various ways in which all three of these sorts of theories might be combined into a hybrid theory, more credible than any one of these standing alone.[82] For present purposes, however, that very stark and sketchy taxonomy will suffice. The aim here, recall, is merely to try to situate theories of institutional design in relation to some larger explanatory menu.

It is often thought that theories which talk in terms of institutional

[82]For case studies see, e.g., Binder et al. (1971) and Almond et al. (1973).

design are necessarily tied to intention-based theories of social change.[83] The source of the thought is easy enough to discern. After all, design and redesign are essentially intentional activities; so it is only natural to suppose that talking in terms of institutional design must be appropriate basically just where the institutions in view have intentionality at their core.

By the same token, it is only natural to suppose that theories conjuring with notions of "design" are out of place absent intentional design or designers. Sometimes institutions just emerge accidentally, in unintended ways, in response to some historical accident or another; sometimes they just evolve naturally, in unintended ways, according to some deeper logic of their own. Insofar as institutions are like that, products of accident or evolution rather than intention, and insofar as theories of institutional design presuppose intention, then theories of institutional design (whether empirical or normative) have a very limited role to play. Or so it is standardly supposed.

That way of thinking is, however, in error across several fronts. First of all, it construes the scope of intentional explanation too narrowly. Institutions are often the product of intentional activities gone wrong – unintended by-products, the products of various intentional actions cutting across one another, misdirected intentions, or just plain mistakes.[84] To explain how those outcomes came about, we must refer essentially to intentions and the interactions among intentions. The explanation is still intentional in form, even if the outcome is not intended. An institution can thus be the product of intentional action, without its having been literally the intentional product of anyone's action.

The Myth of the Intentional Designer (still less the Myth of the Intentional Design) is greatly to be avoided in theories of institutional design. Typically, there is no single design or designer. There are just lots of localized attempts at partial design cutting across one another, and any sensible scheme for institutional design has to take account of that fact. Thus, even within the realm of our intentional interventions, what we should be aiming at is not the design of institutions directly. Rather, we should be aiming at designing schemes for designing institutions – schemes which will pay due regard to the multiplicity of designers and to the inevitably cross-cutting nature of their intentional interventions in the design process.[85]

---

[83]This is at the core of Oakeshott's (1962/1991) critique of "rationalism in politics" and parallel complaints against social planning in Hayek (1973), for just two famous examples.

[84]Merton 1936.

[85]Dryzek's (1990, pp. 40–50) proposals for "discursive designs" for "model institutions" and their real-world approximations are very much in this spirit.

Intentional design of institutions is only part of the story, though. To some extent, it is undeniably true that institutions do come about essentially by accident or that they evolve according to a logic of their own, in ways altogether impervious to intentional intervention and direct human design. Even where direct design is impossible, however, indirect design is often nonetheless feasible. Accidents happen: but the frequency and direction of accidents can be significantly shaped by intentional interventions of social planners.[86] Evolution in the strictest sense may proceed of its own accord, largely independently of the organisms subject to it. But especially in social settings, the criteria of success in the struggle for survival – the things that the analogue of "natural selection" selects for in a social setting, the things that contribute to the longevity of any given institution and the chances for its successors surviving into the distant future – those are all things that can and should be subject to conscious social choice.

Thus, while theories of institutional design undeniably find their primary application in corners of the social world subject to intentional intervention and control, it is simply not true that they are altogether without application to other corners of the social world. Insofar as the social world is accident-prone, we might want to design around the risk of accidents, seeking robust institutions that can withstand the various shocks that will inevitably befall them. Insofar as the social world is subject to evolutionary pressures, we might want to apply design principles to reshape the selection criteria and social reward structures according to which some innovations succeed and others fail.

What theories of social change as accident or evolution are telling us is that social outcomes themselves are not (or not to any great extent) directly subject to intentional change, design, or redesign. Such theories strive to limit the scope for intentionality in descriptive, or hence prescriptive, models of social life. Whatever their aims, however, what these other theories are actually pointing to are possibilities of design and redesign at one level up. Outcomes may be the product of accident, but accident rates might be intentionally altered. Outcomes may be the product of evolutionary forces, but the selection mechanisms that guide that evolution might be intentionally altered. Design and redesign might still have some scope, even in those less intentional social worlds.

When intentional agents cannot work their will directly, they start looking for ways to do so indirectly. In the ways just sketched, they may well succeed in their quest for indirect mechanisms even where direct intentions will inevitably be thwarted. Ironically enough, the less directly intentional the social world in which we find ourselves, the more the appropriate sphere for design principles shifts away from the inten-

[86]Perrow 1984.

tional shaping of level of policies and outcomes, and the more it moves toward the intentional shaping of institutions and practices. Hence, the claim that the social world allows little scope for intentional change and direct design actually expands rather than contracts the scope of theories of indirect – that is, properly *institutional* – design.

Just as theories of institutional design are sometimes thought to imply an intentionalist pattern of social explanation, so too are those theories sometimes thought to imply a "creationist" focus. Talk of "design," this critique complains, seems necessarily to amount to talking of "design de novo," with insufficient appreciation for the ways in which social engineers always work with materials inherited from and to some extent unalterably shaped by the past.

Sometimes, perhaps, institutional designers do indeed come perilously close to such pitfalls.[87] By and large, however, their focus on institutions safeguards theorists of institutional design against any creationist fallacies to which a focus on design might otherwise render them prey. Much of the point of studying institutions, after all, is to explore precisely those ways in which the past leaves traces in the present and constrains our present actions and future options. So designers of institutions, of all people, should be particularly sensitive to the ways in which past inheritances will inevitably constrain them in their own design activities.

It serves as a useful reminder of this point to refer, from time to time, of design and *re*design, shaping and *re*shaping. Those phrases are clumsy, and their frequent incantation would be unduly ponderous. But the larger point for which they serve as markers should be constantly before us: in designing social institutions, we are always doing so against the backdrop of a set of past practices, which brings with it its own peculiar constraints and possibilities.

1.3.3 Theories of Design

So far, this chapter has concentrated heavily on one key word, "institution," at the expense of the other, "design," in the title of the book and of the series which it introduces. The reason is, quite simply, that the same is true of all large literatures across all the several disciplines which this chapter attempts to track.

The phrase "institutional design" is often dropped into these discus-

---

[87]Coleman (1993, p. 2), for example, talks of the legal creation of the "fictional person" of the corporation as a "social invention" – as if it were an utterly new social form, utterly without prior social precedents, when in fact there were precursors aplenty in Roman and medieval canon law (Berman 1983, pp. 215–21).

sions, even into the titles of articles and books on these topics. But the phrase is characteristically dropped relatively casually, with little analysis as to what it means for institutions (or anything else, for that matter) to be "designed" and still less analysis of what principles might properly guide such design attempts. To find any explicit discussions of "design" problems, we must stretch well beyond any narrowly institutionalist focus in search of principles and propositions which we can bring back to bear in that sphere.

Definitions are easily enough come by. Perhaps the most useful states, simply, that "design is the creation of an actionable form to promote valued outcomes in a particular context."[88] But for further discussions, literatures on public policy and political institutions often refer us very far afield indeed – to texts in aesthetics or engineering or architecture or product design or land-use planning.[89] There may well be something to be learned for the study of institutional design from these distant disciplines. But, to say the least, the points of analogy and disanalogy will have to be traced fully and carefully: the objects of design are so very different that there can be no serious thought of wholesale borrowing of the tricks of those very different trades and applying them unreflectively to the design of social institutions. To date, however, those glib analogies to design notions in distant disciplines have remained just that.

Thus, we find ourselves in an awkward position. The paucity of literature specifically on design issues in the study of social institutions forces us to look further afield for guidance – but not too much further afield or we will quickly come to the point where lessons learned might well be utterly nontransferable. Happily, however, we can find much of what we need relatively near to home. There have recently emerged highly useful discussions of "design" problems on at least three distinct levels within cognate social science literatures. In order of increasing generality, these discussions concern the design of policies, of mechanisms, and of whole systems.

There is a modest literature rooted in political science on "policy design." What counts as design in that context varies somewhat. Sometimes it amounts to little more than the generation of policy options: the crafting of new solutions, through a creative combination of recollection and innovation and a serious engagement with both values

---

[88]Bobrow and Dryzek 1987, p. 201. For fuller elaboration on essentially the same ideas, see Alexander (1964).

[89]See, most strikingly, Alexander (1982); but even in texts more sensitive to political context the references to specifically design notions always seem to dredge these same distant waters (see, e.g., Bobrow and Dryzek 1987, p. 200; Dryzek 1990, p. 41; Linder and Peters 1987; Goodsell 1992).

and contexts.[90] Often the central issue in policy design is "feasibility" in some sense or another: the implementability of policy choices, taking due account of the resources and incentives facing various agents and agencies who will have necessarily to be involved in giving effect to policymakers' intentions.[91]

The general purport of the large literature on "mechanism design," a literature rooted in economics, is to prescribe mechanisms for resource allocation quite generally.[92] Such discussions go to the very core of modern economics, amounting to nothing less than the quest for credible models and possible mechanisms to underwrite economic equilibria, the absence of the fictitious auctioneer postulated by Walras.

Within that economics literature on mechanism design, "the major unsolved problem" lies in "the proper integration of the information and incentive aspects."[93] Mechanisms are apparently doomed to fail in their attempts to allocate resources in Pareto-optimal ways if they attempt to respect, at the same time, constraints of "informational decentralization" and "incentive compatibility": producers or consumers or both will have an incentive to deviate from the formal rules of the allocation mechanism (a failure of "incentive compatibility"); and they are able to do so by misrepresenting facts about which (thanks to "informational decentralization") they have unique, privileged information (producers about their production functions, consumers about their preferences).[94] That is the basic shape of the "mechanism design" problem as it appears within economics, and in that form it has given rise to a large literature on the optimal designs of various resource-allocation mechanisms: auctions and bidding systems; contract with imperfect information; and so on.[95]

Parallel mechanism-design problems appear outside these narrowly economic contexts, however. Within politics, there is an analogous theorem about voting schemes. In any voting mechanism that strives to achieve Pareto-optimal outcomes, some voter will always have a strategic incentive to manipulate the outcome by misrepresenting his or her true preferences.[96] Similarly, in the public finance context, there is

---

[90]Alexander 1982. See also Wildavsky 1979 and Bobrow and Dryzek 1987 for less single-minded elaboration on these issues.
[91]Wildavsky 1979. Linder and Peters 1987. Schneider and Ingram 1988. Ingram and Schneider 1988.
[92]Hurwicz 1977.
[93]Hurwicz 1977, p. 32.
[94]Hurwicz 1977, pp. 28–9.
[95]For samplers, see Arrow and Hurwicz 1977 and Hurwicz et al. 1985; for a good survey, see McAfee and McMillan 1987.
[96]Gibbard 1973. Satterwaite 1975.

an analogous problem in surmising "true" demand for public goods. It is no use just asking people how much they would be willing to pay for such goods, and levying a charge upon them accordingly: because the goods are public, people can use them freely once they have been provided by others' payments; given that, people will have a strategic incentive to understate their "true" demand for public goods, if the supply of such goods will be substantially independent of what they say yet what they are charged strictly a function of what they say.[97] In both these more politicized contexts, there have been elaborate proposals for "optimal mechanisms" to circumvent such difficulties.[98]

Finally, there is an even larger literature on "system design." This literature is harder to place, and still harder to contain. For its initial inspiration, it drew heavily on operations research, computer modeling, and artificial intelligence.[99] In the first instance, the primary social scientific applications of those techniques were to problems in military resource allocation during World War II and, from the immediate postwar period, to cognate problems in economics more generally. From this tradition come techniques such as input-output analysis, econometric models (typically, Treasury models) of national economies, and schemes using quasi-markets and shadow prices in more systematic schemes of project planning and appraisal.[100] Latterly, similar techniques have been advocated for "systematic thinking for social action" across a wide range of social programs as well as in the economic and defense applications where such techniques have historically most naturally found their homes.[101]

The sorts of design considerations to which such systematic thinking points us pertain, principally, to issues of comprehensiveness in several dimensions. They invite us to reflect upon larger contexts; to be sensitive to all the various forces in play, and to all the complex interactions among them; to interrogate thoroughly our own values, and to assess carefully the way in which all these interactions might impact upon whatever it is we value and disvalue in social outcomes.

Indeed, something very much like that seems to be what references to "design" considerations point to across this whole range of social-scientific design literature.[102] The reference seems always essentially to be to a notion of "goodness of fit" between the designed object (policy,

---

[97]Samuelson 1954.

[98]Of, e.g., "approval voting" as a solution to the former problem (Brams and Fishburn 1978) and the "Clarke tax" as a solution for the latter (Tideman 1977).

[99]Simon 1969/1981.

[100]Hitch 1958. Hitch and McKean 1960. Leontieff 1982. Little and Mirrlees 1974.

[101]Rivlin 1971.

[102]And beyond: see particularly Alexander 1964.

mechanism, system) and the larger context in which it is set. In the case of a policy, a well-designed policy is one which fits well with the other policies, and the larger political/economic/social systems in which it is set. In the case of a mechanism, a well-designed mechanism is one that works well alongside other features of the social environment in which it is set, including other mechanisms in play there. Insofar as the mechanism works by manipulating incentives to individuals, a well-designed mechanism is one whose internal requirements are "compatible" with other incentives that individuals face, rather than offering people incentives for undercutting the goals (characterized as Pareto-optimality, or whatever) which we were trying to achieve by using the mechanism in the first place. In the case of a whole system, being well designed means that all the pieces fit together well in a harmonious whole: being well integrated, being in equilibrium (and perhaps robustly so, whether homostatically or otherwise).[103]

1.3.4 The Normative/Empirical Interface

Such theories of optimal design – whether of policy, mechanism, system, or institution – are at the same time both empirical and normative. That basic fact is often acknowledged. The details of that connection are rarely explored adequately, however. We are typically left with the general impression that there is and should be some necessary, direct connection between the empirical and normative sides of the design project. But we are rarely given even the sketchiest indication of what makes the connection a necessary, much less a direct, one.[104]

One way the connection might work is this. Let us suppose that those theories of optimal design are essentially normative in their fundamental motivation. They amount to a quest for some ideal state of the world. They are theories about what a good (indeed, perfect: optimal) arrangement would be. But then comes the thought that the ideal may be a pretty good guide to the real. After all (or so the thought goes) it is only to be expected, in the descriptive sense as well as the prescriptive one, that the ideal should be realized. What requires explanation is not doing the right thing, but rather departures from that ideal.

---

[103]On these matters see especially Lockwood's 1964 classic paper, "Social integration and system integration."

[104]That is true even of Arrow and Hahn's 1971 proof of the fundamental theorems of welfare economics: it explains that idealized markets are Pareto-optimal, and thus gives us normative reasons of a kind for desiring them; but absent some other premises, that Pareto-optimality of ideal markets does not in itself explain how markets might empirically have come about.

Greater or lesser departures are common enough, of course, and explanations aplenty are required (and are indeed proffered) by analysts pursuing this basic line of attack. But what they explain is notable: not good outcomes, but bad; not perfectly attaining our goals, but failures to do so. The point is not just that, from certain other perspectives, the explanatory priority (what is "only to be expected" and what demands an explanation) may well be otherwise. That is true too, of course. But, more importantly, we should note the curiosity of taking anything at all for granted in this regard.

How we manage to achieve optimal arrangements requires explanation every bit as much as does our failure to achieve them. It may well be that optimality is self-enforcing, in some way or another. But the ways in which that is true need to be set out specifically. We need to know the explanatory mechanisms at work. They might be intentional rewards and punishments meted out by an angry God or all-powerful Lawgiver; they might be hidden-hand mechanisms guiding us toward a competitive equilibrium. But we need a story. Logically, it is as unsatisfactory to take optimizing for granted as it is to take failures to optimize for granted (saying, perhaps, "it's only to be expected from politics" – or, equivalently for a certain stripe of economist, "rent-seeking is only to be expected in most social affairs").

A second basic way of explaining some connection between the prescriptive and descriptive, the normative and the empirical, in optimal design theories is just this. There is no reason to suppose that agents in the real world will intentionally pursue optimal designs – or even that they will recognize them when they see them (or even that they will ever stumble across them, given how rococo some of those optimal designs are). The prescriptions have explanatory force, not because people internalize and intentionally act upon those prescriptions. Rather, those prescriptions are a good guide to what we will actually find in the real world because the same thing that makes us prescribe them as optimal designs (the "goodness of their fit to the larger context") also makes them well suited to survive in their larger environment.

The reason that optimal designs predominate, on this account, has nothing to do with the frequency with which they are chosen and everything to do with the relative frequency of relatively persistent institutions. Longevity implies frequency, other things being equal. The best bet, at any moment in time, is that most institutions will be the ones that have been around for a while; or equivalently, the best bet a propos any given institution is that it is one which has been around for a while. Institutions which have been around for a while are most likely to be ones that are more nearly optimally designed to fit their environment (or, in older terminology, ones which are "functionally well adapted"). So normative criteria of optimal design can also ground predictions of empirical frequency.[105]

Even that more modest connection between descriptive and prescriptive uses of design theory cannot be sustained without further presuppositions, however. The crucial presupposition, for present purposes, is that there is some mechanism which weeds out ill-fitting institutions over time, either refining and replacing them with ones that fit the environment better or else just disposing of them altogether.[106] There must, in other words, be some selection procedure at work to underwrite the assumption that over time the accumulation of institutions will tend to favor good-fitting ones over ill-fitting ones.

This seems to be a tough sort of claim to sustain. Government organizations, at least, display enormous longevity and persist well after their original reasons for existing have passed away.[107] Insofar as other social institutions are like that, then it seems implausible to postulate any tough competitive environment that weeds out ill-fitting institutions on anything like a systematic basis.[108]

In the end, the best analysis of any necessary connection between descriptive and prescriptive aspects of optimal design theories lodges it squarely in the intentions of social agents. What theories of optimal design try to do is to give social agents good reasons for shaping institutions in some ways rather than others. Insofar as they are convinced of those arguments and moved by those reasons, those social agents will try to act upon those design prescriptions. Insofar as they succeed,

---

[105]"Ground predictions" is an intentional fudge, stopping well short of stronger claims that they "provide explanations"; reasons for this wariness are found in Elster (1983, chap. 2), critiquing early functionalists (notably Merton 1957) and even sophisticated later ones (e.g., Cohen 1978, chap. 9).

[106]Another presupposition, equally crucial to that larger explanatory scheme but less interesting for present purposes, concerns the rates at which new institutions are generated and at which old ill-fitting ones are killed off. If new institutions (some well-fitting, many not) arise at a great rate, and especially if the selection mechanisms work relatively slowly to weed out the ill-fitting among them, then most institutions at any given time might well be ill-fitting newer ones upon which the selection mechanism has not yet had a chance to work.

[107]Kaufman 1976.

[108]Or at least it does so absent some special explanation of the persistence over time of institutions, in this way. Such special explanations might be available: the reason for institutions persisting may be that they have come to acquire new functions to replace their old, and in that way to fit the larger environment well despite their changed focus; or it may be that they have shaped the environment to fit themselves. Some such claim is what must be sustained to save this larger style of explanation of the connection between empirical and normative aspect of optimal design theory.

institutions shaped by their actions will end up bearing something of the mark of those theories of optimal design.

Thus, the connection is there. But the connection comes through effects of the prescriptions on the intentions of agents, and through the effects of those agents' intentions on the social world. To say that is to claim (or ask) a lot. But any more facile claim – that optimal design theories are unreflectively internalized or automatically enforced through competition in a hostile environment – seems far less tenable. It seems far better to admit forthrightly that the point of moralizing (which is after all what we are doing in prescribing optimal social arrangements) is to shape people's values and preferences and, through them, their actions.

1.4 New Institutions for Old, Good Institutions for Bad

In this final section, I turn to larger questions of what sorts of design principles might usefully guide the shaping and reshaping of social institutions. The first issue to address (in Section 1.4.1) is in what sense design criteria track morality: to what extent, or in what sense, "good design" is actually "good" at all. I close (in Section 1.4.2) with a sampler of some design principles that might actually be commended both externally and internally.

1.4.1 Design Criteria and Moral Desiderata

The fundamental notion of design, as explicated in Section 1.3.3, relates to "goodness of fit" of the designed object to its environment. That definition, in turn, provides an obvious "internal" criterion of what it is for a design to be a "good design." A well-designed object is one that fits its environment well. A well-designed institution, in particular, would be one that is both internally consistent and externally in harmony with the rest of the social order in which it is set.

That internal criterion of good design built into the notion of design itself is misleadingly obvious, though. The larger question remains unasked. How well does that "internal" criterion fit with external standards of moral worth? From a larger moral point of view, it is an open question whether goodness of fit is necessarily good at all.

It is a familiar point in moral philosophy that any given individual can have both internal and external reasons for action, and that those two sets of reasons for action might well point in very different directions.[109] Internal reasons, in the individual's case, are reasons derived from that agent's own motivational structure: reasons internal to his existing beliefs and desires, principles and prejudices. External reasons, in the individual's case, are reasons derived from some larger moral truths unconnected with the individual's own extant beliefs and desires: truths about what is right and good and worthy. The latter sorts of reasons offer an external stance for the critique – for reevaluation and reformulation – of internal ones.

The same is true in the case of institutional designs. The internal criterion of good design, central though it is to the very notion of design itself, must be supplemented and held up to judgment against larger external evaluative criteria. From a collective and institutional point of view as well as from an individual moral point of view, there can be external as well as internal reasons for action. There can be good reasons for seeking institutions that fit ill, not well, with the rest of their environment.

The most dramatic instance, of course, is an institution set in the context of an evil social order which morally we ought destroy. Undoubtedly design theories could be applied to concoct an optimal mechanism for overseeing the labor of slaves. But optimality in that context – goodness of fit to *that* environment – constitutes criticism rather than praise from any credible external point of view.[110]

Less dramatic cases are in many ways even more interesting. A natural reading of the "goodness of fit" criterion of good design equates it with "harmony," with "promoting the smooth functioning" of the designed object and the larger system within which it is set. But sometimes disharmony is far from disadvantageous. In designing mechanisms for group decision-making, we are often well advised to designate someone formally to serve as "devil's advocate," challenging our shared presumptions and telling us things we do not want to hear, as a way of improving the quality of the overall decision that we reach.[111] We are often well advised to design institutions so as to encourage disharmony and hence dynamics, to force us to reconsider and perhaps to change

---

[109]Williams 1981, chap. 8.

[110]Of course, if the optimal design enjoins decent treatment of slaves (to protect the slaveowner's capital investment, or to increase morale and hence output) then we might coincidentally concur in the recommendation, at least as an interim step. And if the preferences of slaves themselves were included among criteria to be considered in assessing the "optimality" of such schemes, we might have a further reason for respecting the recommendations. But even then, we might be perfectly prepared to recommend utterly non-Paretian moves in that context – we may well suppose that, in trying to improve the plight of slaves, there is no reason at all to limit ourselves to schemes that would not reduce the welfare of slaveowners.

[111]George 1972.

the way we are doing things from time to time. (Competition, both in economics and politics, is commended on precisely those grounds.) We are often well advised to design institutions in such a way that they allow us to "take one step backward so we may take two steps forward."[112]

Perhaps we might be tempted to say, in all those less dramatic cases, that what optimal designs actually prescribe is the deliberate creation of institutional irritants. In a way that is certainly true. But in so doing these prescriptions appeal to a notion of "optimality" that transcends any narrow reference to the internal criteria of design. The appeal of these larger notions of optimal design is not to smooth functioning, well-ordered internal relations, goodness of fit to the existing local environment, or whatever. The appeal is instead to some notions of "optimal design" that point to the goodness of fit of the institution to some larger objectives than those narrow ones embodied in the internal goals of the institution and its immediate environment.

The appeal is, ultimately, to some larger moral code. There is a sense in which an institution might be said to be well designed if it is internally consistent and externally harmonious with its larger social environment. But that is still an essentially internalist definition of optimal design which must eventually give way to larger external critiques, rooted in normative principles that are at the end of the day themselves independently defensible.

1.4.2 Some Desirable Principles of Institutional Design

What sorts of principles, then, should guide our institutional designs? Clearly, from what has just been said, they should be principles with deeper moral resonance. Good institutional design is not just a matter of pragmatics. It is not just a matter of aesthetic or functional "goodness of fit." Equally clearly, though, we ought not have to suspend our quest for better social institutions until we have reached agreement on all the deeper truths of ethics and metaphysics.

In discussions of institutional design what we often can do, and all we usually ought be trying to do, is seeking principles that trade on "theories of the middle range" in both empirical and normative realms.[113] We can hope to discover, and to embody institutionally, a raft of generalizations of reliable validity, at least within a certain (perhaps tightly circumscribed) sphere.

In the remainder of this section, I shall be sketching a few illustrative

[112]Elster 1979, chap. 1.
[113]Merton 1957.

principles of this sort. None are worked out fully: that is the task for other chapters, and indeed other books. None can be applied universally or commended without qualification: all have a two-edged aspect to them, somehow. Still, it is useful in closing this introduction to offer examples of the sorts of principles that we might be aspiring to adduce, even if this is of necessity a very preliminary cut at that project.

One middle-range social generalization that institutional designers might want somehow to embody in their principles, for example, concerns the twin and connected facts that humans are fallible and that societies change. If we are likely to err about matters either of fact or of value – or if the facts or values upon which our actions are predicated are themselves to some extent specific to situations which might well change – then it is a mistake to set those possible errors in concrete. It is far better to design our institutions in such a way as to be flexible in these regards, to admit of "learning by doing" and to evolve over time.[114] Thus, we might say *revisability* is one important principle of institutional design.

Of course, there is another side to that story, too. We want to have the capacity, sometimes, to bind ourselves to a certain course of action and to ensure that we (or our successors) resist any temptations to deviate from it. Personally, we want to make commitments and stick to them: we want to keep our promises, honor our contracts, respect others' trust and confidences. Politically, we want to make commitments without reneging on them: we want to keep our political promises, to honor our treaties, and so on.[115] Revisability is an important principle of institutional design, then, but it is also one which must somehow be kept within limits.

Just as we want our institutions to be capable of changing in response to relevant changes in the factual or evaluative universe, so too do we want them to be responsive only to relevant changes there. While we certainly do want our institutions to be open to alteration where appropriate, by the same token we want them to be resistant to sheer buffeting by changes in social circumstances that have no bearing upon the assumptions upon which those institutions were predicated.

That points to a further principle of institutional design which might best be termed *robustness*. They should be capable of adapting to new

---

[114]Wildavsky 1979. March and Olsen 1984, pp. 745–77.

[115]In public finance, this appears as the "capital levy" problem: narrowly calculating governments have an interest in luring investors into a jurisdiction with a promise of low tax rates fixed for a specific period, but having induced relatively immobile capital to relocate there then to raise the taxes before the specified period is up. But the same governments, of course, also have an interest in somehow being able to make credible commitments that they will not do any such thing.

situations: not brittle and easily destroyed by them. But they should adapt to new situations only in ways that are appropriate to the relevant respects in which the situations are new – changing fundamentally only where there has been some fundamental change in the factual or evaluative universe, and making only surface accommodations to changed circumstance where there has not.

Of course, what counts as "appropriate" and "relevant" here is again going to be a matter of contention and political controversy. Simple reference to the internal logic of the institutions themselves is insufficient to decide the matter for the same reason that internal standards of "good design" are themselves unsatisfactory. So, again, robustness is a principle of institutional design that is valuable, but only within limits the scope of which cannot in principle be specified.

Another empirical generalization which institutions must respect is the admixture of motives that moves most people, at least in most societies relevantly similar to our own. Within most social actors, self-seeking impulses exist alongside principled and even altruistic motives. In designing our institutions we ought at least take account of that fact, which might (as a further principle) be described as *sensitivity to motivational complexity*.

How exactly institutions might best accommodate that fact of motivational complexity is an open question, turning upon premises that are in part empirical and in part normative. Classic models of separation of powers – checks and balances between branches of government, grants of rights to individuals against the government, and pluralist institutions to ensure centers of countervailing power across society more generally – constitute one style of reaction.[116] But by "designing institutions for knaves" such mechanical solutions risk making knaves of potentially more honorable actors. Depending upon exactly what structure we think people's moral codes take, and exactly what opportunity structure they face, a more trusting model embodying a more direct appeal to moral principles might actually do a better job of evoking high-minded motives for action and of suppressing low-minded ones.[117]

One way to do that might, for example, be through explicit appeal to a Kantian-inspired *publicity* principle, requiring as a test of all institutions and institutional actions that they be (at least in principle) pub-

[116]Grofman and Wittman 1989. Moe 1990. Elster 1993. In the same spirit, Schultze (1977) suggests structuring incentives in more policy-specific spheres so as to make public and private interest coincide.

[117]Goodin 1982, chap. 6; 1992. Brennan and Lomasky's 1993 account of voting in a large electorate is like that, as is Ackerman's (1991; cf. Goodin 1992, chap. 6) account of the "constitutional moment."

licly defensible.[118] The thought underlying this proposal in part turns upon hypotheses in moral psychology: suppositions that people recognize themselves as having higher and lower motives, that they would be ashamed to admit openly to the latter, and that if all action has to be defended publicly only the higher motives would be appealed to as reasons for action.[119] A more frankly political thought paralleling this one is simply this: insofar as we are trying to scare up political support for a project, insofar as we have to do so through open appeals to people's reason, we had better give them reasons that they themselves can embrace; it would clearly be counterproductive, in such situations, to appeal merely to our own narrowly selfish reasons for advocating a project, which of course are reasons that others cannot be expected to share.

But again, of course, publicity protects our public deliberations against only a certain range of contaminating factors. It may block the play of crass self-interest, but it will not do much to block the principled sacrifice of some possibly large segments of the community to the common good or to some "higher" cause. And whether our institutions should be designed with knaves or with potential angels primarily in view depends crucially upon our views as to the relative frequency of each in the population, and as to the relative damage that will be done (or good that will be missed) by making one assumption rather than another given those frequencies. This is a matter of fact, in some sense; but it is in practice usually an empirically undecidable question (we cannot, or cannot afford to, undertake the crucial experiments). Thus, again, whether the publicity principle or the principle of designing institutions for knaves is a good premise for institutional design depends fundamentally upon deeply contentious issues that admit only, in the final analysis, of a political resolution.

Finally, insofar as we are counting on trial-and-error, learning-by-doing processes to perfect our institutional arrangements, we ought embrace as a central principle of design a desire for *variability* in our institutional arrangements. We ought encourage experimentation with different structures in different places; and we ought, furthermore, encourage reflection upon the lessons from elsewhere and a willingness to borrow those lessons where appropriate. Federalism is sometimes defended on precisely this ground, as a "social laboratory" in which different approaches are allowed to emerge in different jurisdictions.[120]

---

[118]This is the subject of Chapter 6; see also Dryzek 1990 and, more skeptically, Goodin 1992, chap. 7.

[119]This is J. S. Mill's argument in *Representative Government* for open voting and against the secret ballot (see Goodin 1992, chap. 7, for a discussion).

[120]Wildavsky 1979, chap. 6.

There are difficulties with all such schemes, though. One is that precisely the sort of "political protectionism" that is required to prevent premature homogenization of arrangements across jurisdictions also gets in the way of borrowing across jurisdictions, once better arrangements have clearly emerged elsewhere. Another more serious danger is that, instead of serving as a "social laboratory" in which other jurisdictions will borrow the best from elsewhere, there will instead be a "race to the bottom." In a whole raft of policy areas, from tax to regulatory policy, we often see the worst practice rather than the best being adopted in neighboring jurisdictions. Whether federal institutions, or other variance-maximizing principles of institutional design, are good ideas thus depends once again upon a fundamentally political judgment as to which is the most likely consequence.

Thus, none of these principles of institutional design are unqualified or sacrosanct. Many more, equally qualified in character, will emerge in the course of subsequent chapters. This short initial list is intended merely as a sampler. These are just a few examples of the sorts of middle-range theories of both empirical and normative import to which we might appeal in designing and redesigning social institutions.

The enterprise is an important one, though. Qualified though our generalizations may be, our institutions are even more influential. If we are to understand how social life works, and how it might work better, fixing our focus firmly upon institutions and their reshaping is one crucial step.

References

Ackerman, Bruce. 1991. *We, the People*. Cambridge, Mass.: Harvard University Press.

Alexander, Christopher. 1964. *Notes on the Synthesis of Form*. Cambridge, Mass.: Harvard University Press.

Alexander, Ernest R. 1982. Design in the decision-making process. *Policy Sciences*, 14, 279–92.

Almond, Gabriel A., Scott C. Flanagan, and Robert J. Mundt, eds. 1973. *Crisis, Choice, and Change: Historical Studies of Political Development*. Boston: Little, Brown.

Arrow, Kenneth J. 1951. *Social Choice and Individual Values*. New York: Wiley.

Arrow, Kenneth J. 1974. *The Limits of Organization*. New York: Norton.

Arrow, Kenneth J., and Frank Hahn. 1971. *General Competitive Analysis*. San Francisco: Holden-Day.

Arrow, Kenneth J., and Leonid Hurwicz, eds. 1977. *Studies in Resource Allocation Processes*. Cambridge: Cambridge University Press.

Arthur, W. B. 1989. Competing technologies and lock-in by historical events. *Economic Journal*, 99, 116–31.

Axelrod, Robert. 1984. *The Evolution of Cooperation*. New York: Basic Books.

Axelrod, Robert. 1986. An evolutionary approach to norms. *American Political Science Review*, 80, 1095–1112.

Barrett, Michele, and Mary McIntosh. 1982. *The Anti-social Family*. London: Verso.

Barry, Brian. 1970. *Socialists, Economists and Democracy*. London: Collier-Macmillan.

Bates, Robert H. 1988. Contra contractarianism: some reflections on the new institutionalism. *Politics & Society*, 16, 187–401.

Becker, Gary S. 1976. *The Economic Approach to Human Behavior*. Chicago: University of Chicago Press.

Becker, Gary S. 1981. *A Treatise on the Family*. Cambridge, Mass: Harvard University Press.

Benton, Ted. 1984. *The Rise and Fall of Structural Marxism*. London: Macmillan.

Berger, Brigitte, and Peter L. Berger. 1983. *The War over the Family*. Harmondsworth, England: Penguin.

Berger, Peter L., and Hansfried Kellner. 1965. Arnold Gehlen and the theory of institutions. *Social Research*, 32, 110–5.

Berger, Peter L., and Thomas Luckman. 1966. *The Social Construction of Reality*. Garden City, N.Y.: Doubleday.

Berman, Harold J. 1983. *Law and Revolution: The Formation of the Western Legal Tradition*. Cambridge, Mass.: Harvard University Press.

Binder, Leonard, et al., eds. 1971. *Crises and Sequences in Political Development*. Princeton, N.J.: Princeton University Press.

Bobrow, Davis B., and John S. Dryzek. 1987. *Policy Analysis by Design*. Pittsburgh: University of Pittsburgh Press.

Bovens, Mark A. P. 1990. The social steering of complex organizations. *British Journal of Political Science*, 20, 91–117.

Brams, Steven J., and Peter C. Fishburn. 1978. Approval voting. *American Political Science Review*, 72, 831–47.

Brennan, Geoffrey, and James M. Buchanan. 1985. *The Reason of Rules: Constitutional Political Economy*. Cambridge: Cambridge University Press.

Brennan, Geoffrey, and Alan Hamlin 1992. Bicameralism and majoritarian equilibrium. *Public Choice*, 74, 169–79.

Brennan, Geoffrey, and Loren Lomasky. 1993. *Democracy and Decision: The Pure Theory of Electoral Preference*. Cambridge: Cambridge University Press.

Bryce, James. 1888. *The American Commonwealth*. London: Macmillan.

Buchanan, James M., Robert D. Tollison, and Gordon Tullock, eds. 1980. *Toward a Theory of the Rent-seeking Society*. College Station: Texas A&M University Press.

Calvert, Randall, Matthew D. McCubbins, and Barry R. Weingast. 1989. A theory of political control and agency discretion. *American Journal of Political Science*, 33, 588–61

Coase, R. H. 1937. The nature of the firm. *Economica*, 4, 386–405.

Cohen, G. A. 1978. *Karl Marx's Theory of History*. Oxford: Clarendon Press.

Cohen, Jean L., and Andrew Arato. 1992. *Civil Society and Political Theory*. Cambridge, Mass.: MIT Press.

Cohen, Joshua. 1982. Book review of G. A. Cohen, *Karl Marx's Theory of History*. *Journal of Philosophy*, 79, 253–73

Coleman, James S. 1990. *Foundations of Social Theory*. Cambridge, Mass.: Harvard University Press.

Coleman, James S. 1991. Constructed organization: first principles. *Journal of Law, Economics & Organization*, 7S (Special issue), S7–S23.

Coleman, James S. 1993. The rational reconstruction of society. *American Sociological Review*, 58, 1–15.

Commons, John R. 1931. Institutional economics. *American Economic Review*, 21, 648–57. Reprinted in Samuels 1988, vol. 1, pp. 18–27.

Commons, John R. 1934. *Institutional Economics*. New York: Macmillan.

Dahl, Robert A. 1963. *Modern Political Analysis*. Englewood Cliffs, N.J.: Prentice-Hall.

Dahrendorf, Ralf. 1958. Out of utopia: toward a reorientation of sociological analysis. *American Journal of Sociology*, 64, 115–27.

Dryzek, John S. 1990. *Discursive Democracy*. Cambridge: Cambridge University Press.

Dunleavy, Patrick. 1991. *Democracy, Bureaucracy and Public Choice*. Hemel Hempstead: Harvester-Wheatsheaf.

Eisenstadt, Shmuel N. 1964. Institutionalization and change. *American Sociological Review*, 29, 235–47.

Eisenstadt, Shmuel N. 1968. Social institutions: the concept. Vol. 14, pp. 409–21 in David L. Sills, ed., *International Encyclopedia of the Social Sciences*. New York: Macmillan.

Ellickson, Robert C. 1991. *Order without Law: How Neighbors Settle Disputes*. Cambridge, Mass.: Harvard University Press.

Elster, Jon. 1979. *Ulysses and the Sirens*. Cambridge: Cambridge University Press.

Elster, Jon. 1983. *Explaining Technical Change*. Cambridge: Cambridge University Press.

Elster, Jon. 1985a. *Making Sense of Marx*. Cambridge: Cambridge University Press.

Elster, Jon, ed. 1985b. *The Multiple Self*. Cambridge: Cambridge University Press.

Elster, Jon. 1989. *The Cement of Society*. Cambridge: Cambridge University Press.

Elster, Jon. 1993. Majority rule and individual rights. Pp. 175–216 in Stephen Shute and Susan Hurley, eds., *On Human Rights.* New York: Basic Books.

Elster, Jon, Claus Offe, and Ulrich Preuss. Forthcoming. *Constitutional Politics and Economic Transformation in Post-communist Societies.* Cambridge: Cambridge University Press.

Elsthain, Jean Bethke. 1981. *Public Man, Private Woman.* Princeton, N.J.: Princeton University Press.

Esping-Andersen, Gösta. 1990. *The Three Worlds of Welfare Capitalism.* Oxford: Polity.

Evans, Peter R., Dietrich R. Rueschemeyer, and Theda Skocpol, eds. 1979. *Bringing the State Back In.* Cambridge: Cambridge University Press.

French, Peter A. 1979. The corporation as a moral person. *American Philosophical Quarterly,* 16, 207–15.

Garrett, Geoffrey. 1992. International cooperation and institutional choice: the European Community's internal market. *International Organization,* 46, 532–60.

George, Alexander. 1972. The case for multiple advocacy in making foreign policy. *American Political Science Review,* 66, 751–85.

Gibbard, Allan. 1973. Manipulation of voting schemes: a general result. *Econometrica,* 41, 587–601.

Giddens, Anthony. 1984. *The Constitution of Society.* Oxford: Polity.

Gintis, Herbert. 1972. A radical analysis of welfare economics and individual development. *Quarterly Journal of Economics,* 68, 572–99.

Goffman, Erving. 1970. *Strategic Interaction.* Oxford: Blackwell.

Goodin, Robert E. 1982. *Political Theory and Public Policy.* Chicago: University of Chicago Press.

Goodin, Robert E. 1992. *Motivating Political Morality.* Oxford: Blackwell.

Goodsell, Charles T. 1992. The public administrator as artisan. *Public Administration Review,* 52, 246–53.

Granovetter, Mark. 1985. Economic action and social structure: the problem of embeddedness. *American Journal of Sociology,* 91, 481–510.

Granovetter, Mark. 1992. Economic institutions as social constructions: a framework for analysis. *Acta Sociologica,* 35, 3–11.

Grofman, Bernard, and Donald Wittman, eds. 1989. *The Federalist Papers and the New Institutionalism.* New York: Agathon Press.

Hardin, Russell. 1982a. *Collective Action.* Baltimore: Johns Hopkins University Press.

Hardin, Russell. 1982b. Exchange theory on strategic bases. *Social Science Information,* 21, 251–72.

Hardin, Russell. 1989. Why a constitution? Pp. 100–20 in Bernard Grofman and Donald Wittman, eds., *The Federalist Papers and the New Institutionalism.* New York: Agathon Press.

Hardin, Russell. 1995. *One for All.* Princeton, N.J.: Princeton University Press.

Hart, H. L. A. 1961. *The Concept of Law*. Oxford: Clarendon Press.

Hayek, Friedrich A. 1973. *Law, Legislation and Liberty*. London: Routledge & Kegan Paul.

Hindess, Barry. 1988. *Choice, Rationality and Social Theory*. London: Unwin-Hyman.

Hindess, Barry, and Paul Hirst. 1977. *Mode of Production and Social Formation*. London: Macmillan

Hirst, Paul. 1994. *Associative Democracy*. Oxford: Polity.

Hitch, Charles J. 1958. Economics and military operations research. *Review of Economics & Statistics*, 40, 119–209.

Hitch, Charles J., and Roland N. McKean. 1960. *The Economics of Defense in the Nuclear Age*. Cambridge, Mass.: Harvard University Press.

Homans, George C. 1964. Bringing men back in. *American Sociological Review*, 29, 809–18.

Huntington, Samuel P. 1968. *Political Order in Changing Societies*. New Haven, Conn.: Yale University Press.

Hurwicz, Leonid. 1977. The design of resource allocation mechanisms. Pp. 3–37 in Kenneth J. Arrow and Leonid Hurwicz, eds., *Studies in Resource Allocation Processes*. Cambridge: Cambridge University Press.

Hurwicz, Leonid, David Schmeidler, and Hugo Sonnenschein, eds. 1985. *Social Goals and Social Organization*. Cambridge: Cambridge University Press.

Ingram, Helen, and Anne Schneider. 1988. Improving implementation through policy design: framing smarter statutes. Paper presented to the American Political Science Association annual meetings, Washington, D.C.

Jackman, Robert. 1972. *Politics and Social Equality*. New York: Wiley.

Kaufman, Herbert. 1976. *Are Government Organizations Immortal?* Washington, D.C.: Brookings Institution.

Kaufmann, Franz-Xavier, Giandomenico Majone, and Vincent Ostrom, eds. 1985. *Guidance, Control and Evaluation in the Public Sector*. Berlin: W. de Gruyter.

Keohane, Robert O. 1984. *After Hegemony*. Princeton, N.J.: Princeton University Press.

Keohane, Robert O., and Joseph Nye. 1977. *Power and Interdependence*. Boston: Little, Brown.

Keohane, Robert O., ed. 1986. *Neorealism and Its Critics*. New York: Columbia University Press.

Key, V. O. 1942. *Politics, Parties and Pressure Groups*. New York: Crowell.

Knight, Jack. 1992. *Institutions and Social Conflict*. Cambridge: Cambridge University Press.

Krasner, Stephen D. 1984. Approaches to the state: alternative conceptions and historical dynamics. *Comparative Politics*, 16, 223–46.

Kymlicka, Will. 1989. *Liberalism, Community and Culture*. Oxford: Clarendon Press.

Leontief, Wassily. 1986. *Input–Output Economics.* 2nd ed. New York: Oxford University Press.

Linder, Stephen H., and B. Guy Peters. 1985. From social theory to policy design. *Journal of Public Policy,* 4, 237–59.

Linder, Stephen H., and B. Guy Peters. 1987. A design perspective on policy implementation: the fallacies of misplaced prescription. *Policy Studies Review,* 6, 459–76.

Little, I. M. D., and J. A. Mirrlees. 1974. *Project Planning and Appraisal for Developing Countries.* London: Heinemann.

Lockwood, David. 1964. Social integration and system integration. Pp. 244–57 in George K. Zollschan and Walter Hirsch, eds., *Explorations in Social Change.* London: Routledge.

Luce, R. Duncan, and Howard Raiffa. 1957. *Games and Decisions.* New York: Wiley.

Lukes, Steven. 1973. *Individualism.* Oxford: Blackwell.

Lukes, Steven. 1974. *Power: A Radical View.* London: Macmillan.

Manis, Jerome G., and Bernard N. Meltzer, eds. 1967. *Symbolic Interaction.* Boston: Allyn and Bacon.

Mansbridge, Jane J., ed. 1990. *Beyond Self-interest.* Chicago: University of Chicago Press.

March, James G., and Johan P. Olsen. 1984. The new institutionalism: organizational factors in political life. *American Political Science Review,* 78, 734–49.

March, James G., and Johan P. Olsen. 1989. *Rediscovering Institutions.* New York: Free Press.

Marshall, T. H. 1949. Citizenship and social class. Reprinted pp. 70–134 in Marshall, *Class, Citizenship and Social Development.* Chicago: University of Chicago Press, 1963.

McAfee, R. Preston, and John McMillan. 1987. Auctions and bidding. *Journal of Economic Literature,* 25, 699–738.

McCubbins, Matthew D. 1985. The legislative design of regulatory structure. *American Journal of Political Science,* 29, 721–48.

McKelvey, Richard D. 1979. General conditions for global intransitivities in formal voting models. *Econometrica,* 47, 1085–1112.

Merton, Robert K. 1936. The unintended consequences of purposive social action. *American Sociological Review,* 1, 894-904.

Merton, Robert K. 1957. *Social Theory and Social Structure.* Glencoe, Ill.: Free Press.

Milgrom, Paul R., Douglass C. North, and Barry R. Weingast. 1990. The role of institutions in the revival of trade: the law merchant, private judges and the Champagne fairs. *Economics & Politics,* 2, 1–23.

Moe, Terry M. 1984. The new economics of organization. *American Journal of Political Science,* 28, 739–77.

Moe, Terry M. 1990. Political institutions: the neglected side of the story.

Journal of Law, Economics & Organization, 6S (Supplement), S213–54.

Moe, Terry M. 1991. Politics and the theory of organization. *Journal of Law, Economics & Organization,* 7S (Supplement), S106–29.

Moravcsik, Andrew. 1991. Negotiating the Single European Act: national interests and conventional statecraft in the European Community. *International Organization,* 45, 19–56.

Nagel, Thomas. 1986. *The View from Nowhere.* New York: Oxford University Press.

Nelson, Richard R., and Sidney G. Winter. 1982. *An Evolutionary Theory of Economic Change.* Cambridge, Mass: Harvard University Press.

Niskanen, William A. 1971. *Bureaucracy and Representative Government.* Chicago: Aldine-Atherton.

Nordlinger, Eric A. 1981. *On the Autonomy of the Democratic State.* Cambridge, Mass.: Harvard University Press.

North, Douglass C. 1990. *Institutions, Institutional Change and Economic Performance.* Cambridge: Cambridge University Press.

O'Donnell, Guillermo, Philippe C. Schmitter, and Laurence Whitehead, eds. 1986. *Transitions from Authoritarian Rule.* Baltimore: Johns Hopkins University Press.

Oakeshott, Michael. 1962/1991. *Rationalism in Politics.* New edition. Indianapolis, Ind.: Liberty Press.

Offe, Claus. 1991. Capitalism by democratic design? Democratic theory facing the triple transition in east central Europe. *Social Research,* 58, 865–92.

Offe, Claus, and Ulrich Preuss. 1991. Democratic institutions and moral resources. Pp. 143–71 in David Held, ed., *Political Theory Today.* Oxford: Polity.

Okin, Susan Moller. 1989. *Justice, Gender and the Family.* New York: Basic Books.

Ordeshook, Peter C. 1986. *Games Theory and Political Theory.* Cambridge: Cambridge University Press.

Ordeshook, Peter C. 1992. Constitutional stability. *Constitutional Political Economy,* 3, 137–75.

Orren, Karen. 1991. *Belated Feudalism: Labor, the Law and Liberal Development in the United States.* Cambridge: Cambridge University Press.

Parfit, Derek. 1984. *Reasons and Persons.* Oxford: Clarendon Press.

Parsons, Talcott. 1937. *The Structure of Social Action.* New York: McGraw-Hill.

Parsons, Talcott. 1952. *The Social System.* London: Tavistock.

Parsons, Talcott, and Edward A. Shils, eds. 1951. *Toward a General Theory of Action.* Cambridge, Mass: Harvard University Press.

Pateman, Carole. 1983. Feminist critiques of the public/private dichotomy. Reprinted pp. 118–40 in Pateman, *The Disorder of Women.* Oxford: Polity, 1989.

Perrow, Charles. 1984. *Normal Accidents: Living with High-Risk Technologies.* New York: Basic Books.

Putnam, Robert D. 1993. *Making Democracy Work: Civic Traditions in Modern Italy.* Princeton, N.J.: Princeton University Press.

Ranny, Austin, ed. 1962. *Essays on the Behavioral Study of Politics.* Urbana: University of Illinois Press.

Rawls, John. 1993a. *Political Liberalism.* New York: Columbia University Press.

Rawls, John. 1993b. The law of peoples. Pp. 41–82 in Stephen Shute and Susan Hurley, eds., *On Human Rights.* New York: Basic Books.

Riker, William H. 1980. Implications from the disequilibrium of majority rule for the study of institutions. *American Political Science Review*, 74, 432–46.

Riker, William H. 1983. *Liberalism against Populism.* San Francisco: W. Freeman.

Rivlin, Alice M. 1971. *Systematic Thinking for Social Action.* Washington, D.C.: Brookings Institution.

Roemer, John, ed. 1986. *Analytical Marxism.* Cambridge: Cambridge University Press.

Rorty, Richard. 1989. *Contingency, Irony and Solidarity.* Cambridge: Cambridge University Press.

Ross, Edward Alsworth. 1901. *Social Control.* London: Macmillan.

Ruggie, John G. 1982. International regimes, transactions and change: embedded liberalism in the post-war economic order. *International Organization*, 36, 379–415.

Samuels, Warren J., ed. 1988. *Institutional Economics.* Aldershott: Elgar.

Samuelson, Paul A. 1954. The pure theory of public expenditure. *Review of Economics Statistics,* 36, 387–89.

Sandel, Michael J. 1982. *Liberalism and the Limits of Justice.* Cambridge: Cambridge University Press.

Sandholtz, Wayne, and John Zysman. 1989. 1992: recasting the European bargain. *World Politics,* 42, 95–128.

Satterthwaite, Mark A. 1975. Strategy-proofness and Arrow's conditions. *Journal of Economic Theory,* 10, 187–217.

Satz, Debra, and John Ferejohn. 1994. Rational choice and social theory. *Journal of Philosphy,* 91, 71–87.

Schattschneider, E. E. 1960. *The Semi-sovereign People.* New York: Holt, Rinehart and Winston.

Schelling, Thomas C. 1960. *The Strategy of Conflict.* Cambridge, Mass.: Harvard University Press.

Schneider, Anne, and Helen Ingram. 1988. Systematically pinching ideas: a comparative approach to policy design. *Journal of Public Policy,* 8, 61–80.

Schneider, Anne, and Helen Ingram. 1988a. Improving implementation through policy design: framing smarter statues. Paper presented to the American Political Science Association annual meetings, Washington, D.C.

Schofield, Norman. 1976. Instability of simple dynamic games. *Review of Economic Studies*, 45, 575–94.

Schultze, Charles L. 1977. *The Public Use of Private Interest*. Washington, D.C.: Brookings Institution.

Sen, Amartya. 1977. Rational fools: a critique of the behavioral foundations of economic theory. *Philosophy & Public Affairs*, 6, 317–44.

Sen, Amartya. 1982. *Choice, Welfare and Measurement*. Oxford: Blackwell.

Sen, Amartya. 1993. Internal consistency of choice. *Econometrica*, 61, 495–521.

Shepsle, Kenneth A. 1979. Institutional arrangements and equilibrium in multidimensional voting models. *American Journal of Political Science*, 23, 27–59.

Shepsle, Kenneth A., and Barry Weingast. 1981. Structure-induced equilibrium and legislative choice. *Public Choice*, 37, 503–19.

Simon, Herbert A. 1957. *Administrative Behavior*. 2nd ed. New York: Free Press.

Simon, Herbert A. 1969/1981. *The Sciences of the Artificial*. Cambridge, Mass.: MIT Press.

Skinner, Quentin, ed. 1985. *The Return of Grand Theory in the Human Sciences*. Cambridge: Cambridge University Press.

Skocpol, Theda. 1979. Bringing the state back in: strategies of analysis in current research. Pp. 3–37 in P. R. Evans, D. R. Rueschemeyer, and T. Skocpol, eds., *Bringing the State Back In*. New York: Cambridge University Press.

Skocpol, Theda. 1992. *Protecting Soldiers and Mothers: The Political Origins of Social Policy in the United States*. Cambridge, Mass.: Harvard University Press.

Smith, Rogers M. 1988. Political jurisprudence, the "new institutionalism" and the future of public law. *American Political Science Review*, 82, 89–108.

Snidal, Duncan. 1985. Coordination versus Prisoner's Dilemma: implications for international cooperation and regimes. *American Political Science Review* 79: 923–42.

Soskice, David, Robert H. Bates, and David Epstein. 1992. Ambition and constraint: the stabilizing role of institutions. *Journal of Law, Economics and Organization*, 8, 547–60.

Spencer, Herbert. 1879. *The Principles of Sociology*. London: Williams and Norgate.

Steinmo, Sven, Kathleen Thelen, and Frank Longstreth, eds. 1992. *Structuring Politics: Historical Institutionalism in Comparative Analysis*. New York: Cambridge University Press.

Stepan, Alfred, and Cindy Skach. 1993. Constitutional frameworks and democratic consolidation: parliamentarianism versus presidentialism. *World Politics*, 46, 1–22.

Stigler, George J., and Gary S. Becker. 1977. De gustibus non est disputandum. *American Economic Review*, 67, 76–90.

Streeck, Wolfgang. 1992. Beneficial constraints: on the economic limits of rational voluntarism. Pp. 5–34 in *Transformation Processes in Eastern Europe–Challenges for Socio-economic Theory*. Seminar papers, no. 16. Cracow: Cracow Academy of Economics.

Taylor, Charles. 1989. *Sources of the Self*. Cambridge: Cambridge University Press.

Taylor, Michael. 1987. *The Possibility of Cooperation*. Cambridge: Cambridge University Press.

Tideman, T. Nicolaus, ed. 1977. Special supplement on the demand revealing process. *Public Choice*, vol. 29, no. 2 (supplement).

Tilton, Timothy A. 1990. *The Political Theory of Swedish Social Democracy*. Oxford: Clarendon Press.

Wagner. Peter. 1994. Survey article: dispute, uncertainty and institution in recent French debates. *Journal of Political Philosophy*, 2, 270–89.

Weaver, R. Kent, and Bert A. Rockman, eds. 1993. *Do Institutions Matter? Government Capabilities in the United States and Abroad*. Washington, D.C.: Brookings Institution.

Weingast, Barry R., and William Marshall. 1988. The industrial organization of Congress; or, why legislatures, like firms, are not organized as markets. *Journal of Political Economy*, 96, 132–63.

Weintraub, E. Roy. 1979. *Microfoundations: The Compatibility of Microeconomics and Macroeconomics*. Cambridge: Cambridge University Press.

Weizsäcker, C. C. von 1973. Notes on endogenous change of taste. *Journal of Economic Theory*, 3, 345–72.

Wendt, Alexander E. 1987. The agent-structure problem in international relations theory. *International Organization*, 41, 335–70.

Wildavsky, Aaron. 1979. *Speaking the Truth to Power: The Art and Craft of Policy Analysis*. Boston: Little, Brown.

Williams, Bernard. 1981. *Moral Luck*. Cambridge: Cambridge University Press.

Williamson, Oliver E. 1975. *Markets and Hierarchies*. New York: Free Press.

Williamson, Oliver E. 1981. The modern corporation: origins, evolutions, attributes. *Journal of Economic Literature*, 19, 1537–68.

Williamson, Oliver E. 1985. *The Economic Institutions of Capitalism: Firms, Markets, Relational Contracting*. New York: Free Press.

Williamson, Oliver E., and Sidney G. Winter, eds. 1991. *The Nature of the Firm: Origins, Evolution, and Development*. New York: Oxford University Press.

Wolf, Charles, Jr. 1990. *Markets or Governments*. Cambridge, Mass.: MIT Press.

Wrong, Dennis. 1961. The oversocialized conception of man in modern sociology. *American Sociological Review*, 26, 184–93.

2

Institutional Design and
Rational Choice

PHILIP PETTIT

IN THIS CHAPTER I look at institutional design from the perspective of rational choice theory. I wish to see what principles of institutional design – what principles of broad, social regulation – are supported under the best construal of the rational choice approach.

The project of looking at institutional design from the perspective of rational choice theory will be attractive for those who are disposed to accept the theory. But is it likely to be of any interest for those who reject that theory? I think it is. Rational choice theory is social science by economistic means and, trained as they often are in the discipline of economics, it is very influential among policy theorists and policy-makers. For that reason alone it is of interest to see what lessons the theory teaches – or should teach – for institutional design.

There is also a further consideration. It is common for regulatory theorists to represent the claims of rational choice theory as simple-minded and sectarian and to assume that the lessons of the theory for institutional design are more or less straightforward. But it turns out that the rational choice approach represents quite a sophisticated viewpoint on human behavior, at least if it is given a sympathetic rendering, and that it offers a nuanced perspective on institutional design which fits well with many of the insights of more sociological approaches.[1]

---

[1] I strongly endorse the spirit of the following remark from Ayres and Braithwaite (1992, p. 51). "Much of contemporary social science is a stalemate between theories assuming economic rationality on the part of actors and theories counterposing action as variously motivated by a desire to comply with norms, to maintain a sense of identity, to do good or simply to act out a habituated behavioral sequence. We think robust policy ideas are most likely to be discovered when we pursue areas of convergence between analyses based on *Homo economicus* and those based on *Homo sociologicus*."

54

The theory gives us reason to countenance some principles of institutional design – spelled out in the final section – which ought to be appealing to theorists from a number of different quarters.

2.1 Institutional Design

When I speak of institutional *design* I do not necessarily have in mind the devising, from scratch, of new social arrangements. The phrase certainly covers that case, but it is meant also to apply to the more commonplace project of examining existing arrangements to see if they are satisfactory and of altering them where necessary: the project of re-thinking and reshaping things – perhaps quite modestly – rather than the project of giving them their initial form. Perhaps it would be better to speak of institutional intervention rather than institutional design; certainly I would be happy to do this, if the word is found preferable.

When I speak of *institutional* design I do not envisage the shaping and reshaping of just formal structures: say, of constitutional structures bearing on the organization of parliament or the courts. I use the phrase to cover interventions in any of the arrangements that coordinate the behavior of individuals in society. Those arrangements include constitutionally and legally established procedures, but they also extend to matters of barely conscious convention and norm and to matters that are fixed by only tacitly and perhaps occasionally registered pressures and prospects.

What is institutional design theory for? Who are the potential designers to whom the theory is addressed? The answer, as I see it, is: all of those who have an interest – as, ideally, every democratic citizen has an interest – in how social life is arranged and who are in a position – again, as every democratic citizen should be in a position – to propose changes designed to effect a rearrangement. In every existing society there are, by all lights, a variety of severe problems and all of those who are moved to think about such problems must have an interest in institutional design; the exercise is not elitist in character.

So much by way of informal introduction. Moving to a more analytical level, I see three assumptions that are tied up with the project of institutional design.

1. The behavior of people in society – their individual behavior, their behavior as the agents of corporate bodies, and their behavior in official capacities – is sensitive to the opportunities and the incentives available to them as a result of their social set-up, as it is sensitive to other factors: for example, to the values and represen-

tations and modes of discourse that they inherit, in good part, from their social background.

2. The opportunities and incentives associated with the social set-up can often be varied – they can be institutionally designed – in such a way that there is a variation in the aggregate behavior of the individuals; in particular, they can often be varied with a more determinate or immediate effect on aggregate behavior than can the other factors relevant to what people do.

3. There are some more or less widely accepted criteria of evaluation for determining that certain aggregate patterns of behavior are more desirable than others and that it may be attractive, therefore, to try to promote those patterns by varying the opportunities or incentives of relevant agents: to try to design things institution-ally so that the patterns get established.

The first assumption postulates certain motors, as we might put it, of human behavior, and it identifies some – opportunities and incentives – that are associated, loosely speaking, with the current social set-up. It does not say that these are the only motors there are. On the contrary, it points us to other factors too: the received values of the agents, their received representations of the situations within which they find them-selves, and the received ways of debating about those situations.

The second assumption says that the motors identified are not only motors, they are also levers (Brennan and Pettit 1991). They are factors which can be varied – in an exercise of institutional design – with a view to varying the aggregate behavior of individuals. Notice that other mo-tors of individual behavior, such as the values and representations and discourses mentioned, may not represent institutional levers of this kind. They may not be easily varied and varying them may only gen-erate long-run and relatively indeterminate effects.[2]

The third assumption suggests that there is point to studying the pos-sibilities and effects of varying certain opportunities and incentives: there is point to institutional design. If there were absolutely no con-sensus on matters of value then the exercise would hardly command general interest. It might command everyone's interest, but it would do so in each case for a different reason: because it showed how things might be altered to suit that person's particular tastes. But I take it that there is a good deal of evaluative agreement, even if there is also a great amount of diversity, in societies like ours. I take it, for example, that we

[2]It may even be that the factors involved are susceptible to disruption – see the discussion of the motivating strategy in Section 2.3 – but not, or at least not reliably, to positive shaping.

would all agree on matters like the following: that politicians should be honest, that the police should not cook up cases against people, that jurors should be conscientious, that factory managers should pay attention to industrial safety, and that no one should do injury to an innocent party. There may be very different political philosophies abroad in our societies, but they converge on a variety of such recommendations.

What measures are envisaged in institutional design as instruments for altering the opportunities and incentives of individual agents and, thereby, their aggregate behavior (Brennan and Pettit 1993)? The most obvious instruments are what we describe, broadly, as sanctions. Sanctions operate on the set of options before an agent, making some options more attractive or less attractive than they would have been had the sanctions not been in place; they affect the relevant incentives. Sanctions come in negative and positive forms, as penalties or rewards. The negative sanction will penalize the agent for the failure to choose appropriately; the positive sanction will reward him for the appropriate choice.[3]

Sanctions are clearly in operation when we can identify an intentional, sanctioning agency. In such a case we focus on the situation that would obtain in the absence of the agency and we see the responses of the agency to the doings of the relevant parties as attempts to affect those doings by imposing suitable rewards and penalties. But sanctions, even sanctions of the sort that the institutional designer contemplates, need not involve the presence of any such sanctioning authority. Suppose that there are certain rewards and penalties on offer to agents in a certain sort of situation and that they make a particular type of choice more likely than it would have been in their absence. In any such situation we want to say that there are sanctions in operation. It does not matter if there is no single agent or agency which imposes the rewards and penalties. It does not matter if the rewards and penalties are not imposed intentionally. It does not matter even if they are not imposed by other agents: they may be the effects of natural causes.

Sanctions in this broad sense will usually be recognized by the parties whom they affect, and may be internalized in their deliberations: the parties may reason that the option supported by the sanctions is the one to choose, given the reward it brings with it or the penalty it avoids. But sanctions may also operate without featuring as reasons in this way and without even entering into the consciousness of the agents they

---

[3]It is almost invariably assumed, of course, that sanctions are based on self-interest, so that it is the person himself and not someone else – even someone he cares for – who is penalized or rewarded. I go along with this assumption. Rational choice theory combines with moral intuition to make it compelling.

affect. Suppose that as things stand in a certain situation agents already have reason enough to choose a particular option but that sanctions are introduced, by whatever instrumentality, to support that option. Even if the agents in question do not become aware of the sanctions, still the sanctions may operate to make the choice of that option more secure than it would otherwise have been. They may mean that were the agents' actual reasons to shift away from the option, so that agents began to choose otherwise, then the agents would generally become aware of the reward forgone or the penalty suffered and would be returned to their original choice. Thus sanctions may operate to make the choice of a certain option more secure without figuring explicitly in the agent's deliberations. They may serve to reinforce a certain form of behavior even though they do not help to produce it.

The notion of the sanction is familiar to all of us· in social life. But there is a second sort of control available to the institutional designer that is not so commonly recognized. This is the filter or screen. The sanctions that an institutional designer may introduce take agents and options as given, and try to influence choice by changing the relative desirability of the options for those agents: by affecting their incentives. The screens that a designer may contemplate operate, by contrast, on the set of agents or options. They are meant to ensure that some agents and not others will get to make certain choices or that in certain choices some options and not others will be available; in other words, they are designed to affect opportunities rather than incentives. As sanctions may be negative or positive, serving as penalties or rewards, so screens may also be negative or positive. They may screen out certain agents or options or, perhaps more surprisingly, they may screen in new agents or options: they may empower individuals who were previously not involved, giving them an opportunity to act that they didn't have before, or they may empower the individuals already involved in the relevant situation, putting a new option on the list of alternatives before them.[4]

The screens which operate on individuals will have the effect, under the ideal institutional design, of recruiting to certain tasks those individuals who are more likely – perhaps inherently more likely, perhaps more likely in the context of certain sanctions – to behave in the manner that is socially valued. Appointment and vetting and search procedures, as well as constraints and desiderata on eligibility for office, exemplify screens of the kind that the institutional designer will try to control. Consider, for example, the procedure whereby members of a

[4]My thanks to John Braithwaite for reminding me of the importance of positive screens.

committee are vetted to ensure that they do not have a personal interest – the interest of a friend or foe – in the outcome to be determined by the committee. Or consider the requirement that members of the committee include representatives of certain groups or that the membership be approved by some independent authority or be subject to appeal by interested parties. All of these measures represent obvious screening devices.

But screens can be used to operate on options as well as agents, putting some options on or some options off the list of available alternatives. We may expect to find such screening devices when the availability of an option depends on access – or can be made to depend on access – to certain resources, social or physical, that are determined by factors within the domain which the institutional designer plans. Whether a researcher gets to pursue a certain project often depends on whether any organization is willing to provide the funds and so the project can be blocked by the refusal of funds or facilitated by their supply. Again whether the researcher can pursue the project usually depends – or can be made to depend – on whether the organization to which she belongs is willing to give its permission, and so the project can also be blocked or facilitated by legal as distinct from financial means. It is no surprise, then, that we find people attempting to design things so that projects of a certain kind or quality are favored and so that only projects that meet certain ethical criteria are possible.

In conclusion to this short discussion of institutional design, it may be useful to indicate the range of cases to which institutional design is potentially relevant. The range is enormous but we can taxonomize the cases on two dimensions, if only for mnemonic purposes. Institutional design may be oriented to the prevention of harm or the promotion of good: the distinction is intuitive, and intuitively important, even if it raises some analytical problems. And again institutional design may be directed toward controlling ordinary agents, personal or corporate – in particular, the powerful and the dangerous – or those agents in whom a certain social trust has been invested: those persons and bodies that are charged with certain public duties. The taxonomy looks like this.

	Harm avoidance	Benefit promotion
Private agents	Sec. 2.1.1	Sec. 2.1.2
Public agents	Sec. 2.1.3	Sec. 2.1.4

The best way of indicating the potential range of institutional design may be to take each of the four categories that this taxonomy gives us – they represent the sorts of results which the institutional designer wants to facilitate – and to give some illustrations of each. In each of the cases illustrated, the institutional designer will want to identify the sorts of devices, screening, or sanctioning that can be put in place to improve the existing level of performance. Looking at cases in this way is a little awkward, since it is necessary to select a few examples from a great range of possibilities, and it will undoubtedly also appear naive: many of the examples are so obvious that it is almost embarrassing to mention them. But looking at cases will at least ensure that we have a good concrete sense of the topic under discussion.

2.1.1 Harm Avoidance by Private Agents

The harm envisaged here includes the injuries that you and I can commit, of the kind that the criminal law normally prohibits. But it also includes the damage that can be done by those in positions of power and influence: the misinformation that the media can disseminate; the negligence in matters of industrial safety that factory managers can display; the ecological damage that various firms can cause; and so on. A prime target of institutional design in any society must be the minimization of such harmful conduct: this, through deploying such screens and sanctions that the power of potential harmers is decreased or perhaps – say, through the screening-in of certain options – the power of potential victims increased.

2.1.2 Benefit Promotion by Ordinary Agents

The classical example here may be the provision of blood for transfusion, which Richard Titmuss (1971) discussed. But there are lots of other examples too. They include conscientious voting, at least on some accounts (Brennan and Pettit 1990); the contribution to worthy causes, charitable or cultural; the establishment of trusts and foundations for the promotion of science or art or religious understanding; and the opening of private art collections to public view. We should probably expect the institutional designer, no matter what political philosophy is in the background, to want to facilitate such beneficence.

2.1.3 Harm Avoidance by Public Agents

It is a commonplace that some of those in public office, in particular the politicians and the judges, the military and the police, can often do the most harm of all to the society they serve; their power gives them the opportunity to advance various private interests, often at a severe cost to the community, and it exposes them to great temptation and pressure. Under ideal institutional design, we will look for suitable measures – a suitable pattern of screens and sanctions – to promote a procedurally conscientious and public-spirited performance on the part of such authorities.

2.1.4 Benefit Promotion by Public Agents

Every public trustee has a task to perform, whether or not the trust invested involves the sort of power just discussed. And so it is also a desideratum of institutional design that this should be done well: that the politicians and judges, the military and police, discharge their official duties to good effect; and also that less powerful functionaries acquit themselves in a satisfactory fashion. The category of functionaries will include many in the medical and caring professions, many in teaching and research and, of course, members of the public bureaucracy. But it should be noticed that it will also include many of those who are given temporary functions to discharge: jurors, who serve in one trial only; members of commissions of inquiry into some specific grievance; and, in general, those who serve on committees that are assigned some particular brief of appointment or promotion or adjudication.

2.2 Rational Choice Theory

Rational choice theory can be described, in a phrase I used earlier, as social science by economistic means (Elster 1986a). It amounts to the attempt to pursue the explanation, not just of market behavior, but also of behavior outside the market, in an economistic manner. The idea guiding the approach is that if economics serves us well in the explanation of how agents behave in more or less marketlike contexts, then equally it should serve us well in the explanation of people's behavior in other areas. The approach has been explored under different names. The rational choice explanation of political behavior has been pursued under the name of public choice theory, for example, and the rational choice explanation of social interaction under the name of exchange theory (McLean 1987; Heath 1976). But the idea remains fairly consistently one of applying economic method in the service of explaining behavior, noneconomic as well as economic.

As I understand it, rational choice theory is distinct from the abstract theory of practical rationality that has been developed in areas of research populated by many economists: decision theory, game theory, and social choice theory (Hargreaves-Heap et al. 1992). The decision theorist tries to say, in the abstract, what it is for an agent to be fully rational; thus the Bayesian decision theorist explicates the notion of the rational agent in terms of the agent who maximizes expected utility (Eells 1982). The game theorist tries to identify the solutions that rational agents may be expected to reach, if there are any, in various situations of interdependent decision: in various games, as they are unhappily called (Luce and Raiffa 1957). The social choice theorist tries to identify the preference ordering, and the choice, which a group ought rationally to endorse – if there is one rationally compelling candidate – given various preference orderings among the individuals who make it up (Sen 1970).

Rational choice theory may draw at different points, and in different ways, on these three bodies of more abstract theory. But it is itself a much more concrete and messy exercise. It is focused on actual people in the actual world, not on ideally rational agents. And it is directed to trying to explain and predict the behavior of those people, not to articulating lessons in what is rationally normative for them (see Pettit 1993a, chap. 5; 1993b, forthcoming).

But if rational choice theory is an explanatory and predictive scheme, what are its central postulates? Following Michael Taylor (1988), I take a short remark of John Harsanyi's (1969, p. 524) as a good expression of the content of the theory: "people's behavior can be largely explained in terms of two dominant interests: economic gain and social acceptance" (see also Becker 1976, chap. 1). When Harsanyi speaks of explaining behavior in these terms, he assumes that the behavior is to be explained as something rationally determined or constrained – given the agent's beliefs – by the self-interested concerns in question. What he tells us then is, first, that rational choice theory makes rational sense of people's behavior; second, that it makes rational sense of people's behavior by reference to self-interest; and third, that the self-interest invoked may represent an interest in economic gain or social acceptance. And he tells us this under an umbrella qualification: that the sense made is not necessarily complete; people's behavior is largely explained in the terms suggested, but not explained completely.

The first strand is not going to attract much dissension. If further explication of what is meant by "rational" is required, then decision theory will probably be introduced to fill the bill. If it is not, then we may instead be offered an informal sense of the sort of rationality – the Humean sort of rationality – that decision theory articulates. The sense of rationality in question is roughly this: that an agent's choice is rational just in case it promotes the satisfaction of his desires better than any of the alternatives, according to his way of looking at things; just in case it serves his desires according to his beliefs. This understanding of rationality means, notice, that the rational choice theorist has to make assumptions about the beliefs of any agents whose behavior is to be explained. Those assumptions will not be dictated themselves by rational choice theory – they may be influenced by other theories, even theories of a very different character – but there will be a question as to whether they are rational in the sense of rationality appropriate to beliefs.

The second strand in the Harsanyi formula will attract some objections. It will be said, as many economists say, that rational choice explanation does not have to postulate self-interest: that it can be neutral on what sorts of desires move agents, as decision theory is neutral on this question, and can be guided simply by the thought that there are some desires or preferences at work such that the behavior is the rational attempt to satisfy them. It can go along with the spirit of revealed preference theory, according to which economics can identify in the behavior of agents the very preferences or desires by reference to which it explains that behavior.

There are three points I would make in defense of the Harsanyi invocation of self-interest. The first is that whatever of the theory, the practice of economists and rational choice theorists is to appeal mainly to self-interested desires in trying to explain and predict human behavior.

The second point is that unless economists and rational choice theorists commit themselves to some substantive postulate about the sorts of desires that human behavior generally serves, their project is likely to lose significance. It is always going to be possible to find some desires and some beliefs such that any piece of behavior can be seen as serving those desires according to those beliefs. In fact, if there are no further constraints on the beliefs and desires that may be invoked, it is always going to be possible to find an indefinite variety of belief-desire sets of this kind (Davidson 1984). Thus the explanatory and predictive project of rational choice theory is in jeopardy in the absence of some substantive postulate about people's desires.[5]

The third point that I want to make in support of Harsanyi's introduction of the self-interest postulate makes use – free and unorthodox use – of an observation of Amartya Sen's (1982, part 1). Sen pointed out that while economists often claim to follow the revealed-preference line, in practice they treat the preferences they ascribe to people as if they were self-interested preferences. They do so to the extent that they assume with any preferences ascribed that it is always better for an in-

---

[5]Standard consumer theory assumptions, which fall short of a self-interested model of motivation – though they fit very naturally with the model – do already represent a certain restriction on people's desires; they suggest, for example, that demand curves are downward-sloping, smooth, and concave.

dividual that his preferences be satisfied: better in roughly a utilitarian sense of making for an increase of well-being. This assumption is not warranted with desires that are not self-interested, as is shown by the old story of the boy who finds two apples and gives the smaller one to his friend. The friend complains, saying that he would have given the larger apple to the other boy, if he had been the one to find them. But the other boy responds that if he would have given away the larger apple in that case – if that is indeed his preference – then he has nothing to complain about in this: his preference is fully satisfied, since he does indeed receive the smaller apple.

Let us assume, then, that it is fair to characterize rational choice theory as the view that people's behavior can be largely explained as something rationally determined or constrained by self-interested desires. The last question about Harsanyi's formulation is whether it is also fair to say that self-interested desires should be taken to be desires either for economic gain or for social acceptance.

The category of economic gain certainly includes the procurement of all forms of money and all forms of tradable goods, but it extends further too. It must also include the enjoyment of the services provided by others, even though these are not tradable; the enjoyment of public goods which everyone enjoys if anyone does; and the enjoyment of material goods that no one provides: goods like a nice climate and a beautiful environment. What do all of these have in common? The supply or accessibility of the goods depends on intentional action, one's own or that of others. The goods are distinctively action dependent.

It may be commonly assumed within the rational choice tradition that there are no goods to desire for oneself other than action-dependent goods, so that the assumption that people are self-interested is equated with the assumption that they seek their own economic gain (Holmes 1990). But the category of social acceptance points us toward different sorts of goods: goods that are attitude dependent, in particular goods that depend on the attitudes of others. Action-dependent goods I get by grace of what I or others do. Attitude-dependent goods I get by grace of what I or others think.[6] They include the good of self-esteem, which I enjoy so far as I come to think well of myself. And, more relevant to social acceptance, they include goods like the esteem, or gratitude, or affection of others, which I enjoy so far as those others come to think well or fondly of me.

The idea that social acceptance engages self-interested agents, on a

---

[6]The cleaner dichotomy, as Rae Langton has persuaded me, may be between goods that are attitude dependent and goods – the economic sort – that are not attitude dependent.

par with economic gain, is not novel (Lovejoy 1961, Lecture 5). Despite his association with the economic and rational choice approach, Adam Smith is one of the most outspoken representatives; indeed he sometimes suggests that it is because of a desire for social acceptance that people often seek economic gain. "Nature, when she formed man for society, endowed him with an original desire to please, and an original aversion to offend his brethren. She taught him to feel pleasure in their favourable, and pain in their unfavourable regard. She rendered their approbation most flattering and most agreeable to him for its own sake; and their disapprobation most mortifying and most offensive" (Smith 1982, p. 115).

I propose that we should follow Harsanyi in taking rational choice theory to posit self-interested desires for social acceptance, side by side with self-interested desires for economic gain. Doing so has the disadvantage of making the theory less exact, particularly since no weighting is given as between the two sorts of self-interested desire. But that disadvantage is outweighed by the overwhelming plausibility of the claim that social acceptance as well as economic gain involves people's self-interest.[7]

To take stock then, we have characterized rational choice theory, after John Harsanyi, as the theory that people's behavior can be explained as rationally determined or constrained by certain self-interested concerns: in particular, concerns with economic gain and social acceptance. But now we must turn to the umbrella qualification implicit in the characterization: that people's behavior can at least be partially explained in this way. What can it mean to say that the interests "largely" explain people's behavior, as Harsanyi puts it: this, as distinct from explaining it in some more total fashion? The escape clause signals that rational choice theory leaves some explanatory slack. But what kind of slack can the theory countenance? In answering the question, I shall try to offer

---

[7]An objection. There is clearly going to be no problem in introducing social acceptance, if self-interested agents desire social acceptance quite independently of their desire for economic gain: if both goods are desired for their own sake. But suppose that either good is desired only because it promises more of the other. Suppose for example, as many rational choice theorists may suggest, that social acceptance is desired only because one has a better chance of enjoying certain economic benefits at the hands of others – perhaps in some indefinite future – if one is socially more accepted by them. Doesn't that mean that if we look separately to the economic gain and the social acceptance promised by an option, then we may be double counting: we may be counting twice the economic gains associated with the acceptance? I don't think we need worry about this. Whatever prospective economic gains are associated with an option in virtue of its promise of increased social acceptance, they are unlikely to be counted into our sums independently of our looking at the promise of social acceptance.

an interpretation of rational choice theory that leaves enough slack in place for the theory to be empirically plausible, while not leaving so much that it becomes empirically empty. (Pettit 1993a; forthcoming) The interpretation is entirely my own responsibility, I should say; it is not offered as a paraphrase of what Harsanyi may have had in mind.

There are two sorts of cases for which we need to consider the question. The first is the situation where people often overtly discuss and deliberate about their options – they overtly manage their behavior – in more or less self-interested terms. This situation is exemplified in marketlike contexts. It is a matter of common expectation in such contexts that anyone will be attracted to a certain option just to the extent that it does better for him – usually better in terms of economic gain – than any of the alternatives. The discourse of those contexts, as we may put it, is predominantly a bargaining discourse. If one party recommends an option to another, that is always on the grounds that it does better for the other in self-interested terms than any feasible alternative.

What does it mean to say that human behavior in such marketlike situations can be largely explained in self-interested terms? It means, most plausibly, that the considerations that move people deliberatively to action in such situations are predominantly considerations of self-interest. It may be that every individual is subject in some degree to other considerations than those of self-interest and it may be that some individuals give those nonegocentric reasons quite a large place in their deliberations. But the point is that egocentric considerations play a major part in determining, in aggregate, what people do. And so the theory will predict a change in aggregate behavior on the basis of any change in the self-interested payoffs available to the agents; the theory will make any such comparative-static shift intelligible.

But the question as to what explanatory slack is left by rational choice theory is much more complicated for situations that are not marketlike in character. In most social contexts the discourse in terms of which people deliberate and discuss their options is nonegocentric. People take their decisions and manage their behavior not – or not just – by reference to their own welfare but rather by reference to the welfare of their family, their friends, or one or another body to which they belong. And sometimes they take their decisions and manage their behavior without reference to any welfarist considerations at all. They think about what to do, and come to a conclusion about what to do, in the light of considerations as to what is fair or just, what would be aesthetically pleasing or amusing, what would make a mark or advance understanding, what would be contextually appropriate, and so on. The possibilities are endless.

How can rational choice theory, which invokes only self-interested considerations, hope to explain behavior that is managed and generated – exclusively, as we may suppose – in the light of nonegocentric forms of reflection and justification: in terms of discourses that direct us to the interests of others or discourses that are relatively disinterested (Hindess 1988)? How can it hope to explain this behavior in any part, let alone completely? In other words, how can we find a suitable interpretation here for the qualification that it "largely" or at least partially explains such behavior?

One way of responding to the difficulty would be to deny that people do ever deliberatively manage their decisions – exclusively or otherwise – in nonegocentric terms. But this is not persuasive. Outside the market it is rarely taken as acceptable for agents to reach their decisions on the basis of self-regarding considerations alone. The friend, adviser, or politician who defends certain initiatives on the grounds that they are personally advantageous loses all claim to affection, attention, or respect. And it is unlikely in areas where it is socially unacceptable to choose on the basis of self-regarding considerations that people, nonetheless, make their choices on such grounds. Of course we all recognize that people may sometimes act on considerations that are not socially acceptable: say, that politicians may act with a view to their reelection even when they invoke more high-minded grounds for their policies. But if we are not to take an entirely jaundiced view of human beings, we must think that in many cases people are really attending to the socially acceptable grounds which they invoke in justification of what they do.

A second way of responding to the difficulty is more commonly adopted but is not much more attractive. It would consist in saying that while people outside the market do not deliberate explicitly in self-interested terms, they do so implicitly or unconsciously, and that that is why it is possible to explain their behavior by reference to their self-interest. Gary Becker (1976, p. 7) suggests that he is sympathetic with this point of view: "the economic approach does not assume that decision units are necessarily conscious of their own efforts to maximize or can verbalize or otherwise describe in an informative way reasons for the systematic patterns in their behavior. Thus it is consistent with the emphasis on the subconscious in modern psychology." (See too McCullagh 1991.)

This response may not fly in the face of appearances in the manner of the calculative line, for it does not say that we attend only to self-regarding considerations in managing our behavior. But it requires us to accept a very controversial story about what actually moves us in deliberation and affects the management of our behavior, a story which runs counter to our immediate sense of ourselves and one another. No doubt that story sometimes applies; no doubt the best of us are subject to occasional self-deception about the things that move us. But the idea that the story applies to most of us most of the time is extravagant and implausible. Under this approach, the epistemic cost of coming to accept rational choice theory would surely be too high; it would require too deep a revision of the view we spontaneously take of most human beings.

I wish to offer a third and more plausible way of responding to the difficulty raised and of understanding the qualified nature of rational choice theory as it applies in the relevant contexts (Pettit 1993a, chap. 5; 1993b; forthcoming). This response denies that agents have to deliberate explicitly or implicitly in terms of self-interest in order for rational choice theory to be relevant to their behavior. It holds that rational choice theory will be relevant to the extent that self-interested considerations are virtually present in the deliberations of the agents: virtually, as distinct from actually, present in their management practices.

Self-interested considerations will be virtually present in the deliberations of agents if the following scenario obtains.

1. The agent does what he or she does for certain nonegocentric reasons, so that self-interest has no actual presence, explicit or implicit, in his or her deliberations.
2. But what the agent does is more or less satisfactory – the criterion of satisfactoriness may be a variable – in self-interested terms; it serves self-interest reasonably well.
3. Moreover, if what the agent did as a result of nonegocentric considerations were not satisfactory in this way, then this would cause the agent to begin thinking in self-interested terms and, in all likelihood, to adjust his or her behavior accordingly.

How could the third clause be true? How could it be the case that if an agent's nonegocentrically generated behavior did not serve his or her self-interests satisfactorily, then the agent would begin to rethink what he or she is doing? It would have to be that as the behavior becomes egocentrically unsatisfactory, this registers in the consciousness of the agent, and the red light goes on. Suppose that the behavior is egocentrically satisfactory if and only if it enables the agent to maintain, without special effort, the life-style of those in his or her reference group (Runciman 1972). Were that so, then the fact that the agent was apparently falling behind his or her fellows in certain ways, or the fact that great efforts were apparently necessary in order to keep up, would put on the red light and cause the agent to rethink behavior that is generated in deliberation by nonegocentric considerations: to rethink his or her contributions to charity, scrupulous payment of taxes, generosity to relatives, or whatever.[8]

The best interpretation of rational choice theory for marketlike contexts – the interpretation that keeps it plausible without making it empty – takes the theory to ascribe a partial influence to self-interest in the generation of behavior. The best interpretation of the theory for nonmarket contexts, so I now suggest, takes it to ascribe a virtual influence to self-interest in the shaping of behavior: a virtual influence in the deliberations of all or at least many people. The interpretation requires support from something like the reference group approach, since it needs a story as to when a pattern of behavior will be egocentrically satisfactory: will not put on the red light. I say nothing further on that matter here, assuming only that there is content to the notion of the egocentrically satisfactory.

But is a virtual influence sufficient for explanatory relevance? That self-interest is virtually influential – that it has a virtual presence in people's deliberations – means that it is only a standby cause, not an actual one; it means that it is there, ready to play a causal role if the red light goes on, but that actually it has no causal effect at all. How can self-interest be explanatorily relevant to nonmarket behavior, if actually it plays no role in producing it?

Consider a relevant example. Take the now familiar rational choice explanation as to why slavery remained firmly in place in the South of the United States prior to the Civil War: that it was an economic arrangement which suitably rewarded the plantation holders. The explanation is suggested, for example, in the classic text by Fogel and Engerman (1974, p. 4). "Slavery was not a system irrationally kept in existence by plantation owners who failed to perceive or were indifferent to their best economic interests. The purchase of a slave was generally a highly profitable investment which yielded rates of return that compared favorably with the most outstanding investment opportunities in manufacturing." Suppose that the plantation owners did not actually think much in economic terms about their commitments. Suppose that they stuck to what they did out of mere habit or because of conceiving of those commitments, as some have suggested, in moral, quasi-religious terms. Suppose in other words that economic self-

---

[8]Being virtually self-interested in this sense is compatible, notice, with being also, for example, virtually moralistic: with being such that if the agent's deliberation leads toward certain forms of immoral behavior then other red lights will go on and cause the agent to rethink. Problems will arise with the dispensation envisaged only if there are situations where the agent cannot simultaneously honor the two sorts of constraint.

interest had at most a virtual presence in their deliberations. Can we still invoke such self-interest in explanation of their behavior?

We cannot invoke self-interest to explain why the behavior emerged or was reproduced, if we assume that the behavior was actually managed by habit or by nonegocentric deliberation. But we can introduce self-interest in another, still important explanatory role. We can invoke it to explain why the behavior and the system it generated remained resiliently in place: why there was a robustness about it which enables us to say that even if plantation owners had begun to rethink or revise what they were doing – as some must of course have done – still, the behavior and the system would probably have remained in place. The idea is that given the way it served economic self-interest, any plantation owner who began to change his behavior would have quickly faced a serious downturn in economic fortunes and, in face of that prospect, would have been inclined to return to the status quo. Suppose, to take the contrary possibility, that slaveholding had not been in the economic self-interest of the plantation owners. The implication of the model is that as individual owners randomly or experimentally gave up slaveholding, the fact that they began to fare better than their erstwhile colleagues would probably have given rise to a general exodus from the slaveholding system.

This is enough, I hope, on rational choice theory. The theory is a heuristic or schema of explanation which suggests that self-interest, economic or social, has an important role in the production of human behavior. People often entertain self-interested considerations in their deliberations, as in marketlike contexts, and when they do, such considerations have at least a partial – though no doubt large – influence on their behavior. And when people do not entertain such considerations, when they decide what to do on the basis of other sorts of deliberations, still self-interest has a virtual influence on their decisions; it means in general that their behavior will be at least satisfactory in self-interested terms; their behavior will not flout their self-interest to the point of putting on the red light.

2.3 Rational Institutional Design

If we assume that institutional design has any role to play in human life, then we assume that people in general are not inevitably motivated, absent possible screening or sanctioning initiatives, to comply with the relevant norms of behavior. If they were so motivated, then there would be no point to trying to alter the institutional variables. Indeed it would be positively hazardous to risk any such intervention, for the institutional tinkering might have a negative effect on an already satisfactory level of performance.

Rational choice theory has a ready explanation to offer for why institutional compliance, as we may call it, is not inevitably forthcoming on a spontaneous basis. The preferred explanation is not that people are stupid and don't see that compliance would be for the general good, as we may assume it is. Nor is it that people are liable to such excesses of emotion or passion that they deviate from the institutional norms in a more or less spasmodic way. The explanation that rational choice theory offers – at least as a partial story – is that people's self-interest often dictates noncompliant behavior. The conduct required for the general good is not always the sort of conduct that promotes individual self-interest; on the contrary, it may sometimes require a degree of self-sacrifice.

In making this point rational choice theorists can call upon what game theory has to tell us about the Prisoner's Dilemma. In this dilemma the payoffs are structured so that it is better for each of two prisoners to confess to a joint crime, whether the other confesses or refuses to confess; confessing is an equilibrium outcome from which neither can depart with benefit: more strongly, indeed, it is an outcome from which neither can depart without loss. But despite this fact, it is better for each of the prisoners that both should refuse to confess than that both should confess: joint confession is Pareto-inferior to joint refusal to confess. And so we can see that a form of behavior – joint refusal to confess – can be to the general good without being individually motivating for the self-interested individuals involved.[9]

Given this explanation of noncompliance, what does rational choice theory suggest by way of remedy? What does it suggest in the way of institutional design? There are two general strategies that it might lead us to investigate, depending on whether it focuses in the first place on the fact that with most norms of behavior there are some deviants or noncompliers or on the fact that, while noncompliance does occur, there are also many who comply with any relevant norms or who are at least disposed to comply with them. The first sort of strategy may be described as deviant centered, the second as complier centered. I shall argue that while the first is the more salient possibility, rational choice theory ought to go for the second.

---

[9]It should be noted, for the record, that even altruists can get themselves into a Prisoner's Dilemma (see Parfit 1984; Pettit 1985). Self-interested individuals are individuals whose motivation is agent relative: each seeks a good identified by reference to who he or she is. Altruistic individuals – in particular, perfectly altruistic individuals – may also be motivated in an agent-relative way, and with a Prisoner's Dilemma effect, as each seeks exclusively the good of the other.

2.3.1   The Deviant-Centered Strategy

The deviant-centered strategy begins from the thought that if self-interest leads people – some people, at any rate – away from compliance, then we should make such institutional interventions that ensure that, on the contrary, compliance becomes the self-interested option for such deviants. We should increase people's motivation to comply by rigging the payoffs in favor of compliance. If the expected self-interest score for deviating is X and the expected self-interest score for complying is something less, then we should introduce sanctions which ensure that the balance is redressed, at least in some measure. Institutional design should be guided by the aim of putting such motivators in place as will keep more and more potential deviants on the desired track.

The ideal way to implement the deviant-centered strategy would be to identify the motivator, if any, that is required for each individual and to make sure that it is in place. But of course that custom-built approach is not going to be feasible in our world; we cannot have different sanctions for different individuals. So how then should we proceed with the strategy? The obvious reply is that we should consider the perfectly self-interested individual and put in place sanctions which ensure, at the least, that if such an individual is convicted of deviation, then the sanction will be enough to cause him or her to regret doing what he or she did. I say that we should ensure this "at the least," because the aim of deterring such individuals – deterring them under uncertainty as to whether deviators will be apprehended and convicted – will require even heavier sanctions.

The general idea with the deviant-centered strategy, then, will be to provide more motivation than is necessary for most – certainly, more than would suffice to cause regret in someone convicted – in order to make sure that the motivation is sufficient for all. The idea connects the approach with the knaves strategy that is defended by the likes of Hume and Mandeville. As Hume (1875, pp. 117–18) puts it, in "fixing the several checks and controls of the constitution, every man ought to be supposed a knave, and to have no other end in all his actions than private interest." Or as Mandeville (1731, p. 332) had earlier said, the best sort of constitution is the one which "remains unshaken though most men should prove knaves." The deviant-centered strategy comes down in practice to what is sometimes known as the knaves strategy.

But the deviant-centered strategy is subject to two major difficulties, especially within the perspective on rational choice theory developed in the last section. (See Ayres and Braithwaite 1992; Brennan and Buchanan 1981; Goodin 1992.) One of these is the generic difficulty that if we are to put in place the extreme penalties or rewards that may be required to motivate the knaves – if we put deviant-centered sanctions in place – then we shall need to rely on a centralized system of sanctioning that gives great power to those responsible for centrally administering the sanctions. But if we have to do this, then we are likely to create more problems than we solve. For we shall be faced in a particularly dramatic guise with an age-old challenge. "Quis custodiet costodes?," – Who will guard against the guardians? In particular, who will guard against the guardians who have been given such great powers of penalty and persuasion?

Even if we suppose that this problem can be avoided, however, a second, more specific difficulty presents itself. The difficulty is entailed by three plausible propositions, all of which are predictions of the view – the virtual, rational choice view – presented in the last section.

1. Absent extreme, deviant-centered sanctions, many agents will comply with the relevant patterns of behavior on the basis of a nonegocentric regime of deliberation: compliance will leave them sufficiently well off not to put on the red light and thereby activate egocentric reconsideration of the behavior.
2. An egocentric regime of deliberation would be less likely to generate the same level of compliance among relevant agents: and this, even in the presence of deviant-centered sanctions.
3. But the introduction of deviant-centered sanctions would tend to switch agents from a nonegocentric to an egocentric mode of deliberation.

Conclusion: The introduction of deviant-centered sanctions is likely to do more harm than good.

The first proposition directs us to the fact that in many relevant areas, as discussed in the last section, people conduct themselves in the light of nonegocentric considerations that offer categorical reason for complying with the patterns in question. "Why forgo a holiday to help these people? They are my parents." "Why spend so much time on those exam papers? I have to be fair to the students." "Why go to such a boring meeting? It's expected of members." "Why not steal the watch? I'm not a criminal." I do not mean to suggest that such considerations are always found compelling. And I do not mean to imply that they can be effective in the total absence of supporting sanctions: more on this later. But I do say that often they are the only sorts of considerations that register with people and that they can serve to keep people more or less automatically on the paths to which they point. If there is a single lesson that sociology has taught us – if, indeed, it needed to be learned – then that is that often we do act under the control of nonegocentric, role-related pilots; often we do conform to the profile of *Homo sociolo-*

gicus. Thus, to take a relevant example, it is a widely substantiated view that so far as people avoid crime, they do so because the considerations that guide them make crime unthinkable; they put it off the list of relevant alternatives (Braithwaite 1989).[10]

The second proposition bears on the likely effect on compliance of an increase in egocentric deliberation: in the egocentric management of behavior. The claim is that, even if there are heavy egocentric sanctions that favor compliance, still a regime of egocentric deliberation would generate lower levels of compliance. Here there are two particularly telling considerations. One is that at best egocentric considerations support compliance only conditionally, not categorically. Under a nonegocentric, role-related mode of reasoning, compliance is more or less automatically supported, as we just noted, and the question of whether it is worthwhile complying does not even arise (Durkheim 1961). But under an egocentric regime of deliberation, the question of whether to comply would generally make itself felt. And while the question might often receive a positive answer, the very fact that it arises in every case would make noncompliance a more salient and likely possibility.

The other consideration is that not only do egocentric considerations support compliance only conditionally, one of the conditions for support is that the chance of detection is believed to be appropriately high. This is a particular weakness, since there are so many cases, in all areas of life, where it is possible for the wrongdoer or the nonperformer to avoid detection and where a little reflection – egocentrically focused reflection – ought to make that obvious. If people were directed by an egocentric pattern of deliberation to look in every case to whether noncompliance is likely to be detected, then they would be all too likely to to deviate. The habit of checking on the probability of detection, given that that probability tends to be low, would easily give rise to habits of deviance (Zimring and Hawkins 1973).

The third proposition says that if the deviant-centered strategy were implemented, and if the harsh penalties and high rewards that it would support were put in place, then this would be likely to switch many nonegocentric deliberators to egocentric mode. One way in which it would effect this switch is by putting on the red light, suggesting to

---

[10]Under rational choice theory, as interpreted in the last section, this pattern will be resilient just so far as it is egocentrically satisfactory enough, or apparently satisfactory enough, not to put on the red light: just so far as it appears to serve self-interest appropriately. It is worth noting that, for all that we have said, the pattern may actually serve self-interest better than egocentric deliberation would do; as honesty may be the best policy, so a regime of virtual self-interest may be egocentrically optimific.

people that their established patterns of behavior do not serve them as well as they might. Suppose I find that the salary for my sort of work goes up dramatically or that the penalty for cheating on the sort of tax return that I have to make is drastically increased. One effect of this may be to make me wonder about whether I haven't been selling myself short: whether I haven't been putting in an excessive level of effort at work or ignoring opportunities for tax avoidance that my fellows regularly exploit. Making me wonder about those questions, the new sanctions might make me attentive in a novel degree to the promotion of my own advantage.

But there are other ways too in which the third proposition might be borne out, consistently with the perspective of virtual egocentrism. One is that the introduction of the new sanctions – the high rewards or harsh penalties – might make egocentric considerations salient in a way in which they just weren't salient before, even if they didn't put on the red light, and that they might drive out or marginalize nonegocentric thoughts. Sanctions are all paid in egocentric currency, representing self-interested rewards or penalties. The fact that they are introduced in a given situation can have the effect, in itself, of turning people's minds in an egocentric direction. Economic or social sanctions that are sufficiently high or harsh to motivate the knave may be so high or harsh that they eclipse or undermine other considerations in the deliberations of ordinary agents. Accustomed to think and make their decisions in more or less professional or conscientious terms, for example, such agents may be triggered into thinking in a more self-interested, outcome-centered way by the appearance of the sanctions (Lepper and Greene 1978; Ayres and Braithwaite 1992, pp. 49–51).

A further possibility is that deviant-centered sanctions do not drive out or displace nonegocentric thoughts so much as render those thoughts less gripping. They may do this, so far as they serve for agents as a signal of the attitudes held by others, in particular by authorities. The fact that certain extreme sanctions are introduced for people generally in a given area of behavior suggests an expectation that the relevant agents are so egocentric in their deliberations that they will not comply in the absence of such rewards and penalties. And the projection of such an expectation can be self-fulfilling. It can serve to legitimate the egocentric management of behavior, by representing it as statistically normal, and this legitimation of egocentric deliberation may cause people to become more egocentric in their habits of management. This effect will be reinforced if the sanctions are taken to signal distrust or low regard on the part of those responsible. It requires no great imagination to envisage a situation where someone who is extremely professional and punctilious about levels of performance –

say, about something as trivial as putting in enough time at the office – is led by the imposition of harsh penalties for certain failures – for being late at work – to think in the self-interested mode projected by those penalties. "If they think I'm a self-server, then let them see how a self-server behaves" (Braithwaite and Makkai 1994; see too Williamson 1983).

We have looked so far at three ways in which deviant-centered sanctions may switch nonegocentric agents to an egocentric mode of deliberation. They may put on the red light, they may drive out or marginalize nonegocentric thoughts, or they may signal demoralizing attitudes on the part of others: that is, attitudes that undermine nonegocentric deliberation. These are all effects whereby the sanctions reduce the impact of nonegocentric considerations on otherwise well-disposed agents and there are two more effects of the same kind that we should also notice. Both are signaling effects similar to the last possibility mentioned.

The fourth is the effect whereby agents have their attention directed to the accessibility of the defect option – this may have struck them before as only a marginal possibility – or to some specific ways of defecting. Take the worker who is turned into a clock-watcher by the imposition of harsh penalties for being late to the office. On becoming a clock-watcher, he will not only lose the commitment he had prior to demoralization, he will also be alerted to loopholes for the satisfaction of self-interest that he hitherto ignored: he may begin to discover less and less demanding ways of satisfying or seeming to satisfy the requirements on his time.

The fifth and last effect I wish to mention is the signaling effect whereby complying agents learn from the introduction of deviant-centered sanctions that others are not, or at least have not always been, compliant in the same measure. This information will itself undermine compliance, so far as compliance has a tacitly contractual element: an element of doing one's bit on the understanding that others are doing their bit too (Levi 1987). If the introduction of bigger rewards or tougher penalties signals to a complier that up to now she has been taken for a ride by others – she has been doing more than her bit – then it may cause her to ease off on the efforts she has been making, despite the increased sanctions that have been put in place.

Besides these five effects of reducing the impact on compliers of nonegocentric considerations, the introduction of deviant-centered sanctions may also have certain adverse selectional effects: tougher penalties may put off the spontaneously compliant from entering a certain area of activity – it may reduce the idealistic profile of the activity – and higher rewards may attract into the relevant area egocentrically minded agents who might previously have considered it an inappropriate domain for the likes of them.[11] Assume, to illustrate the rewards effect, that there are some people who are more inclined than others to commit themselves in a wholehearted and deliberative way to the role of doctor or researcher, administrator, or politician. Other things being equal, we may expect such people to be more attracted toward the relevant positions than less suitably disposed individuals. But if we make the rewards attached to those positions relatively high, then other things cease to be equal and we may well find that those attracted to the positions, and those who succeed in getting the positions, include a greater and greater proportion of those not particularly well disposed to internalizing the relevant roles. We may find that the positions come to be filled by a higher and higher number of money seekers and honor hunters. The point is reminiscent of the proposition that Richard Titmuss (1971) emphasized in his defense of blood donation as distinct from the sale of blood: those attracted to donate may be a better bet as a source of healthy blood than those attracted or driven to sell.

I hope that the various effects discussed here will be found fairly plausible. It is easy to see how the effects might materialize across a variety of areas of social and institutional life, under the imposition of deviant-centered penalties. We can see how a person who abides unthinkingly with the criminal law might cease to see the law as something with which he or she identifies and might begin to look for strategic opportunities to flout it (Braithwaite and Pettit 1992). We can see how the politician who is given the self-image of someone untrustworthy – so hemmed in is the politician by regulations and threats – might begin to live up to that image, seeking out occasions to advance his or her own interests. We can see how the researcher who is badgered and alienated by an officious ethics committee might come to be less conscientious than hitherto in adhering to ethical principles (Pettit 1992). And we can see how the factory or restaurant manager might take the position of adversary of inspectors – an adversary bent on winning some rounds – if the rule of the inspectorate is too draconian (see Bardach and Kagan 1982 and Ayres and Braithwaite 1992 for other illustrations).

The spread of our various effects can be illustrated also with reference to high rewards rather than harsh penalties. Here is an example from the area of scientific or scholarly research. The normal inclination of the dedicated researcher is to invest his energy in problems that interest him or that look intellectually promising. This may be disrupted by high rewards and may give way to a tendency to be strategic and speculative

---

[11]Here I am grateful for discussions with Geoffrey Brennan. See Brennan and Pettit 1991.

about what projects are taken on. An investment market of the kind associated with traditional research may be replaced by a market that is speculative in character. A market in which each goes in the direction that is intellectually attractive, without more than cursory attention to prices – in effect, to self-interested rewards – may give way to a market in which each tries to go in the direction that, as things now seem, will earn the highest prices later on. The distracting prices or rewards may be economic, as each tries to get into the area, for example, that funding agencies are likely to favor. Or the distracting rewards may be social, as each seeks to be ahead of the herd in espousing ideas that promise to become fashionable and to earn public attention and applause. Paris intellectual culture, at least as it has often been parodied, may constitute a speculative market of this latter kind: a speculative market, dominated by anticipations of where the herd will go, as distinct from the investment market represented by more traditional scholars.

So much for our three propositions and the difficulty they entail for the deviant-centered strategy of institutional design. I realize that none of the propositions has been established here; they all make more or less vulnerable empirical claims. But the very fact that the difficulty they point us toward is a real possibility should raise doubts about proceeding with the deviant-centered strategy. It should lead us to ask whether there is any other strategy that might avoid the difficulty. I turn now to consider an alternative that would seem to do so.

2.3.2 The Complier-Centered Strategy

The deviant-centred strategy is driven by the need to deal with the knave: that is, with the most explicitly self-interested person around. The complier-centered strategy is driven by the need to deal with a more ordinary sort of individual: someone who deliberates in most contexts in a nonegocentric way and who is self-interested only in the manner associated with the virtual presence of self-interest. The idea is that institutional design should look in the first place to building on the positive dispositions of this sort of person and only consider in the second place how to cope with those who are more explicitly self-interested. It should build to strength, looking for the means to stabilize compliant dispositions, and only look later at how to compensate for weakness: how to guard against the problems to which the deliberative regimen of self-interest can give rise.

Kant was pessimistic about whether anything quite straight could be made out of the crooked timber of humanity. Even if his pessimism is well placed, it should be clear that we are more likely to approximate straightness with some samples of the human timber than with others.

The complier-centered strategy takes that lesson to heart, arguing that we should fix our attention on the better or more pliable samples and only later worry about how to keep the particularly crooked pieces in position. I described the first strategy as the deviant-centered strategy, because it is driven by the assumption that compliance primarily requires the provision of extra motivational resources to control the deviants or knaves. I describe the second strategy as the complier-centered strategy, because the assumption here is that the first requirement for compliance is not to disturb the deliberative or management practices that keep compliers or nonknaves on track.

I will present the complier-centered strategy in three principles. The first says that possibilities of screening should be explored prior to considering the options for sanctioning; the second that the sanctioning devices introduced should be, so far as possible, supportive of nonegocentric deliberation; and the third that the sanctioning devices should also be motivationally effective.

2.3.3 First Principle: Screen before Sanctioning

The first principle is that in institutional design we should look at possibilities of screening before we investigate sanctioning prospects. The principle is supported by our reflections on the problems to which excessive sanctions, be they penalties or rewards, can give rise. If the population of agents relevant in a given piece of institutional design can be screened so that those who appear there are generally not deliberatively moved by self-interest – they are inclined to deliberate about their choices in whatever currency is contextually appropriate to the choice on hand – then it may be possible to ensure the desired degree of compliance without resort to heavy and hazardous sanctions. Again if the damaging options relevant in a piece of institutional design can be taken off the list of alternatives, or more attractive, suitable options put on the list, then it may be possible to induce people to act appropriately without such sanctioning interventions. Of course screening opportunities will not always be available and, even when they are, they may be too costly to be really feasible. But if they are available, and if they are really feasible, then the first principle says that institutional designers should try to exploit them.

The more commonly recognized screening device is the agent-centered one that tries to vet the individuals relevant in a given setting. A good example is the procedure whereby the members of a jury are vetted, so as to ensure that no friends or enemies of the accused, and no one prejudiced for or against him, is included in the group. If we are dealing with such a screened group of people, then we can be fairly optimistic that they will conform to the norm of trying conscientiously to determine whether the evidence establishes guilt beyond reasonable doubt. If we are not, then all sorts of dangers present themselves and it may seem that only a draconian form of sanctioning – with all the attendant difficulties discussed earlier – can offer any hope of keeping the jurors in line.

How to screen a group will be determined in good part by the sorts of motors – including the sorts of sanctions – that we expect to influence the agents in question. Suppose we hope that jurors will generally be moved by the value of conscientious deliberation, with the virtual voice of self-interest quietened, and that if they are not, then they will be sanctioned by the disapproval that is likely to be aroused in others by a more cavalier approach (Pettit 1993a; Brennan and Pettit 1993). In this case, we will not just screen for the elimination of anyone with a special interest in the outcome. We will also try to ensure that there is a mixed group of jurors, so that it is really a cavalier attitude that attracts disapproval and really conscientiousness that wins approbation; we will try to screen in appropriate jurors. If the group of jurors is of a similar background, and if a certain judgment in respect of the accused would generally be expected from someone of that background, then there may be more approval to be won by conforming to that expectation than there is by being conscientious.

The second screening possibility is to screen for options rather than agents. Such screening may occur via the funding or authorizing body, via the operation of rules or criteria of eligibility, or in a number of other less obvious ways. The ethics committee plays a screening role relative to certain sorts of research. The rule that no one can be president of the United States for three consecutive terms plays a similar role relative to certain political projects. And other devices exercise the same sort of function in yet other areas. Consider, for example, the balance-of-powers device, which requires that any measure of law must be approved by each of two or more bodies: two or more bodies that represent quite opposed interests. This ensures that there is a screening against any options that deeply harm or offend one of those interests.

These are all examples of arrangements for screening out certain options. But the screening-in of various options also represents a salient possibility for institutional design. Consider arrangements whereby people are given resources for whistle-blowing on certain authorities or, more generally, resources for lodging complaints and appeals; these represent devices for screening-in options on the part of ordinary folk that should serve as important controls on the behavior of authorities (Peters and Branch 1972; McCubbins and Schwartz 1984). The principle involved points us toward a range of other possible examples of the same effect. Consider all the arrangements, for example, whereby ordinary people are protected against interference or exploitation by ensuring that certain options remain available to them: the option of legal representation, via legal aid; the option of entering hospital, via Medicare; the option of learning what influenced some official decision, via freedom of information laws; and so on.

Like agent screening, option screening would allow us to avoid recourse to excessive sanctions. It would seem to be the merest common sense, given the line of argument pursued against the deviant-centered strategy, to explore all such measures of screening fully before looking to what sanctions are necessary.

James Madison gives expression to the spirit of our first principle when he writes in Federalist Paper no. 57: "the aim of every political constitution is or ought to be first to obtain for rulers men who possess most wisdom to discern, and most virtue to pursue the common good of the society; and in the next place, to take the most effectual precautions for keeping them virtuous, whilst they continue to hold their public trust" (Wills 1982, p. 289). The first principle implements what Morton White sees as Madison's guiding idea in institutional design: that we should take the different motivation of different individuals and groups as given and then try to allocate opportunity to motivation in the manner that best promotes the common good (White 1987).

2.3.4 Second Principle: Sanction, but in a Deliberatively Supportive Way

So much then for the proposition that in institutional design we should look to screening initiatives prior to making any sanctioning interventions. The second principle that I associate with the compliercentered strategy is that we should look for sanctioning as well as screening devices but, in particular, for sanctioning devices that are deliberatively supportive. By deliberatively supportive sanctions in any area, I mean sanctions that tend to reinforce the sort of deliberative habits which constitute or produce the desired behavior.

Given the importance of screening, does it enable us to avoid sanctions completely in our design of institutions? It could do so in the unlikely event of putting all damaging choices off the list of available alternatives or putting all dangerous individuals out of the court of agents. But could it do so in more run-of-the-mill situations, where there is always some room for noncompliance? I do not think so. Two considerations show us, from within the perspective of rational choice theory, that it is always going to remain necessary to rely on sanctioning as well as screening devices.

The first consideration is this. Even though certain agents are disposed to deliberate in a fashion that reliably generates the behavior desired in some context, the absence of any sanctions – any interest-based sanctions – against behaving otherwise may lead him away from that path. Consider the story of the ring of Gyges, the story in which we are asked to imagine whether we would remain committed to virtue even if we possessed a ring that made us invisible and that enabled us to resort with impunity to more vicious ways. The absence of sanctions envisaged in this story is what makes it so plausible that even a very virtuous agent could be corrupted. The absence of sanctions in the purely screening dispensation which we are asked to envisage should equally give us pause about endorsing the proposal in question. It can be true both that an agent ignores existing sanctions in finding reason to adopt a certain desired form of behavior and that the absence of those sanctions would cause him to depart from that course of conduct. The point will be obvious under our virtual model of self-interest. The absence of any sanctions would make it salient that there is an alternative form of behavior under which self-interest is better served – it would put on the red light – and, that being salient, it is all too possible that the agent will be attracted toward noncompliance (Braithwaite and Pettit 1990, pp. 139–40).

There is a second reason why we should resort to sanctions as well as screens and it also commands attention within the sort of rational choice perspective that we have adopted. Suppose that a certain agent is deliberatively led to adopt a certain form of desired behavior in a context where all sanctions that support that behavior have been removed. Even if the absence of sanctions does not lead the agent to wonder whether to advance his or her self-interest by deviation, it may lead the agent to wonder whether others will continue to do their part. The absence of sanctions may mean that the agent loses any sense of assurance about this and that the futility of making a solo contribution – such a contribution will be futile in many cases – leads the person to depart from the original path. The point is reinforced by the recollection of Chester Bowles, a commercial regulator in the United States during World War II: 20% of firms would comply unconditionally with any rule, 5% would attempt to evade it, and the remaining 75% would tend to comply, provided – and only provided – the deviant 5% were exposed to a credible threat of apprehension and punishment (Bardach and Kagan 1982, pp. 65–66; see too Levi 1987).

But if sanctioning devices of some kind are necessary, the second proposition insists that they should be deliberatively supportive in character. I argued earlier that high rewards and harsh penalties can activate self-interested deliberation on the part of agents who would otherwise be guided by nonegocentric considerations – considerations, we may assume, that would support compliance – and that in doing this, it can lead agents toward noncompliance. The lesson of that argument is that institutional design should try to avoid the high rewards and harsh penalties that are likely to have such a deliberatively disruptive effect. It should seek out sanctions that tend to retain and even reinforce nonegocentric deliberation.

Our discussion of the ways in which deviant-centered sanctions can disrupt nonegocentric deliberation gives us constraints that sanctions should satisfy. Whether they are rewards or penalties, the sanctions should be quantitatively and qualitatively such that conditions like the following are avoided.

1. The sanctions put on the red light for agents, presenting their actual situation under compliance as egocentrically unsatisfactory.
2. The sanctions marginalize or drive out nonegocentric thoughts: they rivet the attention of agents on more self-regarding concerns.
3. The sanctions render nonegocentric thoughts less gripping by suggesting to agents that others, in particular others in authority, think badly of them or distrust them.
4. The sanctions direct the attention of agents to possibilities of noncompliance that may never have struck them previously.
5. The sanctions suggest to some agents that others have not been doing their bit and that they are bearing the burdens of compliance without the support of others.
6. The sanctions have selective effects whereby the naturally less compliant are attracted into the relevant area or the naturally more compliant driven out.

The best way of showing how sanctions can be deliberatively supportive, and can avoid conditions like those listed, may be to go to an example. Take any committee where the desired pattern of behavior is conscientious voting. Suppose that we have vetted the body in question, so that ideally no one has a special interest in the outcome; and suppose that we have ensured that the doings of the committee are confidential, so that no one is particularly moved by fear of those with such an interest. These screening moves make it likely that most members of the committee will spontaneously apply themselves to the brief before them and seek to make a conscientious decision: that, with the voice of self-interest dampened, people will display the contextually relevant sort of nonegocentric deliberation that ensures conscientious voting.

What sorts of sanctions might be supportive of this pattern of deliberation? It is the custom with any committee that the chair will call on members to declare their inclinations and to defend them to others. Assume that when the members defend themselves, they must do so in terms that do not depend for their appeal on holding a particular, sectional perspective: this, because the committee is not stacked in favor of any such perspective. Unless members can give a good justification of how they are inclined to vote – a justification that is persuasive across different perspectives – they will lose face with the others; they will look silly or prejudiced. Thus we can see that in the situation described there are sanctions at work that can be expected to keep in line anyone who is inclined to stray: for example, anyone who is impatient of the time given to the meeting and who announces his views in a peremptory fashion (Brennan and Pettit 1990, 1993).

The approval-based sanctions in play here offer a good example of sanctions that support the deliberation which will normally produce the desired result. If someone expects to lose face by any deviation from serious reasoning, or to gain face by successful efforts in that direction, the observation should not tend to disrupt the deliberation and discoursing in question. On the contrary, if the person is moved by the sanction in question and is sensible about how best to achieve the relevant reward and avoid the penalty, then he or she should embrace the practice that earns those results. The person should not be led, for example, to focus explicitly on the good regard of others, seeking it by whatever means available, in a process of egocentric deliberation. Doing that would likely lead to being detected, and the surest way of losing the regard of others is to present oneself as someone who is actively seeking it. "The general axiom in this domain," as Jon Elster (1983, p.66) says, "is that nothing is so unimpressive as behavior designed to impress."[12]

The sort of sanction at work in the committee case is of a kind that can in principle be mobilized in any forum where there is a debate to be conducted and a collective decision to be made. It may be the sanction to which Jürgen Habermas looks – perhaps with too much optimism – as he envisages the effects of the ideal speech situation. He imagines that as different parties come to present reasons for and against different options, they will be obliged to argue in nonsectional terms of the kind that can appeal to anyone; and that as they do this, they will tend more and more to internalize the habit and become truly detached, senatorial contributors to the debate (Elster 1986b; Pettit 1982; Goodin 1992, chap. 7). One reason that they may be obliged to

---

[12]In this case, then, the way to maximize on the self-interest involved may be to avoid egocentrically deliberating in terms of the interest; it may be to keep the self-interest virtual. See footnote 8.

argue in these terms – even if they are not spontaneously inclined to do so – is that otherwise they cannot enjoy the acceptance and approval of their colleagues in the forum.

Short of recourse to the discursive sanctioning envisaged here – and that sort of sanctioning may not often be available – there are other ways of trying to ensure that the sanctions deployed in institutional design are supportive of suitable deliberation. Consider, for example, the sanctions envisaged in systems of criminal law. These have traditionally been very unsupportive, at least in Western countries, of the more or less moralistic deliberation that keeps most of us on the right side of the law (Braithwaite 1989). But there is no reason in principle why the criminal law should not begin to explore possibilities of sanctioning that have a reprobative aspect and that tend to support the deliberation that keeps most people on track. John Braithwaite and I argued in this vein for recourse to "the socialising institution, which seeks to bring home to people the shamefulness of crime and thereby induce in them, not just the behavioural dispositions, but the deliberative habits of the virtuous citizen" (Braithwaite and Pettit 1990, pp. 88–89).

2.3.5. Third Principle: Structure Sanctions to Cope with Occasional Knaves

We have seen that under the complier-centered strategy of institutional design, rational choice theory would recommend that screening options should be investigated prior to possibilities of sanctioning and that, so far as possible, sanctioning interventions should be supportive of suitable deliberation. However there is one further and more or less obvious lesson that rational choice teaches. This is that since there are liable to be explicitly self-interested agents present in any area of social life, it is important in the institutional design of that area that we put in place sanctions that are motivationally effective for such people: sanctions that are sufficient to motivate the knaves on whom Mandeville and Hume and their successors concentrate.

The complier-centered idea, as represented in the first two recommendations, is that in institutional design we should try to ensure that people are reinforced in a pattern of behavior that they have independent, deliberative reasons to adopt; we should do this, rather than trying to motivate them, as if from scratch, to adopt that pattern. The principle that we now add comes of the recognition that this idea may not apply well to some people: it may not apply to the knaves who are more or less explicitly and exclusively self-interested in their deliberations and who lack independent inclinations to behave in the manner for which we want to plan.

But the principle raises a problem. The sanctions that we introduce in support of the deliberation of nonknaves will not generally be appropriate to the control of knaves. So what are we to do? How are we to ensure that even knaves can be motivated? No system is going to be wholly satisfactory, to be sure; knaves will never be contained completely. But any system of sanctioning that is worthy of consideration must put some restraints on those who are independently inclined to be noncompliant. It must be able to reduce the potential damage that deviants can do and it must be able to reassure compliers that their efforts are not undermined, exploited or derided by those of a different cast.

The problem is pressing for someone who follows the complier-centered strategy. It appears that any sanctions that are suited to motivate knaves are likely to be disruptive of the deliberation that keeps most people on track. So what then are we to recommend? Is there any way of putting institutional motivators in place that won't disturb the habits of the majority?

John Braithwaite has elaborated an approach to sanctioning that gives us an answer to this question. The idea is that sanctions, in particular penalties, can be devised in an escalating hierarchy. At the lowest level, we find sanctions that apply to everyone and that are ideally supportive of deliberation. But if the sanctions at that level prove incapable of keeping someone in line – if the person is found to breach the relevant regulation and proves to be something of a knave – then sanctions are invoked at a higher, more severe level. The process can go on for a number of stages, advancing up a hierarchy toward what Braithwaite likes to describe as the big stick or the big gun (Ayres and Braithwaite 1992).

In the absence of this proposal for imposing sanctions in an escalating hierarchy, it would be hard to uphold the complier-centered strategy that I have described. The system envisaged in the first two principles would seem to be fatally vulnerable to the damage that a knave could do. It could scarcely recommend itself to rational choice theorists, whatever the demerits of the alternative, deviant-centered strategy. But with the escalation proposal in hand, I think that we can be reasonably sanguine about the complier-centered strategy. We can keep our focus on ordinary individuals, as that strategy recommends, while having a clear conscience about the provisions for dealing with knavish outliers.

I hope that the considerations mustered in this last section show why the complier-centered strategy in institutional design ought to be much more attractive to rational choice theorists than the more traditional, deviant-centered strategy: than the strategy, in effect, of designing a world fit for knaves. The complier-centered strategy neatly avoids a problem to which the deviant-centered strategy gives rise and, on balance, it looks to be far the better option. But in conclusion there is a last question I would like to signal. I said that there were two problems with the deviant-centered strategy. One is that it would tend to undermine spontaneous compliance and the other – a more generic difficulty – is that it exacerbates the problem of guarding against the guardians, providing assurance against the assurers. The complier-centered strategy is explicitly designed to deal with the problem of undermining compliance. But how does it do in regard to the other issue?

It certainly does not exacerbate the difficulty in the manner of the deviant-centered strategy, for it does not call for any particularly heavy centralized sanctioning and does not need to empower any group of officials excessively. On the contrary, in this regard as in regard to the problem of undermining spontaneous compliance, the complier-centered strategy directs us to ways beyond the difficulty; it points us toward a variety of measures by which we might hope to keep the guardians on track. The strategy suggests that we should look in the first place to screening measures: to measures of screening for individuals and of screening for options. And it suggests that there may be ways of sanctioning any individuals empowered that would reinforce the sorts of deliberations we look for in public officials; in particular, there may be ways of doing this that can also allow for escalating the sanctions applied to those who prove themselves unsuitable candidates for such reinforcement. But I must leave the suggestions unexplored in any further measure. Here, as on so many other matters in the paper, there is scope for a great deal more reflection and research.[13]

References

Ayres, Ian, and John Braithwaite. 1992. *Responsive Regulation.* New York: Oxford University Press.

Bardach, Eugene, and Robert A. Kagan. 1982. *Going by the Book: The Problem of Regulatory Unreasonableness.* Philadephia: Temple University Press.

Becker, Gary. 1976. *The Economic Approach to Human Behavior.* Chicago: University of Chicago Press.

Braithwaite, John. 1989. *Crime, Shame and Reintegration.* Cambridge: Cambridge University Press.

Braithwaite, John, and Philip Pettit. 1990. *Not Just Deserts: A Republican Theory of Criminal Justice.* Oxford: Oxford University Press.

[13]My thanks to the participants at two workshops where this material was discussed: one in the ANU, Dec 1992, the other in Cerisy, Normandy, June 1993. I should particularly acknowledge helpful comments received from John Braithwaite, Geoffrey Brennan, Peter Drahos, John Ferejohn, Bob Goodin, Claus Offe, and an anonymous referee.

Braithwaite, John, and Toni Makkai. 1994. Trust and compliance. *Policing and Society*, 4, 1–12.

Brennan, Geoffrey, and James Buchanan. 1981. The normative purpose of economic "science": rediscovery of an eighteenth century method. *International Review of Law and Economics*, 1, 155–66.

Brennan, Geoffrey, and Philip Pettit. 1990. Unveiling the vote. *British Journal of Political Science*, 20, 311–33.

Brennan, Geoffrey, and Philip Pettit. 1991. Modelling and motivating academic performance. *Australian Universities' Review*, 34, 4–9.

Brennan, Geoffrey, and Philip Pettit. 1993. Hands invisible and intangible. *Synthese*, 94, 191–225.

Buchanan, James. 1975. *The Limits of Liberty*. Chicago: University of Chicago Press.

Davidson, Donald. 1984. *Inquiries into Truth and Interpretation*. Oxford: Oxford University Press.

Durkheim, Émile. 1961. *Moral Education: A Study in the Theory and Application of the Sociology of Education*, trans. E. K. Wilson and H. Schnurer. New York: Free Press.

Eells, Ellery. 1982. *Rational Decision and Causality*. Cambridge: Cambridge University Press.

Elster, Jon. 1983. *Sour Grapes*. Cambridge: Cambridge University Press.

Elster, Jon, ed. 1986a. *Rational Choice*. Oxford: Blackwell.

Elster, Jon. 1986b. The market and the forum: three varieties of political theory. Pp. 103–28 in *Foundations of Social Choice Theory*, ed. J. Elster and A. Hylland. Cambridge: Cambridge University Press.

Fogel, Robert W., and Stanley L. Engerman 1974. *Time on the Cross: The Economics of American Negro Slavery*. Boston: Little, Brown.

Goodin, Robert E. 1992. *Motivating Political Morality*. Oxford: Blackwell.

Hargreaves-Heap, Shaun; Martin Hollis; Bruce Lyons; Robert Sugden; and Albert Weale. 1992. *The Theory of Choice*. Oxford: Blackwell.

Harsanyi, John. 1969. Rational choice models of behavior versus functionalist and conformist theories. *World Politics*, 22, 513–38.

Heath, Anthony. 1976. *Rational Choice and Social Exchange*. Cambridge: Cambridge University Press.

Hindess, Barry. 1988. *Choice, Rationality and Social Theory*. London: Unwin Hyman.

Holmes, Stephen. 1990. The secret history of self-interest. Pp. 267–86 in *Beyond Self-interest*, ed. Jane J. Mansbridge. Chicago: University of Chicago Press.

Hume, David. 1875. Of the independence of Parliament. Vol. 3 in *Philosophical Works*, ed. T. H. Green and T. H. Grose. London.

Lepper, M. R. and D. Greene. 1978. *The Hidden Costs of Reward*. Hillsdale, N.J.: Erlbaum.

Levi, Margaret. 1987. *Of Rules and Revenue*. Berkeley: University of California Press.

Lovejoy, Arthur O. 1961. *Reflections on Human Nature*. Baltimore: Johns Hopkins University Press.

Luce, R. D., and Howard Raiffa. 1957. *Games and Decisions*. New York: Wiley.

Mandeville, Bernard. 1731. *Free Thoughts on Religion, the Church and National Happiness*. 3rd ed. London.

McCubbins, Matthew D., and Thomas Schwartz. 1984. Congressional oversight overlooked: police patrols vs. fire alarms. *American Journal of Political Science*, 28, 165–79.

McCullagh, C. Behan. 1991. How objective interests explain action. *Social Science Information*, 30, 29–54.

McLean, Iain. 1987. *Public Choice: An Introduction*. Oxford: Blackwell.

Parfit, Derek. 1984. *Reasons and Persons*. Oxford: Oxford University Press.

Peters, Charles, and Taylor Branch. 1972. *Blowing the Whistle: Dissent in the Public Interest*. New York: Praeger.

Pettit, Philip. 1982. Habermas on truth and justice. Pp. 207–28 in *Marx and Marxisms*, ed. G. H. R. Parkinson. Cambridge: Cambridge University Press.

Pettit, Philip. 1985. The Prisoner's Dilemma and social theory: an overview of some issues. *Politics*, 20, 1–11.

Pettit, Philip. 1992. Instituting a research ethic: chilling and cautionary tales. Academy of Social Sciences Annual Lecture, 1991, University House, Canberra. Reprinted, with slight amendments, in *Bioethics*, 6 (1992), 89–112 and *Bioethics News*, 11 (No. 4) (1992).

Pettit, Philip. 1993a. *The Common Mind: An Essay on Psychology, Society and Politics*. New York: Oxford University Press.

Pettit, Philip. 1993b. Normes et choix rationnels. *Reseaux*, No. 62, pp. 87–112.

Pettit, Philip. Forthcoming. The virtual reality of *Homo economicus*. *Monist*.

Runciman, W. G. 1972. *Relative Deprivation and Social Justice*. Harmondsworth, England: Penguin.

Sen, Amartya. 1970. *Collective Choice and Social Welfare*. Edinburgh: Oliver & Boyd.

Sen, Amartya. 1982. *Choice, Welfare and Measurement*. Oxford: Blackwell.

Smith, Adam. 1982. *The Theory of the Moral Sentiments*, ed. D. D. Raphael and A. L. Macfie. Indianapolis, Ind.: Liberty.

Taylor, Michael. 1988. Rationality and collective action. In *Rationality and Revolution*, ed. Michael Taylor. Cambridge: Cambridge University Press.

Titmuss, Richard. 1971. *The Gift Relationship*. London: Allen & Unwin.

White, Morton. 1987. *Philosophy, the Federalist, and the Constitution*. New York: Oxford University Press.

Williamson, Oliver E. 1983. Credible commitments: using hostages to support exchange. *American Economic Review*, 71, 519–40.

Wills, Garry, ed. 1982. *The Federalist Papers*. New York: Bantam Books.

Zimring, Franklin E., and Gordon J. Hawkins. 1973. *Deterrence: The Legal Threat in Crime Control*. Chicago: University of Chicago Press.

3

Second Best Theories and the Implications for Institutional Design

BRUCE TALBOT CORAM

3.1 Introduction

Social theorists have recently given considerable attention to the problem of designing institutions which ensure that individuals seeking their own interests maximize welfare or serve the interests of some principal, such as the government.[1] By institutions is meant the rules that cover such things as decision-making procedures, property transfers, bargaining processes, or voting schemes. So far, however, very little attention has been given to some of the implications of problems of the second best for institutional design.[2] Such problems concern the optimal policy when all the conditions required for a first best solution are not present. They are well known in the literature on welfare economics (Mishan 1981; Ng 1983; Bos and Seidel 1986).[3] The main point of interest in this literature is that, contrary to our intuitions, when the conditions required for a first best do not apply in one sector of the economy, the next best solution may not be to get all other sectors as close as possible to the conditions that were required for a first best solution. It may be better to have all other sectors also deviate from the

I am grateful to Bob Goodin for suggestions on the argument and for drawing out the implications of this paper. I am also grateful to an anonymous referee for the series.

[1] The question of rules is dealt with at the general level by Brennan and Buchanan (1985).

[2] The one exception seems to be Goodin 1995, which relates problems of second best to the question of the appropriate ends for institutions and political practice. For a discussion of some game theory problems in the design of institutions and control mechanisms see Binmore and Dasgupta 1986, Kreps 1990, and Nurmi 1993.

[3] For a brief history of the second best, see Streissler and Neudeck 1986.

first best settings (Lipsey and Lancaster 1956),[4] moreover, in ways that are difficult to predict (Mishan 1981). The purpose of this chapter is to explore some of the more general implications of this aspect of the second best. It is particularly concerned with the question of whether, in political institutions, it can be assumed that small changes in initial conditions or rules can be ignored.

The importance of the question of the relation between conditions and consequences is that, if small changes always have small consequences, then it is safe to borrow off-the-shelf institutional solutions from other places.[5] In addition, small changes in the conditions under which, say, a constitution was drafted can be accommodated by tinkering with the original document. On the other hand, if small changes do not always have small consequences, then institutional borrowing without due regard to this possibility may be dangerous. Moreover, radical alterations in institutions may be required to accommodate small shifts in initial conditions.

It will be argued here that, especially in the case of political and legal institutions, slight deviations in initial conditions may cause the second best to depart radically from the first best. As a consequence it is suggested that thinking about some familiar problems in terms of second best may help in avoiding a number of pitfalls in institutional design. In particular, it is suggested that one of the most desirable characteristic of institutions may be robustness against small changes in conditions. This is a preliminary inquiry into these questions and does not consider a number of issues, such as that of the appropriate measure of a best result.

3.2 The General Problem of the Second Best

Second best considerations affect both the ends that institutions might pursue and the institutions and rules that are designed to pursue these ends. The implication of the question of ends for ideals in political philosophy has been considered by Goodin (1995). The problem here is that of what is to be done when the conditions desired in the ideal state of the world cannot be met in every dimension simultaneously. Examples are provided by Sen's (1970) argument about the impossibility

---

[4]Technically, the deviation from the conditions required for the first best result in an optimization problem with additional constraints. The solution of this problem with additional constraints may not be close to the previous solution. The widespread use of this notion in economics depended on the application of the Lagrangian approach.

[5]I owe this expression of the problem to Bob Goodin.

of being a Paretian liberal, or Arrow's (1963) impossibility theorem. In these cases the question is that of the deviations from first best outcomes that might result from attempting to pursue ideals that cannot be simultaneously attained. The question of the institutions that might be set up in pursuit of some end involves problems like designing a set of voting rules to ensure that politicians act in the public interest, or agents such as the military or politicians or lawyers or taxpayers act in a way that brings about a desired result, or designing an enforcement mechanism to avoid excessive pollution. The end might be stability, or peace, or legislation that is responsive to the wishes of the population. In this case the problem is that of what is to be done when all the conditions or rules required for a first best institution cannot be attained simultaneously. It is this problem of institutional design that is of concern in this chapter.

The difficulty of applying the notion of first and second best to problems in the design of institution lies in choosing an appropriate standard for the first best. In the literature in economics on the second best, the first best is often taken to be a model of optimization under perfect conditions. In other words, it is what could occur in the absence of impediments like imperfect information, or the existence of interest groups or unions.[6] Second best problems are thus first best optimization problems with the addition of some extra constraints. Although this notion of a perfect world might make sense if a perfect market is taken as the starting point, it is less useful for broader social institutions.[7] In such cases, a more flexible interpretation might be required.

The most natural application of the first best in the cases of nonmarket institutions would be to use it to refer to the set of rules being used for the model of the best arrangement. The model might, for example, be either an idealized version of an institution that is successful in a different society or setting or some actual institution that has been successful. Alternatively, it might be a simplified model of mechanisms and outcomes that has been constructed under certain assumptions about information or preference revelation. In either of these cases, the first best is being used in the more general sense of an ideal, or benchmark, or unit of comparison, that has to be specified for each case.[8] This

---

[6]See Wickstrom 1986 for the assumption that the existence of interest groups constitute a departure from the first best.

[7]It may not even be appropriate in the context of markets. In particular, it is not clear that endogenous constraints imposed by the maximizing behavior of individuals should be treated as a deviation from first best conditions. For a discussion see Streissler and Neudeck 1986.

[8]The question of optimality in institutions is obviously being fudged for the purpose of this discussion since first best only means the model that is used as the basis

benchmark allows us to think in terms of optimization and variations in constraints. One benefit of thinking in these terms is that it links the debate about political institutions to well-known theorems and techniques in economics. In addition, it retains the possibility of applying optimization theory to manageable subsets of the problem being considered.

The advantage of using an approach in terms of the language of the second best can be illustrated with the following example. Problems of institutional change are often thought of, and debated, in terms of radical and conservative positions. In caricature these positions look something like this: The conservative position is that, if change is necessary, it should consist of small departures from what is known or proven elsewhere. Underlying this is the notion that smaller changes involve much less uncertainty than larger changes. The radical approach is more comfortable with large-scale changes or departures from existing institutions.

In contrast, what the theory of the second best suggests is that the problem of choosing an appropriate set of rules to achieve some desired outcome should be approached in a somewhat different manner. Since departure from any one condition in the institution used for the model means that all the other conditions may not be desirable, it is not clear whether the optimum choice is to get as close to the original as possible, or to construct a completely different institution. It also follows that, if the rules are changed in one respect, it may not be desirable to maintain them in all other respects. Further, it is not necessarily the case that the extent of the deviations in initial conditions gives a good guide. A large deviation might be benign, whereas a small deviation might be such as to bring about large changes in the outcome.

It follows that the presentation of the problem in terms of the second best does not fit into either a conservative or a radical approach to institutional change. If the effect of deviations in conditions may lead to large differences in outcomes, institutional design is intrinsically difficult. This may seem to be grist for the conservative mill. But, if small changes in initial conditions may lead to large differences in outcomes, it is also the case that there is no argument for favoring incremental to more radical approaches.

The general feeling among welfare economists, and the one that seems to accord with our intuitions, is that problems of the second best

---

for the design. This does not preclude that the second best may produce results that are in some sense "better" than the first best. Similarly, the second best in welfare economics may produce results that are in some non-Paretian sense better than the first best. These are important problems, but are somewhat tangential to the main point.

in markets will not, in the normal course of events, require extreme deviations. That is to say, when there is a deviation from the first best condition, the second best will only involve nonradical adjustments to get something like a near first best outcome (Rowley and Peacock 1975, p. 21; Mishan 1981, p. 112).[9] This is not necessarily the case for other types of institution, however. Game theorists seem to have been particularly aware of the potential of small changes in things like information to have a large effect on outcomes. There is already a large and growing literature on problems of mechanism and institution design that implicitly recognizes this tendency for outcomes to be jumpy (Kreps 1990; Nurmi 1993). Nonetheless, the broader implications of this tendency have not been widely discussed.

In order to think about the implications of the theory of the second best more systematically, it is useful to identify two sorts of mistakes that might be made about the consequences of changes in either initial conditions or rules. They are:

> *i. The fallacy of continuity.* This is the idea that similar initial conditions will give similar results. In mathematics continuity roughly means that, if a function of x, say $f(x)$, is continuous, then two points close to each other are mapped close to each other. In other words, small changes in the xs do not lead to big jumps in the output, the $f(x)$s. In this case f can be thought of as the rules and x as the conditions. Thus a rules function f would map conditions into outcomes. It would be continuous if, by analogy, small changes in the initial conditions did not cause large changes in the output.
> *ii. The fallacy of stretchability.* This is the idea that rules can be stretched and that small changes in the rules will lead to small changes in the results. A set of rules or an institution, say parliamentary democracy or a voting system, could be thought of as stretchy if small changes in the rules did not cause jumps in the output.

It is probably the assumption of continuity that is the most common and the most appealing of these errors. It gets some of its impetus from the tendency in much of neoclassical economics to work with continuous functions which have the property of mapping small changes into small changes. It implies that the same institution will work where conditions are almost the same. Stretchability has a similar intuitive appeal, but applies to the rules rather than the conditions. It has obvious connections with the usual conservative position. It implies that institutions that look somewhat the same will produce results that look somewhat the

---

[9]Rowley and Peacock (1975) argued long ago that welfare economists make this assumption, and the recent book on welfare economics by Johansson (1991), for example, does not mention second best problems.

same. Thus, a small or incremental change in the rules should not cause outcomes to deviate very much from established patterns.

In order to illustrate these possibilities, some examples are given. The first three cover the case where payoffs are sensitive to initial conditions. The third is of rules that do not stretch.

3.3 Some Examples

The following examples are made as transparent as possible by keeping them at the level of simple toy models. Insofar as some of these toy mechanisms appear in real-world processes the examples suggest, but do not prove, that the condition they indicate might also appear.

3.3.1   Case 1: Sensitivity to Initial Conditions or Continuity

The first case is where the rules do not change, but slight changes in the initial conditions lead to large changes in output. In other words, the mapping is discontinuous. The three examples that will be considered here are a voting game, a bargaining game, and a dynamic system. The first two have been chosen because they are familiar from other analyses. They are thus useful for illustrating the second best implications of some well-known material.

I. VOTING. The most well-known cases where the same rules might give quite different outcomes with changes in initial conditions are those found in the literature on voting. In order to begin, this will be illustrated in its simplest form. To do this, consider an example of the sequence in which votes are taken in a committee or a legislature. This is covered in most public choice textbooks. All that is needed here is the simple Condorcet paradox. Similar results extend to more general cases, but are not necessary to make the point. It goes as follows.

Consider a voting system in which there are three voters and the majority wins. The preferences are listed from top to bottom for the voters 1, 2, and 3 and outcomes x, y, and z. The outcomes can be as distinct as you wish. They might be war, peace, and surrender, or communism, social democracy, and laissez-faire.

1	2	3
x	y	z
y	z	x
z	x	y

The logic here is straightforward. Let $x > y$ stand for "x defeats y." In any contest between two possibilities the ordering is $x > y$, $y > z$, and $z > x$. It is easy to see that if the sequence starts at x the outcome is z. If it starts at y the outcome is x and if at z the outcome is y.

In this case, variations in the starting point for a round of voting are exogenous to the system and might be considered small with reference to the differences in the outcomes. This simple idea extends to any number of more complex cases where voting or collective choice mechanisms have equilibria that are sensitive to exogenous initial conditions. Obvious illustrations would be variations in the costs of coalition formation or party financing.

II. BARGAINING. To see that the sorts of changes in outcomes just analyzed are not confined to voting systems, consider a bargaining game in which two players are bargaining over some fixed amount of money. Let this be s and be, say, one million dollars. The players are rational. Each round in the bargain costs the players something. This is so for two reasons. The first is that it is assumed that players discount their future returns. The second is that the bargaining process might be costly. Maybe the players have to organize, or travel, or hire lawyers, or pay to have contracts printed, or make telephone calls.

To emphasize the point about discontinuities, the cost of bargaining will be the only factor considered. Discounting might also be taken into account by assuming that it imposes a constant fixed cost. Consider a Rubinstein bargaining game in which one player makes an offer, and the other accepts or rejects. If she rejects, she then makes an offer and it is the first players turn to accept or reject, and so on.

Suppose that it costs player two slightly more than player one for each round of the game, say two cents. For example, it might cost the first player one cent per offer and second player three cents. Imagine that player one makes the first offer. Let the payoffs to players one and two be v_1 and v_2. In this case the outcome is

$$v_1 = s$$
$$v_2 = 0$$

That is, player one proposes that she gets the million dollars and player two gets nothing, and player two accepts. This result is proven by Rubinstein (1982). It can be illustrated in an informal manner as follows. Each round of the game costs player one a and player two b, where $a < b$. Player one offers player two $v_2 = 0$. If player two rejects this offer, she must offer player one $v_1 = s - a - a + \varepsilon$, where ε is small or player one will reject the offer. This is because it only costs player one an amount a to wait until the next round where she can offer

$v_2 = 0$ in order to get $s - 2a$. If player one accepts player two gets $v_2 = -b - \varepsilon + a < 0$. Hence player one should accept the first offer.

Imagine that the costs are altered, so that it costs player one more than player two. Now $v_1 = 0$ and $v_2 = s$.

It follows that slight changes in the condition of the bargainers might make major changes to the outcome for the parties, even though the bargaining rules remain the same. In this case, the only change required to reverse the outcome was a two-cent shift in the cost of bargaining.

III. DYNAMIC SYSTEMS. The problem of noncontinuity can be explored for a more general case by considering a dynamic process. Once more the point is to illustrate the way in which small deviations from an initial position may cause cumulative changes in outcomes. Although the following analysis is quite general, it is given some context by telling a story about the dynamics of fund-raising and expenditure on elections by political parties. In this case it is supposed that there are two societies that have the same institutions and organizations but differ slightly in their starting point. Each society wishes to hold expenditure to some acceptable level.

The rules are that political parties are free to raise any sum of money they wish, maybe through tax-assisted organizations like political action committees (PACs), and government reduces the assistance as the total amount of expenditure increases. It is assumed that the expenditure of each party will increase as the expenditure of the opposition party increases. Let x stand for the level of expenditure of party 1 and y for the level of expenditure of party 2. x' and y' stand for the rate of change in this expenditure. This gives a system of linear differential equations for each society that looks like this:

$$x' = -ax + by + c$$
$$y' = gx - hy + k$$

In these equations, the terms a, b, c, g, h, and k are constants, with a, b, g, h positive (c and k may be positive or negative). Since each party increases expenditure as the opponent does, we have $+b$ and $+g$. The rate of expenditure might be expected to slow as the level increased, so we have $-a$ and $-h$. The constants c and k indicate the strength of political division. If the society is deeply divided, individuals will contribute, and parties will spend, large amounts. In this case c and k will be positive. It will be seen that the higher the values of c and k the faster the rate of increase in expenditure. If the society is reasonably homogeneous, and the stakes in victory are low, c and k may be negative.

Now, the question is, what effect will small changes in conditions have on the outcomes. Imagine that, in the first society there is a great

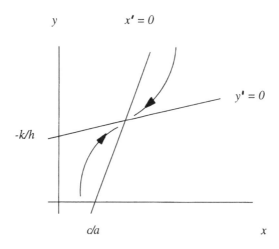

Figure 3.1. A stable dynamic system.

deal of political division and c and k are positive. In this case, it is easy to prove that the outcome looks something like Figure 3.1.

What is important in this case is that, regardless of the initial levels of fund-raising and expenditure, the institution produces a stable outcome since there is a tendency to converge on some equilibrium point.

Now consider society 2. In this case political divisions are slight and the tendency to raise funds and spend money is less. c and k are negative. In this case it is easy to prove that the rules do not produce a stable dynamic. One possibility is something like Figure 3.2.

If we assume that the stable equilibrium for society 1 is the first best, in the sense that this is the outcome to be emulated, it can be seen that the same institutions in society 2 produce very different results. This toy example also illustrates the point that the deviations are not easy to predict. It would have been more natural to predict less stability in society 1, where political divisions were greater.

3.3.2. Case 2: Rules That Are Not Stretchy

The case where initial conditions stay the same and slight changes in the rules bring about jumps in the outcome is now considered. This is where the rules cannot be stretched. The illustration is of voting to give another perspective on the more general social choice problem considered in case 1. It shows that an institution almost like the insti-

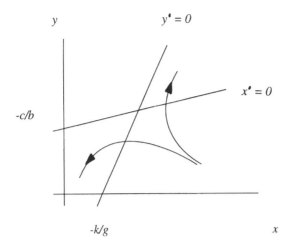

Figure 3.2. An unstable dynamic system.

tution being copied may not give almost like results. Hence there are some dangers in what appear to be slight modifications.

Consider the following pirates' game. In this game pirates have some treasure to divide among themselves, and it is decided that this should be done by vote. The captain is asked to propose a rule. She suggests the following procedure. The pirates are ranked in order from the captain down. The lowest starts, then the next lowest, and so on through to the captain. Each pirate offers a division. If it is not accepted by everyone, this pirate is thrown overboard. The next pirate then makes an offer. A pirate will vote for a proposal that makes her no worse off than the next alternative.

If this voting procedure were adopted, the lowest pirate would propose that the captain gets all the treasure and everyone would accept. To see this, start with the last pirate and work forward.[10]

The pirates are asked to accept or reject the procedure, and they reject it. The question is, what is the captain's second best proposal?

One proposal that seems as close as possible to the first proposal, or first best, is that the division must be accepted by all the pirates except one. However, if this rule is adopted, the lowest pirate would propose

---

[10]Imagine two pirates. In this case the first must propose that all the treasure be given to the second, or the second will not agree and the first is thrown overboard. Now imagine three pirates, and so on.

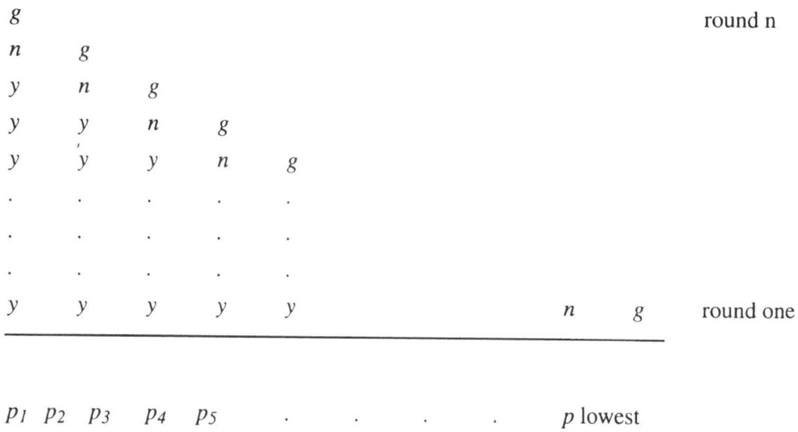

```
g                                                              round n
n    g
y    n    g
y    y    n    g
y    y    y    n    g
.    .    .    .    .
.    .    .    .    .
.    .    .    .    .
y    y    y    y    y                        n    g        round one
```

```
p1   p2   p3   p4   p5    .    .    .    .        p lowest
```

Figure 3.3. Pirates' voting game.

that she be given all the treasure and everyone would accept. This can be proven as follows.

Start with the case of two remaining pirates. Call the treasure g and number the pirates $p_1, p_2, \ldots, p_n$. The captain is p_1. Then p_2 proposes a division $(0, g)$ which does not require p_1's vote. Hence p_2 gets g and p_1 gets zero. For three pirates p_3 proposes $(0, 0, g)$. p_2 might oppose this but p_1 would accept, because she is no worse off. For four, p_4 proposes $(0, 0, 0, 4)$. p_1 and p_2 accept, because they can do no better on the next round. This continues for any number of pirates. Let n stand for an opposing vote and y or g be a vote for that proposal, where g also indicates the voter who gets the good. Then, counting backwards from the captain, the voting pattern looks like Figure 3.3. In this diagram the top line shows how the captain would vote in the last round, if it were reached. The second line shows how the captain and the remaining pirates would vote, and so on.

In the same manner, it can be shown that, for any other voting procedure in which half or more of the pirates must accept the proposal, the lowest pirate gets all the treasure. Thus the captain's second best is not to get as close to the first best as possible. In this case it is to deviate considerably. For example, she might propose any of the preceding procedures and reverse the order in which the offers are made.

A real-life example of the consequences of small changes in rules is given by the results of what was seen as a technical change to the electoral system for the Australian Senate. The shift was from plurality to proportional voting.[11] This had major consequences such as increasing the bargaining power of small parties and independent senators, altering the conduct of parliamentary business and shifting control of the legislative agenda. It also altered the organization of committees and the pattern of regional representation (Sharman 1986).

3.4 Conclusion

The examples presented here have illustrated some implications of thinking about institutional design in terms of the second best problem. They have suggested that small deviations from the conditions, or structure, of the first best, or whatever model is being used, may be extreme in the case of political institutions. The most important implication of this is that it may not be prudent to borrow institutions from similar contexts without considering this possibility. Another is that small changes in conditions might make institutions that were optimal no longer so. Further the alterations necessary to restore optimality may require large deviations from the previous set of rules. As with the pirates game, the conservative injunction to make small changes may not be good advice. What the dynamic model suggests is that it may be the case that the most desirable attribute of an institution is stability. That is, rather than seek optimality for some set of static conditions, it may be better to design institutions with outcomes that either converge to some desirable equilibrium or remain in some near vicinity of a desirable equilibrium when the conditions are perturbed. Such institutions are most likely to safeguard against suboptimalities that may otherwise result from inevitable changes in circumstances.

Since these problems may occur in a large variety of different institutional settings, there is no single design rule that is likely to emerge from considerations of second best. This does not mean, however, that all discussion is forced back into the position that the world is complex and very little can be done. What it does mean is that there is a need to systematically investigate the possibilities of small perturbations mapping into large consequences. This possibility is, no doubt, considered in an ad hoc way in comparative analyses and historical studies. What may be required is for these approaches to be supplemented with more formal analyses directed specifically at this prospect.

References
Arrow, Kenneth J. 1963. *Social Choice and Individual Values*. 2nd ed. New York: Wiley.

[11]I am grateful to Campbell Sharman for this example.

Binmore, Ken, and Partha Dasgupta. 1986. *Economic Organizations as Games*. Oxford: Basil Blackwell.

Bos, Dieter, and Christian Seidl, eds. 1986. *Welfare Economics and the Second Best*. New York: Springer-Verlag.

Brennan Geoffrey, and James Buchanan. 1985. *The Reason of Rules*. Cambridge: Cambridge University Press.

Goodin, Robert E. 1995. Political ideals and political practice. *British Journal of Political Science* 25: 37-56.

Johansson, Per-Olov. 1991. *An Introduction to Welfare Economics*. Cambridge: Cambridge University Press.

Kreps, David. 1990. *A Course in Microeconomic Theory*. Princeton, N.J.: Princeton University Press.

Lipsey, Richard, and Kelvin Lancaster. 1956. The general theory of second best. *Review of Economic Studies* 24: 11–33.

Mishan, Ezra. 1981. *Introduction to Welfare Economics*. Oxford: Oxford University Press.

Ng, Yew-Kwang. 1983. *Welfare Economics*. London: Macmillan.

Nurmi, Hannu. 1993. Problems in the theory of institutional design. *Journal of Theoretical Politics* 5: 523-40.

Rowley, Charles, and Alan Peacock. 1975. *Welfare Economics*. London: Martin Robertson.

Rubinstein, Ariel. 1982. Perfect equilibrium in a bargaining model. *Econometrica* 50: 97-109.

Sen, Amartya. 1970. The impossibility of a Paretian liberal. *Journal of Political Economy*, 78: 152–7.

Sharman, Campbell. 1986. The Senate, small parties and the balance of power. *Politics* 21: 20-31.

Streissler, Erich, and Werner Neudeck. 1986. Are there intellectual precursors to the idea of second best optimization? In Dieter Bos and Christian Seidl, eds., *Welfare Economics and the Second Best*. New York: Springer-Verlag.

Wickstrom, Bengt-Arne. 1986. Transfers, collective goods and redistribution. In Dieter Bos and Christian Seidl, eds., *Welfare Economics and the Second Best*. New York: Springer-Verlag.

4

The Informal Logic of
Institutional Design

JOHN S. DRYZEK

WHEN ASSESSING or contemplating interventions in processes of institutional design we should attend closely to the way these interventions reinforce, reshape, or undermine particular discourses. This is what I mean by the informal aspect of institutional design. A discourse is a framework for apprehending the world embedded in language, enabling its adherents to put together diverse bits of sensory information into coherent wholes. These adherents therefore share assumptions and capabilities, which they will typically take for granted, often unaware even of the possibility of alternatives to them.

"Discourse" in this sense was popularized by Michel Foucault, who made a career out of exposing contingency and discontinuity in discourses about criminality, insanity, illness, sex, and so forth. To Foucault, individuals are largely the creations of the discourses which they engage, and so generally incapable of rational choices across discourses. A Foucauldian commitment to the general impenetrability and hegemony of discourses implies scornful dismissal of the idea of institutional design, on the grounds that any such project would either perpetuate old kinds of repression, or at best institute new ones. Foucault himself softened the severity of these commitments toward the end of his life. Here, I will depart from a Foucauldian position to suggest that while discourses do indeed exist, they are rarely hegemonic, that more than one discourse is normally available in any particular setting, that they are only partially incommensurable, that they are open to informed scrutiny and reconstruction at the margins, and that rational choices across them can indeed be made.

Society's discourses are intertwined with its institutions. If, as Goodin suggests in his introduction to this volume, institutions are meta-behavioral entities featuring continuity, longevity, and stable contexts

103

for action; or if they are, in Philip Pettit's words, "arrangements that coordinate the behavior of individuals in society"; or if they are, as Talcott Parsons defined them, sets of regulatory norms; then discourses and institutions have much in common. No institution can operate without an associated and supportive discourse (or discourses).

Discourses may best be treated as institutional software. Institutional hardware exists in the form of rules, rights, operating procedures, customs, and principles. Given that this hardware generally exists at a conscious level of awareness, it is unsurprising that this is where institutional analysts and designers have concentrated their attention. The discourses which constitute institutional software are more often taken for granted – until they are uncovered by discourse analysts.

To illustrate this distinction, consider recent attempts to introduce the institutions of a capitalist market in Eastern Europe. This introduction has run into difficulties in large measure because people simply do not know what to make of these institutions, or what it means to behave as an instrumentally rational, maximizing market actor. In other words, the hardware of the capitalist market lacks a supportive discourse. In the discourse of the capitalist West, people who accumulate personal wealth are entrepreneurs; in the popular discourse of Russia, they are mafia.

In a context like that in Eastern Europe (or for that matter Thatcher's Britain in the 1980s), institutional designers can press ahead and hope that recalcitrant discourses will eventually follow. But this is a recipe for dictatorship. Moreover, it might not work; there is no simple and unidirectional causality from institutions to discourses, as the experience of the imposition of Soviet institutions upon Eastern Europe should have made clear. Institutional interventions can have all kinds of effects in their interactions with the prevailing constellation of discourses.

These effects are not beyond comprehension or analysis. In this essay I argue that institutional design is largely a matter of reshaping the constellation of discourses in society. I shall explore some systematic methods for the analysis of this constellation, and for identifying alternatives to presently dominant discourses and any institutional status quo which they support (though, as Eastern Europe again demonstrates, disjuncture between dominant discourses and institutional status quo is also possible). These methods are political discourse analysis, essentially a set of procedures for laying bare the elements of discourses, and Q methodology, an approach to the study of human subjectivity which can be deployed in the empirical identification and scrutiny of discourses.

4.1   Formal and Informal Logics

I shall, then, suggest that the informal aspects of institutional design can be approached systematically – so there is some logic involved. But it is not a formal design logic, by which I mean one which possesses three characteristics. First, it embodies a single fixed paradigm of personhood, or what it means to be a human being. Second, it treats interactions among persons as governed by explicit rules. Such rules need not be legal prescriptions in any sense, but they must be amenable to unambiguous statement. Third, its methodology is deductive; it reaches conclusions, especially institutional prescriptions, by deducing how its persons will act under particular systems of rules. Empirical evidence can be adduced here, but deduction is the core.

Many formal approaches will embody a single social scientific frame of reference, though more theoretically eclectic formalisms can and do exist. Examples of formal approaches include microeconomics (and its offshoots such as public choice), Darwinism (as it appears in biopolitics and sociobiology), traditional Weberian organizational theory (which would cover Soviet-style approaches to planning too), the "Benthamite, deductive, geometric method" for the design of social welfare delivery systems whose demise is celebrated by Klein in this volume,[1] behaviorist psychology (especially as deployed by B. F. Skinner), cybernetics, and (more speculatively) "maternalist" feminism. I add the last to underscore the fact that it is not quantification or a commitment to hard (phallocentric) science that defines the formal category.[2]

I will argue that formal approaches fail to recognize the real multiplicity of discourses surrounding any complex institutional setting. They focus on institutional hardware and ignore discursive software. Unwarranted simplification often means that the interventions they prescribe produce surprising effects when inserted in the interplay of competing discourses. At a minimum, my intent is to warn formalists about discursive pitfalls. More positively, I want to advocate an informal logic of institutional design as an alternative to misplaced formalism.

[1] Klein takes the quote from Letwin (1965).
[2] Strictly speaking, maternalism counterposes one formalism to another. Maternalists (for example, Ruddick 1980; Gilligan 1982) postulate a model of female personhood defined by a concern for the concrete needs of particular individuals, as opposed to liberalism's emphasis on the general rights of abstract individuals. Maternalists have generally emphasized the criticism of institutions such as markets and liberal politics that embody models of man, and have spent less time on developing the constructive institutional implications of their model of woman. But their favored institutions would presumably feature face-to-face interaction in small scale settings, though such interactions could be matriarchal as easily as they could be democratic (Dietz 1985).

In terms of the three dimensions I used to characterize formal approaches, an informal approach to institutional design may be characterized as follows. First, it allows multiple dimensions of human subjectivity (which cannot be subsumed as "preferences" under a paradigm of instrumental rationality). Second, it can tolerate extensive ambiguity in interactions among persons and the rules that govern interactions. Third, its methodological commitments can be elastic, though I shall suggest they may be subsumed most fruitfully under the heading of critique: the idea that we seek the new world through criticism of the old.[3]

At first sight, the informal approach might seem like nothing more than a vernacular domain of common sense, everyday talk, and at best journalistic analysis. Professional social scientists are often dismissive of such efforts as belonging to a prescientific past; so, for example, Riker (1982, p. 753) in advocating a particular formalism (though not in a design context) refers scathingly to the "belles lettres" practiced by political scientists who do not share his methodological dispositions. However, when it comes to design, there may be much to be said for everyday, nonscientific knowledge. Charles Lindblom has argued at length (e.g., Lindblom and Cohen 1979; Lindblom 1990) in favor of "ordinary knowledge" in social problem solving, on the grounds that social science expertise is typically too limited and partial, not to say false, to constitute anything more than expensive, unnecessary, and frequently counterproductive noise in social problem-solving processes. And if we draw a parallel with architectural design, Prince Charles is far from alone in concluding that vernacular design has over the years produced far better living environments than the best efforts of professional architects.

My purpose here is not to line up with Lindblom and Prince Charles in praise of common sense and ordinary knowledge in opposition to theoretical and professional expertise. Social science applied to social problem solving, be it in policy design or institutional design, can indeed be decidedly problematic, and it would be easy to recount horror stories. But what passes for common sense can be problematic too, and subject to all kinds of ideological distortions. The informal approach to institutional design I shall explore would take into account the role and limitations of both ordinary knowledge and professional expertise. Indeed, I would suggest that the formal/informal distinction is as fruitful

---

[3]This tolerance for ambiguity and affinity for critique implies substantial divergence from philosophers such as Taylor (1961, p. xi), whose "informal logic" is concerned with the clarification of the rules followed in different areas of discourse.

as the professional expertise/ordinary knowledge one.[4] But rather than proceed further on this metatheoretical plane, let me get some bearings from concrete examples. My first case concerns policies and institutions for dealing with environmental problems.

4.2   Designing Instruments for Pollution Control

Most industrial societies rely on the promulgation and enforcement of regulations as the primary means of pollution control. There can be considerable cross-national variation in how regulation proceeds – contrast, for example, the adversarial, legalistic, and relatively open style of the United States with the more cooperative, secretive relationships that prevail between regulators and polluters in the United Kingdom. However, the basic regulatory idea is common: pollution is restricted by limits upon how much of each pollutant can be emitted by each source, or specifications as to what technology should be installed to restrict emissions. This approach to environmental policy used to be called – accurately and simply enough – "regulatory." More recently, the description "command and control" has been adopted by environmental policy analysts who prefer a different system. The significance of this redescription may be implicit recognition on the part of these analysts that their formal argument against regulation has failed to convince. Thus they turned to a rhetorical strategy (and the informal realm). In this democratic age, and following the manifest failure of centrally controlled economies, who could possibly favor "command and control" of anything (except perhaps the military)?

Policy analysts who have contemplated pollution control have almost universally concluded that systems of regulation are necessarily inferior

---

[4]A related distinction is drawn in an institutional design context by Linder and Peters (1994), who describe "decisional" and "dialogic" traditions. Their decisional tradition bears some relation to my formal category, in that it views design as a technical matter of expert engineering of institutions. The ends for the engineers are given either by some policy elite or by liberal moral philosophy (be it Kantian or utilitarian). My depiction of the formal category is slightly different in that it is silent on where these ends come from, stressing instead the use of particular frameworks and deductive methodology. But there is nothing to prevent Linder and Peters's decisional designers using what I call formal design logic, though decisional designers would have other options too. According to Linder and Peters, dialogical designers engage in open-ended institutional reconstruction guided by principles of free discourse in which the designer is at most catalytic. Dialogical designers could use the informal approach as I describe it; but again, they have other options. The informal logic I advocate may be interpreted as an attempt to push the dialogical tradition in a particular direction.

to quasi-market incentive systems. There is now two decades or so of exhortation on this score (see, for example, Kneese and Schultze 1975; Anderson et al. 1977; Baumol and Oates 1975; Pearce, Markandya, and Barbier 1989). For the most part, this is microeconomics speaking. For if polluters themselves are allowed to calculate the least-cost combination of particular technological measures for pollution control, then obviously the results are going to be more efficient in terms of both the firm's profit-maximizing proclivities and social welfare than if governmental specifications are followed. Such calculation is not allowed under regulatory systems. But it is allowed, even required, under incentive systems. The latter category includes a "standards and charges" approach in which government sets an emissions limit for (say) a river and then imposes per-unit pollution charges designed to achieve the requisite level of pollution reduction. Firms for which pollution reduction is costly will cut back a little. Firms for which reduction is relatively cheap will cut down a lot, and all firms have a continuous incentive to find low-cost means of emission reduction. A more radical incentive system would have government establish markets in pollution rights. Auctions would be held for polluters to bid for the number of rights established for a particular lake, river, or airshed (see Anderson and Leal 1991).

Incentive schemes of this sort have been adopted occasionally. So, for example, pollution charges have been applied in Germany, though the motive there is as much to raise revenue as it is to efficiently control pollution (Weale 1991, pp. 166–67), and the U.S. Environmental Protection Agency has sponsored some limited experiments in emissions trading across firms. And following the British government's 1990 White Paper on the environment, *This Common Inheritance*, it became conceivable that incentive mechanisms might be adopted more widely in Britain too (though the Treasury's opposition to new taxes effectively blocked pollution charges). However, for the most part the virtually unanimous advice of policy analysts in favor of incentive mechanisms has met political rejection. The same twenty years that have seen uninterrupted analytical exhortation on behalf of incentive mechanisms have also seen expansion and entrenchment of regulatory pollution control throughout the industrial world (Opschoor and Vos 1988). An examination of the reasons for this result can point to some inherent limits to formal logics of institutional design.

Doubtless bureaucratic inertia plays some part here. But more important may be the reaction of key environmentalist constituencies to incentive schemes. These reactions range from the guarded to the hostile, and no amount of efficiency-based argument could change them. The reason for such negative reactions is, according to Kelman (1981), that incentive schemes fail to stigmatize pollution as morally wrong. Markets in pollution rights, in particular, imply that pollution is a morally neutral commodity just like anything else that is made, sold, and bought in the marketplace. Emissions charges are only slightly less nefarious in this respect, for they too imply that if you are wealthy enough you can pay for the right to pollute. Goodin (1994) offers another angle on this issue, drawing a parallel between rights to pollute sold by government and indulgences sold by the medieval Catholic Church. Just as the Church had no right to sell places in heaven (which were for God or St. Peter to allocate – and then not for money), so governments have no right to sell the environment to polluters.

The issue here is not simply one of choosing among different policy instruments in terms of their likely performance across different criteria, or even in terms of their intrinsic moral rightness or wrongness. There are broader questions at issue pertaining to what kind of world – and what kind of institutions – we are helping to create by our seemingly limited policy choices. As Tribe (1973) notes, we should therefore learn how to reason constitutively in public policy, rather than instrumentally.

It is perhaps easier to envisage "reconstitutive" rather than "constitutive" reasoning when it comes to the impact of limited choices of policies and other practices. For any assumption to the effect that we can begin contemplating design of policies and institutions with a blank slate, free from established institutions and policy commitments, is a formalist error that should not be copied. One way to reason in reconstitutive terms, consistent with an informal approach to institutional design as defined earlier, is to think in terms of the discourses that particular choices help to reinforce or undermine. And discourses always have a history and a context.

I have already noted that a discourse is a system of possibility for knowing; it embodies capabilities that in turn enable us to assemble otherwise unintelligible bits of sensory input into coherent wholes (or "texts" as postmodernists would have it). More formally (based on Dryzek 1988, p. 711), any politically interesting discourse contains:

1. An ontology, or set of entities whose existence is recognized.
2. Ascription of agency to some entities: these entities, be they individuals, groups, institutions, wood nymphs, or social classes can act; other entities can only be acted upon.
3. For agents, some ascription of motive, and concomitant denial of other motives.
4. Taken-for-granted relationships (especially hierarchies) across agents and other entities.

We can use these four elements to uncover and scrutinize particular discourses. In these terms, it is not hard to analyze the discourse associated with incentive instruments in environmental policy. The entities recognized are governments, firms, environments, and individuals. Governments and firms have agency; ordinary people and the environment do not, as they are only acted upon, be it as victims of pollution or beneficiaries of cleanup. Governments are motivated by efficiency considerations, and perhaps by some other determination of what level of pollution is acceptable; firms are motivated by material self-interest. Relationships across firms are competitive, and there is also an implicit hierarchy in which government knows better than ordinary people (because the calculation of charges and the design of markets is a technical matter).

As instructive as what this discourse contains is what it does *not* contain. There is little or no room for active citizenship, relationships based on talk and persuasion rather than material incentives, and moral virtue (still less heroism) as a motivating force. The importance of citizenship in an environmental policy context is highlighted by Sagoff (1988), who notes that individuals typically have preferences as both consumers and citizens. These preferences often conflict. His own running example is that of individuals who as consumers would love to take advantage of a ski resort, but as citizens do not think the resort should be constructed because it will spoil a wilderness area. Sagoff's language of preference as opposed to subjectivity and identity is a bit restrictive here, but his point should be well taken: citizenship identity should not be excluded from public policy discourse. And when it is so excluded, as when economic discourse informs policy proposals, strange and unexpected things can happen.

Proposals for quasi-market incentive mechanisms in environmental policy do, then, draw upon and reinforce a particular discourse, and this does much to explain their political fate. I am not sure of the best name for this discourse; "economic rationalism" may capture it well enough. The general point is that a formal logic (microeconomics) points in one policy direction: incentive-oriented policy instruments are always best. But an informal logic (discourse analysis) points to some reasons why such instruments may not be so desirable after all, for these instruments help to constitute a discourse, and a world, which many environmentalists and others do not find very congenial.[5]

---

[5]This is also a world in which democratic politics of any sort is highly improbable. Microeconomic logic as embodied in public choice theory has itself demonstrated the incoherence of a democratic politics where everyone acts in economically rational fashion. Rather than simply accept the power of this dismal result, anyone interested

A discourse analysis of regulatory instruments would yield the following results. The entities whose existence is recognized would probably be the same as for incentive schemes: governments, firms, environments, and individuals. However, individual government officials may be recognized in the way they are not in incentive schemes, where government is treated as a unitary, efficiency-seeking whole. When it comes to agency in the discourse associated with regulation, only governments and their officials possess the power to act; firms are now only acted upon. The motives of government regulators would be recognized as public spirited, if in somewhat imprecise terms (i.e., it is not clear how the public interest is defined). There is a clear hierarchy in which governmental regulators stand above both firms and ordinary individuals (remember we are talking about a discourse here, not the actual relationship that obtains between government officials and polluters, which may put polluters on top).

Now, this is not exactly a Green discourse, and it contains little of which democrats might approve. But there are reasons why it might be more attractive to environmentalists than the economically rationalist discourse associated with incentive mechanisms. For at least the discourse associated with regulation is open-ended when it comes to the motivation of public officials, and it excludes firms *as agents*. Thus self-interest and profit maximization are excluded as legitimate considerations in the environmental domain.

So far, I have contrasted incentive mechanisms and regulation in terms of the discourses they support and undermine. To underscore the differences between formal and informal approaches here, consider how a formal comparison of the two approaches to antipollution policy would proceed. I have already noted that the formalism of microeconomics backs incentive schemes. But regulation too can be backed by a formal framework: a Weberian one in which expertise is embodied at the apex of a bureaucratic hierarchy, and instructions are communicated to officials responsible for formulating the details of regulations and applying them to particular cases. The hierarchy should be so organized as to enable the unambiguous transmission of principles and goals from top to bottom. The formal logic of microeconomics can be used to attack regulation by demonstrating the likely inefficiencies resulting from discretionary judgments on the part of government officials who have no stake in the profitability of private enterprises. Microeconomic offshoots in public choice theory can be deployed to show how government officials with discretionary authority are likely

in (democratic) institutional design would do better to explore the contingency of the discourse which gives rise to it. For greater detail on this issue, see Dryzek 1992b.

to pursue their own benefit rather than the public interest, which might involve (for example) sweetheart deals with polluters or excessive money spent on the environmental bureaucracy's own operations.

Two formal logics point in different directions: which one is right? Anyone committed to a formalist epistemology of institutional design would presumably have to choose one or the other.[6] In contrast, an informal orientation can tolerate ambiguity in the sense that actions and interactions can take on a variety of meanings. Are employees of environmental agencies self-interested maximizers, "commanders and controllers," or servants of the public interest? An informal approach would allow that they can be all of these things, or none of them. To a formalist, any such admission would probably mean throwing one's hands up in despair at the impossibility of institutional design. To an informalist, it is business as usual.

The upshot of this environmental policy example is that in designing policies and institutions one of our first concerns should be to determine what kinds of discourses are reinforced or, conversely, undermined by particular proposals. Formal designs, even if they have no direct effect on policies or institutions, can have some effect in the informal realm, by reinforcing or undermining discourses. The nature of that effect will depend on the prevailing constellation of discourses. So incentive schemes for pollution control may have contributed (however little) to the kind of naked individualist, economically rationalistic discourses which reached their height in the United States and United Kingdom in the 1980s (and whose demise seems a bit belated in Australia). Such schemes may be manifestly efficient and effective, but we might still want to reject them if the kind of world they help to (discursively) constitute or reconstitute strikes us as undesirable. And a world populated by *Homo economicus* as opposed to *Homo civicus* strikes many environmentalists (and, for that matter, socialists, communitarians, and republicans with no particular environmental concerns) as an undesirable place.

4.3 Reshaping Democracy

Recognition of the discursively constituted dimension of collective life can easily be assimilated to a conservative view of the world. For it would seem that in proposing novel alternatives for policy and institutions one always has to cope with the grip of established discourses,

---

[6]Note the difference between explanation and design here. In explanation, plurality in frameworks is far more easily tolerated (and, in postpositivist philosophy of science, encouraged).

which can rarely be shaken. Proponents of incentive mechanisms in environmental policy might easily interpret their failure in this light.

It would also be easy here to fall into a pit of poststructuralist despair, a Foucauldian pessimism in which life is just one damn discourse after another. However, I have already alluded to the possibility of reconstituting discourses, even as we can never escape them completely. So change is possible, even though it is rarely so straightforward a matter as formal approaches generally imply. The key here is to map the prevailing constellation of discourses with a view to identifying locations in which the existing political order is vulnerable. Now, it might indeed turn out to be the case that no such locations exist, such that there is no point at which to apply levers for change. Again, if poststructuralists such as Foucault are correct in ascribing hegemony to dominant discourses (about sex, criminality, economics, governmentality, and so forth), then little can be done.

I believe it is possible to test empirically such contentions of hegemony (and that most such tests so far have shown a striking lack of it). Discourse analysis need not be confined to armchair critique of the sort in my environmental policy example. Instead, some empirical social science can be brought to bear. The case for an informal approach to institutional design rests in part on the access it provides to some social scientific tools, most notably those of Q methodology as guided by elements of discourse analysis.

Q methodology may be unfamiliar to social scientists led astray by the false gods of survey research, so let me describe it briefly (for greater detail, see Brown, 1980, 1986). Q is concerned with modeling individual subjects in their entirety, and with seeking patterns across individuals – unlike the R methodology of survey research, which is concerned only with patterns across variables. Q begins by modeling each subject in terms of his or her reaction to a set of statements about a particular topic. He or she is asked to order these statements according to specified conditions of instruction, such as "most agree" to "most disagree," or "most like me" to "most unlike me." Usually forty to sixty statements are used, and the ordering requested is quasi-normal (i.e., more statements in the middle of the distribution than at the extremes). The ordering a subject produces is called a Q sort, and it models the subject in the entirety of his or her orientation to the domain ("concourse") from which the statements are drawn. The concourse might refer to a particular issue area, conflict, religious experience, game, market, or any other area of human life where subjectivity is at issue. The Q sorts of different subjects can be summarized and compared using statistical techniques such as correlation and, most fruitfully, factor analysis. Individuals loading heavily on a common factor exhibit a high level of similarity with one another, and dissimilarity with individuals loading heavily on other factors (or negatively on the same factor). Each factor can be interpreted by computing a Q sort (statement ordering) for a hypothetical individual loading 100% on that factor and zero on any other factor.

To illustrate the uses to which Q methodology and discourse analysis can be put in institutional design, let me introduce a recent mapping of discourses of democracy present in the United States, with a view to showing how these results might be useful to anyone interested in reshaping the institutions of (American) democracy. A fuller presentation of the research, but without any connection to institutional design, may be found in Dryzek and Berejikian (1993).

The motivating principle behind the study of discourses of democracy was reconstructive. That is, we tried to ascertain how ordinary people and political actors actually conceptualize democracy, giving the researchers as little leeway as possible to impose their own categories and conceptualizations. To this end, we gathered several hundred statements relevant to democracy made by ordinary people, political activists and leaders, and writers (but not by academics). These statements came from published sources (such as letters columns in newspapers, and ethnographic studies that report verbatim what their subjects say) and from discussion groups for which we recruited individuals through newspaper advertisements. Examples of such statements were "Democracy can make mistakes, but it has the unique advantage of a way to make corrections before it is too late" and "If you want the state off your back, put your feet to the pavement." A sample of sixty-four statements was isolated through a fairly elaborate sampling procedure informed by the four elements of discourse analysis discussed earlier. We then sought subjects based on the principle of maximum diversity in terms of age, sex, race, occupation, social class, region, and political ideology. Each subject was asked to order the sixty-four statements into thirteen piles from "most agree" to "most disagree." Thirty-seven subjects were recruited. Q methodology always works with a small number of subjects. Unlike large-n methods such as survey research, Q has confidence in its individual observations. We factor analyzed the Q sorts of the thirty-seven subjects, and isolated four meaningful factors. The hypothetical Q sort associated with each factor was then interpreted to give the description of a discourse of democracy.

Both impressionistic and social scientific accounts of the political culture of the United States often describe a single discourse centered around the idea of liberal democracy – this is the essence, for example, of Louis Hartz's (1955) *The Liberal Tradition in America*, of *The Civic Culture* celebrated by Almond and Verba (1963), of the supposed "end of ideology" in the 1950s, and of the "end of history" in the early 1990s.

However, our results suggest that there exists no simple, let alone hegemonic, discourse of liberal democracy. Matters are more complex than that. In the factor analysis we identified four discourses of democracy prevalent in the United States (of course, different countries will produce different results). We cannot guarantee that these four discourses exhaust the range of possibilities, nor can we say how many people in the population of the United States subscribe to each one of them. But what we can say with confidence is that these four discourses have a real existence in the population out there, such that they are not the analyst's or theorist's invention, and that their *content* is generalizable to the population at large. If the subject group is sufficiently diverse, then we can be secure in generalizing the results to the larger population. But our units of analysis when it comes to generalization to this population are discourses, not individuals. The four discourses may be characterized briefly as follows. In Table 4.1 they are summarized in terms of the four elements for the scrutiny of political discourses which I introduced earlier.

Contented republicanism. Democracy is a way of life, the best form of government, and existing institutions and practices closely match this ideal. Government does listen to ordinary people; it is not an adversary, but the body in which citizenship is embedded. However, some constitutional limits are necessary to prevent government from becoming too big and intrusive. Political equality and active citizenship are both important and unproblematical; there is no such thing as too much participation. It is citizenship which unites the people, not shared traditions. Politics is not properly about the pursuit of self-interest, and it is possible in public debate to reconcile personal and public interests. To facilitate this debate, there should be no restrictions on the free exchange of ideas.

Deferential conservatism. Democracy as such is hard to define, which means that it is not necessarily undesirable, but not particularly desirable either. Politics is properly for an elite only, for ordinary people such as myself are incapable of making good judgments, or even of really knowing what we want; politics is distant and confusing. So increased participation would be undesirable. Society is unequal and class-divided, but this does not matter, and we should rely on honest elites to govern. There is no need to fear such government, and no need for a free press or independent judiciary to limit it.

Disaffected populism. Power is in the hands of repressive corporate and governmental elites, and so we do not live in a democracy. Political equality and true freedom and democracy are desirable and possible, but only if the people rises up against these elites. We should have great faith in the political capabilities of ordinary people, who should

Table 4.1. *Analysis of Four U.S. Discourses of Democracy*

Discourse	Ontology	Agency	Ascribed Motivation	Relationships Seen as Natural
Contented republicanism	the people, individuals	everyone	public good	political equality, harmony between public and private interests
Deferential conservatism	society, elites	elites	mysterious	hierarchy
Disaffected populism	corporate/ governmental elites, the people	presently elites, properly the people	elite – own interest; people are properly radical	presently class conflict, properly political equality
Private liberalism	individuals, government	individuals (but not necessarily in politics), government	material self-interest	separateness of individuals, conflict between individuals and government

Source: Dryzek and Berejikian (1993, p. 56)

attend more to politics. Confronting government is more important than occupying roles within it. A free press is essential.

Private liberalism. Democracy as such is not particularly valuable, as it allows for undesirable kinds of government (such as socialism) as well as more desirable forms. Thus we should not be concerned that we do not live in an especially democratic society. It is private life which really matters, and democracy does little to secure the freedom of individuals to pursue their private interests. Government is currently too big and too active; it should be as small and unintrusive as possible, and subjected to constitutional limits and separation of powers. Active citizenship and public debate are unimportant and undesirable. Politics should not be central to life. There are no limits to my own political capabilities, but my energies, and those of others, are best directed elsewhere: to work, family, and the market.

These four discourses represent both constraints upon, and resources for, anyone interested in reshaping American political institutions. They act as constraints because any normative theory of democracy – or political life more generally – that relates to none of these discourses (or no combination of these discourses) thereby becomes both infeasible and implausible. Some of the theories so ruled out are unsurprising; so, for example, Leninist democratic centralism finds no comfort anywhere in these four discourses, and neither does European-style corporatism (though "corporatism without labor" might be connected to deferential conservatism).

Other theories which fare badly are more surprising. So, for example, pluralism as normative theory finds little support here. For pluralism as normative theory stresses the aggregation and articulation of preferences through organized interest groups, leavened by a democracy that can only be representative, and never direct. But none of the four discourses has much faith in elected representatives, and so none is really a discourse of representative democracy. The two discourses with the most profound commitment to democracy (contented republicanism and disaffected populism) stress a citizenry far more active and committed than that sought by pluralists – indeed, a level that most pluralists would regard as dangerous. The other two discourses (deferential conservatism and private liberalism) seek far less in the way of citizen activity than pluralists would favor, indeed, hardly any such activity at all. These results fit oddly with Lowi's (1979) claim that pluralism is *the* ideology of the "second American republic." Our analysis suggests that even if Lowi is right about the ideology of intellectuals, he is wrong about ordinary people; either that, or his second republic has already passed into history (our study was carried out in 1991; the first edition of *The End of Liberalism* appeared in 1969).

Other prescriptive theories can draw more comfort from our findings. Consider, for example, the conservative intellectuals who gave voice in the late 1970s to the problems that an excess of citizen demands was causing for the very governability of the United States and other Western societies (e.g., Crozier, Huntington, and Watanuki 1975). These conservatives favored a more authoritarian kind of politics which would, however, retain some democratic forms. American paleoconservatives continue this political tradition into the 1990s, though arguably their commitment to popular control of government is even thinner than that of ungovernability theorists. (Inasmuch as some of the latter were sponsored by the internationalist Trilateral Commission, they would be regarded with horror by paleoconservatives.) But whatever the precise degree to which popular control is subordinated to central authority in the conservative mix, any such mix could draw comfort from its congruence with the deferential conservative discourse we have identified.

The very different kind of prescriptive democratic theory advanced by participatory enthusiasts such as Barber (1984) should find our contented republicanism discourse interesting, because of the level of civic virtue and active participation which this discourse expects and requires. One puzzle for participatory theorists might be that this discourse sees little need for the kind of reforms Barber and others would advocate. The disaffected populism discourse is more energized by the need for change in a participatory mode, but that energy is largely contingent on the amount of repression existing in the system, about which Barber, for one, is unconcerned.

These examples of potentially fruitful connections between political theories and discourses of democracy demonstrate that these discourses constitute resources for, and not just constraints upon, anyone interested in reshaping institutions. For our results indicate that discourses which are not simple apologies for the institutional status quo, and which may indeed challenge it quite radically, can and do exist. This finding is contrary to the expectations of (among others) Edelman (1987), for whom political language is mostly a cloak for the exercise of power. Such oppositional discourses offer promising springboards for anyone interested in institutional change, and so would-be institutional innovators would do well to seek them out. Even discourses which do seem like apology for the status quo can be rearranged by creative reformers in pursuit of a changed institutional order. Note, for example, how Martin Luther King, Jr., put the principles of U.S. liberalism to work on behalf of a civil rights agenda in the 1950s and 1960s. Political innovation can, then, involve creative interaction between discourse and prescriptive theory, for the discourses we have identified do not fix rigid limits upon what is possible in political change, and may themselves be open to reconstitution through imaginative theoretical contributions.

4.4   Critique and Autonomy in Institutional Design

Earlier I suggested that the methodological commitments of an informal approach to institutional design could be related most fruitfully to the idea of critique, and both the environmental policy and democracy examples contain hints as to what kinds of critique are possible and defensible. Let me now try to be a little more explicit, and so pin down rather more precisely just what critique as a methodology entails here.

At a minimal level, critique can explicate the discourses that are drawn upon, reinforced, or undermined by particular policies, policy designs, structural proposals, formal logics, or other contributions to the conversation of institutional design. My earlier account of the discourses that are reinforced by market-type and regulatory instruments in antipollution policy is an example of this kind of critique. This level of critique is minimal because it implies no judgments or evaluations concerning the worth of the discourses in question. All it does is attempt to expose some otherwise hidden aspects of a situation to public light.

A somewhat more forceful kind of critique would involve the identification and explication of marginal or subversive discourses that imply institutional arrangements different from the status quo. My sketch of alternative discourses of democracy falls into this category. In fact, if liberal democracy is the status quo, all four of these democratic discourses embody such alternatives (of varying degrees of radicalism). There is no necessary suggestion here that alternative or marginal discourses are better than the status quo, only that they are different. This level of critique might therefore sit well with postmodernists, who deny that there is any solid ground on which one can stand in order to conduct critique, or judge any one discourse better than any other. The image here is a conversation to which both established discourses and more novel ideas can contribute, the upshot of which is the reconstitution of theories, discourses, and perhaps even institutions. Within this conversation, discourses are always being shaped or reshaped, strengthened or undermined in open-ended interplay.

The next issue that arises is whether or not to hold this interplay up to any critical standards, and here there is substantial room for divergence. My own view is that one can and should apply such standards, and that the standards involved have broad applicability. Others, notably poststructuralists, postmodernists, (some) feminists, Burkean conservatives, and strong communitarians, would deny the possibility that any such standards can be found outside of *particular* discourses.

It is difficult to resolve this issue without recourse to some fairly complex metatheoretical debates. Rather than enter these debates here (for my own contribution, see Dryzek 1990, chap. 1), let me just state a position on how the critique central to an informal approach to institutional design may be fruitfully assimilated to (modernist) critical theory.

Conversations surrounding institutional design may be conducted by more or less competent individuals, under more or less undistorted conditions. Participants are autonomous to the extent that they are capable of making informed choices. Now, autonomy in this sense does not mean merely the capacity of the person to make effective, goal-directed choices – in other words, to behave like a microeconomic man. This is autonomy at its thinnest. A thicker notion of autonomy involves judicious selection of ends as well as means, what Dahl (1989, pp. 91, 99) terms "moral autonomy."[7] However, it is unnecessarily restrictive to

---

[7]Dahl develops his ideas about autonomy in the context of a justification of de-

work solely within a paradigm of instrumental rationality, under which even Dahl's morally autonomous individual may be subsumed. What I will call "full autonomy" allows that individuals can reflectively choose to invoke different kinds of action principles as circumstances warrant: communicative, socially integrative, dramaturgical, playful, emotional, or intuitive, as well as instrumental. We are now in a position to criticize institutions, discourses, or processes of institutional reshaping which repress autonomy, or instill one kind of subjectivity at the expense of others. Examples of this kind of critique might involve showing how markets suppress alternatives to instrumental subjectivity (see, e.g., Lane 1978; Marcuse 1964), or how bureaucracy creates attitudes of subservience and dependence (e.g., Hummel 1987), though these examples often proceed at excessively high levels of abstraction and ratios of rhetoric to evidence.

Full autonomy's counterpart at the intersubjective level is communicative rationality, as specified (for example) in Habermas' notion of an ideal speech situation free from deception, self-deception, political power, and strategizing. For obvious reasons, such an ideal is especially appropriate to apply to the evaluation of processes of institutional reshaping conceived of as conversations. It should be remembered that communicative rationality does not embody any particular theory of human needs, beyond the need to communicate and understand, nor does it determine any particular way of life, still less any utopia for which to aim. Rather, it is best thought of as a procedural standard for resolving disputes and arguments (Habermas 1979, p. 90; Dryzek 1990, pp. 17–18). Thus, contrary to the charges leveled by the postmodern opponents of critical theory, it allows for continued plurality in ways of life, paradigms of personhood, dimensions of subjectivity – and discourses relevant to political institutions.

4.5 Realist Constraints

The analysis of this chapter so far has been idealist, in the sense that it has assumed that the world is constituted by what people think, be it in terms of ideologies, discourses, theories, or (relatively) autonomous reflection. But this realm of thought and talk is constrained by some

---

mocracy over authoritarianism. Dahl presumes that people really are the best judges of their own interests, and that "guardians" or others who claim to know better are mistaken. Dahl's defense of democracy here is actually a formalist one. For he starts with a single, fixed paradigm of personhood – moral autonomy – and then proceeds to deduce the implications for political systems. As formal approaches to institutional design go, this is pretty loose, given that Dahl allows considerable scope for variation in the kind of democracy justified by his presumption of moral autonomy.

very real material forces. So the kind of conversation I have described has practical import only within such constraints.

These constraints can be quite severe. When it comes to reshaping political institutions, most of these constraints stem from the fact that the dominant form of political organization in the contemporary world is the state, which may be defined as the set of individuals and organizations legally authorized to make binding decisions for a society. All states in the industrial world must do the following:

1. Avoid economic downturn, for such downturn means both government unpopularity in the eyes of the populace and a shortage of tax revenue to finance whatever it is that government wants to do. Downturn can result from businesses deciding to disinvest; thus the first task of any state must be to maintain business confidence. This point is stressed by structural Marxists (e.g., Block 1977) to explain why states must favor capital even in the absence of direct instrumental control of the state by the ruling class. It is echoed by someone with liberal credentials as impeccable as those of Lindblom (1982).

2. Stay afloat in the international system, both militarily (Skocpol 1979) and, more importantly in today's world, economically. Any state that runs afoul of the international trade regime and its institutions is in serious trouble.

3. Keep order internally, either through effective repression or operation as a welfare state. The latter can ease the discontent of those who would otherwise suffer from the vicissitudes of the capitalist order, and so contribute to the legitimation of the capitalist political economy. Measures occurring in the presence of the state which threaten any one of these essential maintaining functions will be punished automatically; there is no need to look for conspiracy or control by some nefarious ruling elite. So, for example, attempts to expand state control of industry, introduce industrial democracy (as in the case of the Swedish wage-earner funds), or extend the quantity of liberal interest group participation (for example, to the very poor, or disadvantaged ethnic minorities) are likely to founder in the face of the "disinvestment" constraint.

Institutional reshaping can only fruitfully proceed in the spaces that remain once these constraints are taken into account. These spaces can sometimes prove distressingly small, though an active theoretical imagination can help to expand them. Elsewhere (Dryzek 1992a) I have enumerated both state-related constraints and the resultant spaces for institutional innovation in more detail. To cut a long story short, such spaces may be found in connection with

- war;
- depression;
- autonomous public spheres that confront the state but do not seek a share of state power;
- revolution (but only ephemerally);
- collapsed peripheries of otherwise stable societies;
- functional indeterminacy (for example, when two different constraints – e.g., the need to prevent disinvestment and the need to supply an adequate amount of welfare – point in different directions, or when some deviation is allowed from what is most functional, or when alternative institutional structures might be equally functional);[8]
- the international system (which has no state at the system level);
- local politics.

To put it crudely, any talk of fundamental institutional reshaping (whether or not it has the informal characteristics I have described) has no practical import outside of these spaces. All the world is not a text, and it cannot be rewritten at will.

4.6 Conclusion

Processes of political innovation are necessarily limited by both the state-related constraints just described and the prevailing constellation of discourses. Thus institutional reshaping is always going to be an uphill struggle. It is likely to prove fruitful to the extent that (a) these constraints are recognized and identified, and (b) contributions to the conversation are imaginative in terms of locating or creating islands of freedom in seas of structural necessity and discursive hegemony.

I have argued that institutional designers should focus on the discursive software as well as the formal hardware of institutions. Formalists who hope that supportive discourses will simply fall into place once the hardware has been established are likely to be disappointed. In the face of recalcitrant discourses, their commitment to reform can be sustained only by recourse to dictatorship.

This kind of recognition does not imply that attention to the informal logic of institutions should be thought of as just a reality check or feasibility test for the proposals generated by more formal approaches.

---

[8]The institutional reconstruction associated with the introduction of quasi-market reforms in the British National Health Service discussed by Klein in this volume falls into the functional indeterminacy category. On Klein's account, this situation is one in which lack of knowledge as to what will work best (prove most functional) virtually mandates institutional self-reinvention.

Discourses do more than just get in the way. The informal approach points to a realm of possibility in which institutional design can operate. For in uncovering, describing, and criticizing the discourses permeating institutions we can provide resources for both imaginative reconstruction of discourses and a democratic conversation about institutional futures.

References

Almond, Gabriel A., and Sidney Verba. 1963. *The Civic Culture: Political Attitudes and Democracy in Five Nations*. Princeton, N.J.: Princeton University Press.

Anderson, Frederick, et al. 1977. *Environmental Improvement Through Economic Incentives*. Baltimore: Johns Hopkins University Press for Resources for the Future.

Anderson, Terry L., and Donald R. Leal. 1991. *Free Market Environmentalism*. San Francisco: Pacific Research Institute.

Barber, Benjamin. 1984. *Strong Democracy: Participatory Politics for a New Age*. Berkeley: University of California Press.

Baumol, William J., and Wallace E. Oates. 1975. *The Theory of Environmental Policy*. Englewood Cliffs, N.J.: Prentice-Hall.

Block, Fred. 1977. The ruling class does not rule: Notes on the Marxist theory of the state. *Socialist Revolution*, 33: 6–28.

Brown, Steven R. 1980. *Political Subjectivity: Applications of Q Methodology in Political Science*. New Haven, Conn.: Yale University Press.

Brown, Steven R. 1986. Q Technique and method: Principles and Procedures. Pp. 57–76 in William D. Berry and Michael S. Lewis-Beck, eds., *New Tools for Social Scientists: Advances and Applications in Research Methods*. Beverly Hills, Calif.: Sage.

Crozier, Michel J., Samuel P. Huntington, and Joji Watanuki. 1975. *The Crisis of Democracy: Report on the Governability of Democracies to the Trilateral Commission*. New York: New York University Press.

Dahl, Robert A. 1989. *Democracy and Its Critics*. New Haven, Conn.: Yale University Press.

Dietz, Mary G. 1985. Citizenship with a feminist face: The problem with maternal thinking. *Political Theory*, 13: 19–35.

Dryzek, John S. 1988. The mismeasure of political man. *Journal of Politics*, 50: 705–25.

Dryzek, John S. 1990. *Discursive Democracy: Politics, Policy, and Political Science*. Cambridge: Cambridge University Press.

Dryzek, John S. 1992a. The good society versus the state: Freedom and necessity in political innovation. *Journal of Politics*, 54: 518–40.

Dryzek, John S. 1992b. How far is it from Virginia and Rochester to Frankfurt? Public choice as critical theory. *British Journal of Political Science*, 22: 397–417.

Dryzek, John S., and Jeffrey Berejikian. 1993. Reconstructive democratic theory. *American Political Science Review*, 87: 48–60.

Edelman, Murray. 1987. *Constructing the Political Spectacle*. Chicago: University of Chicago Press.

Gilligan, Carol. 1982. *In a Different Voice: Psychological Theory and Women's Development*. Cambridge, Mass.: Harvard University Press.

Goodin, Robert E. 1994. Selling environmental indulgences. *Kyklos*, 47: 573–96.

Habermas, Jürgen. 1979. *Communication and the Evolution of Society*. Boston: Beacon Press.

Hartz, Louis. 1955. *The Liberal Tradition in America*. New York: Harcourt, Brace.

Hummel, Ralph P. 1987 *The Bureaucratic Experience*, 3rd ed. New York: St. Martin's.

Kelman, Steven. 1981. *What Price Incentives? Economists and the Environment*. Boston: Auburn House.

Kneese, Allen V., and Charles L. Schultze. 1975. *Pollution, Prices, and Public Policy*. Washington, D.C.: Brookings Institution.

Lane, Robert E. 1978. Autonomy, felicity, futility: The effects of the market economy on political personality. *Journal of Politics*, 40: 2–24.

Letwin, Shirley. 1965. *The pursuit of certainty*. Cambridge: Cambridge University Press.

Lindblom, Charles E. 1982. The Market as Prison. *Journal of Politics*, 44: 324–36.

Lindblom, Charles E. 1990. *Inquiry and Change: The Troubled Attempt to Understand and Shape Society*. New Haven, Conn.: Yale University Press.

Lindblom, Charles E., and David K. Cohen. 1979. *Usable Knowledge: Social Science and Social Problem Solving*. New Haven, Conn.: Yale University Press.

Linder, Stephen H., and B. Guy Peters. 1994. The two traditions of institutional designing: Dialogue versus decision? In David Weimer, ed., *Institutional Design*. Boston: Kluwer.

Lowi, Theodore J. 1979. *The End of Liberalism*, 2nd ed. New York: Norton.

Marcuse, Herbert. 1964. *One Dimensional Man*. Boston: Beacon Press.

Opschoor, J. B., and H. Vos. 1988. *The Application of Economic Instruments for Environmental Protection in OECD Member Countries*. Paris: OECD.

Pearce, David, Anil Markandya, and Edward R. Barbier. 1989. *Blueprint for a Green Economy*. London: Earthscan.

Riker, William H. 1982. The two-party system and Duverger's law: An essay on the history of political science. *American Political Science Review*, 76: 753–66.

Ruddick, Sara. 1980. Maternal thinking. *Feminist Studies*, 6: 342–67.

Sagoff, Mark. 1988. *The Economy of the Earth.* Cambridge: Cambridge University Press.

Skocpol, Theda. 1979. *States and Social Revolutions.* Cambridge: Cambridge University Press.

Taylor, Paul W. 1961. *Normative Discourse.* Englewood Cliffs, N.J.: Prentice-Hall.

Tribe, Laurence H. 1973. Technology assessment and the fourth discontinuity: The limits of instrumental rationality. *Southern California Law Review*, 46: 617–60.

Weale, Albert. 1991. *The New Politics of Pollution.* Manchester: Manchester University Press.

5

Institutional Morality

5.1 Introduction

A central problem in the design of institutions is the assignment of responsibility. Almost all moral theories are about the morality of individuals, not of supra individual entities such as organizations or societies.[1] Hence, in those theories, an account of institutional responsibility must be subject to unpacking down to the level of individuals. This raises questions of composition: Who is how much responsible for which part of what? It is these compositional problems that are the focus of discussion here.

In general, we may say of an institution as a whole that its morality is reasonably well defined by its purpose and its likely effects. In this sense, an institution's morality is inherently consequentialist. It might not be utilitarian, however, because its purpose could be the support of equality, justice, or autonomy, and not necessarily the support of welfare.[2] Once the institution's morality is defined, we may infer or deduce

An earlier version of this chapter was presented at the conference, "Institutional Design," Research School of the Social Sciences, Australian National University, Canberra, 16–17 July 1992. I thank the organizers of the conference for stimulating this paper, John Braithwaite for extensive written commentary, Michael Stocker for extensive oral commentary, and participants in the Russell Sage Foundation seminar, New York, 21 October 1992, a colloquium at the Department of Politics, New York University, February 1993, the Legal Theory workshop at Columbia University Law School, and the joint workshop in Economics and Political Science at the University of Western Ontario. And I thank the Russell Sage and Mellon foundations for general support.

[1] The same is true of law in, at least, the United States. See Dan-Cohen 1986.

[2] The political institutions in John Rawls's theory are clearly intended to achieve consequences: "to maximize human achievement in art, science, and culture" (Rawls 1971, p. 325). Also see Scanlon 1977, esp. pp. 61–65.

the morality of individual office holders in the institution as derivative from the purpose of the institution. Or, we may say, the rules and procedures that guide the actions of individual officeholders are determined by the functional relation of their actions to the general purposes of the institution (Rawls 1955; Hardin 1988, pp. 100–5). Institutional morality is structurally similar to some variants of virtue theory: Its content is functionally determined by the purpose it is to serve. And it is analogous to the problem of legal justification. We may first seek justification *of* the law and then justification *in* the law. The latter depends on the former for much of its content. It also depends on social scientific facts of the way incentives and institutions can be made to work.

The consequentialist evaluation of institutions might seem to fit ill with many moral theories, which, as their proponents assert, are not consequentialist. But these theorists often evaluate institutions by how well they achieve or support autonomy, justice, fairness, and so forth. For example, one must grant that John Rawls's theory of justice is consequentialist when it focuses on institutions for achieving justice even if one supposes that, in its later Kantian variant, it is grounded in nonconsequentialist concerns. One might suppose it fine to have institutions for the achievement of various consequences, including welfare enhancement, while still insisting that nonconsequentialist considerations also play a role in a particular moral theory. In all of these cases, as well as in fully consequentialist theories such as utilitarianism, the problems addressed here are central to the moral assessment of institutional design. Indeed, it may be difficult to give a compelling nonconsequentialist justification of an institution.

Problems of composition in institutional morality take at least three forms, one of which is special to institutions. There is the problem of collective action, especially for large numbers of actors, on which there is a vast literature (Olson 1965; Hardin 1982). There are stochastic problems of probabilistic effects that are common in policy issues that are often handled by institutions (Hardin 1989). And there is the problem of relating institutional to individual action, which is the focus of the present discussion. It is especially important in applied moral theory and public policy debates. It often involves the other two compositional problems.

5.2 Morality by Design

When an institution fails to accomplish its purpose, we may charge the failure to one of two causes: (1) misdesign of the institution for that purpose and (2) failure of particular people within the institution. I am concerned with institutional design and therefore with the first class of problems. The second class of problems is of interest for design only to the extent it should be taken into account in the institutional design – for example, through creation of incentives to control individual failure or design of selection or training procedures to reduce the incidence of such failure. (The one problem of individual failure to be considered here is potential conflict between the dictates of individual and institutional morality, especially when these are ostensibly guided by the same moral vision.) But this just means the problem is again one of design. Institutional morality is in this sense a design issue: Morality must be built in.

In the extreme case of misdesign, we may even suppose that a particular purpose cannot be served by any institution. If we take seriously the dictum that "ought" implies "can" we may wish to give up on that purpose. For example, Lon Fuller argued against the attempt to create adjudicative regulatory agencies to handle allocative decisions, such as setting fares and allocating routes for the airlines. Such agencies, Fuller thought, cannot be designed to do the job well enough to justify government interference (Fuller 1969, pp. 170–77). In a similar move, John Rawls has recognized the possibility that we must give up on the achievement of equality of income and wealth in order to achieve mutual advantage. The reason for doubting income equality is that actual people may well be differentially motivated in part by the rewards they get for producing goods and benefits. Hence, unequal rewards may be necessary for general productivity.

In the extreme case of apparent irresponsibility within an institution we may not be able to assign specific responsibility to anyone. The standard problems of collective responsibility arise. If the institution's failure cannot be adequately regulated through the assignment of responsibilities, the institution may fall under the censure of misdesign rather than internal irresponsibility.

If an institution's morality is defined by its purpose or likely effects, then its morality might be judged harshly from a particular moral perspective if its purpose is one that is judged immoral from that perspective. For example, from almost every Western moral perspective the institutions of Nazi genocide had a morally reprehensible purpose. But the functional relation between the actions of various officeholders in those institutions to the purposes of the institutions might have fit very closely. It might seem to be only a matter of definitional convention whether we say that the functionally fit actions were moral in those institutions or whether we say, by inference from the larger morality of the institutions' purpose, that they were immoral simpliciter. The choice, however, may not be trivial. We cannot say without confusion that the competence of a superb secretary is immoral simpliciter. Yet, the actions of such a secretary may be necessary for the success of an organization with a heinous purpose.

Much of the debate over the inherent morality of the law seems to have been a debate at cross purposes from these two quite different linguistic conventions. Fuller, assuming that law is to have some function or purpose, then argued that it has an internal morality. Much of his argument was muddled, but it makes relatively clear sense if it is seen as an argument from functional fit within the law rather than as an argument for specific moral content in the law. He blurred these two categories somewhat when he further assumed bits of human psychology to argue that certain purposes could not readily be achieved by law and were therefore generally not consistent with the morality of law, and when he assumed specific content for the external morality of law, which he thought must be to facilitate human interaction.

Institutions typically have the structure of law roughly as Fuller saw it. Again, this means merely that the rightness within an institution of a particular action by one of its officeholders is determined contingently by the functional fit of that action with the institution's purposes. This need not allow an Eichmann defense against personal responsibility for one's actions within an institution, because one's personal moral responsibility may be to oppose an institution's purpose and the means it uses to achieve that purpose. The discussion here will focus on the internal problem and will simply assume that the purposes of the institutions under discussion are externally justifiable.

Note that the internal morality of an institution is, as Hume called duties of justice, artificial. That is, it depends for at least part of its content on what humans have first created. In this sense, the morality of a profession is artificial and what Fuller roughly called the internal morality of law is artificial. What it is right for a professional or an officer of the law to do depends on how the profession's services or the law's institutions are organized. Hence, the argument for institutions more generally has its more specialized counterparts in professional ethics and the internal morality of law (Hardin 1991; 1994).

5.3 Collective Responsibility

No one would want to live in a world in which just anyone could have significant effect on major policy issues. For example, if, during the recent superpower standoff, just any individual American or Soviet citizen could have had major impact on whether nuclear weapons would be put to use, all of us would have been at much more grievous risk even than what one might suppose we did face from those weapons. There is even a logical problem in supposing that each of us could have a major impact. What could it mean to suppose that you and I could each individually have great impact on whether the weapons were to be used this week if it is not logically precluded that my impact would be to cause their use and yours would be to prevent their use? Yet, despite the obvious sense in which it is absurd to suppose many of us can have substantial impact on such policies, many of us were inclined to think we were somehow partly responsible for those weapons. If "ought" implies "can," as we generally believe it does, then our sense of responsibility in such cases is typically wrong.

In common usage and in much of our moral concern with it, responsibility is a causal notion. This is not the only sense of the word "responsibility." Dictionaries typically make casual notions the first sense of "responsible." One or something is responsible that is the primary cause, motive, or agent – the cause or explanation, for example, of an accident. Dictionaries then include a second sense, which generally applies only to persons or collective persons. One is responsible if one is able to answer for one's conduct and obligations, able to choose for oneself between right and wrong. Hence, by taking on ambivalent meaning, responsibility plays a role in both consequentialist and deontological moral theories.

In a utilitarian moral theory "responsibility" is inherently a causal notion. To say, on a utilitarian account, that I am responsible for result x is to say that I caused or helped to cause x. It follows that a proper assignment of responsibility requires a relevant assessment of causal effects. But causal assessments are notoriously difficult in many contexts, perhaps most especially in social contexts. Difficulties in making causal claims may be epistemological or informational in large part but the more important difficulties are conceptual in the following sense. If my action is one of many contributions to a result, there may be no compelling way to resolve the full cause of that result into its partial causes. The collection of causes may violate John Stuart Mill's principle of the composition of causes (Mill 1974 [1843], book 3, chap. 6).

It is often supposed that the possibility of doing experiments has been the major reason for the relative success of certain of the hard sciences as compared to the social and behavioral sciences. A far more important consideration may be differences in the causal structures of the phenomena of interest in these sciences. For many physical laws, especially in classical physics, the principle of the composition of causes is valid or approximately so. For example, a classical electron may be accelerated by the combination of gravitational and electrical forces, each of which can be partialed out from the sum of the two forces. It is because the effects of gravitational and electromagnetic forces are straightforwardly separable that the Millikan oil-drop experiment for determining the charge of the electron was possible.[3]

For much, perhaps most, of what interests us in the social sciences and, hence, in moral theory, the principle of composition of causes is clearly not valid. There have been theories, such as Arthur Bentley's group theory of politics (Bentley 1949), that presumed such simple relationships. But the once commonplace phrase, "the vector sum of forces," has rightly fallen out of vogue in the social sciences. We are now too accustomed to the importance and pervasiveness of threshold and other complex effects in social causation to suppose lightly that the result of a large number of actions by many people is somehow merely a vector addition of the results of the actions taken singly.

Suppose my institution is badly designed and it does harm (or it fails to do the good it could do) or that it is well designed and it does good. And suppose I fulfill my role in the institution as I am supposed to do. What is my responsibility for the harm or the good that my institution now does? This question is merely an instance of the common question of how causal weights should be assigned in cases of plural causation. To keep the general question clear, let us consider varied contexts in which it might arise, contexts that display strategic as well as substantive variety.

5.3.1 Some examples

In an election, many of us may vote. Some of us vote for the losing side. Do we share responsibility for the result? The votes of many of those who vote for the winning side may be otiose – victory does not depend on them, given the other votes cast. Many of us may not vote. If the victor wins by, say, a million votes, does any particular nonvoter bear any responsibility for letting the loser down? Do a million and one nonvoters bear any responsibility? During the Watergate scandal that followed Richard Nixon's landslide reelection as president in 1972, there was a widely appreciated bumper sticker that said, "Don't blame me, I'm from Massachusetts." While every other state went for Nixon in his reelection, 54 percent of voters in Massachusetts voted against Nixon.[4] Was someone in Massachusetts who voted for Nixon less responsible than someone in Illinois who voted with a state majority for

---

[3]Mill makes this point with reference to differences between chemistry and physics (Mill 1974, sec. 1).

[4]The District of Columbia voted 78% for McGovern. No state other than Massachusetts topped 47%.

Nixon? Less responsible than someone in Illinois who voted, forlornly, for George McGovern? One might have said, with Bentley, that the Nixon and McGovern causes were like two forces in opposition and that the greater force prevailed, as though politics were merely social physics in its classical variant. But the question of the prior composition of each of those forces is much messier.

Between crossing the Niemen River into great Russia in June 1812 and leaving Moscow in despair some months later, Napoleon's army declined from 422,000 to merely 100,000; by the time they recrossed the Niemen, they were down to 10,000.[5] These numbers trumpet defeat. We may suppose that many of the losses were from desertion; many were from disease and exposure in an unusually early and harsh winter and some were even from battlefield casualties. Suppose at Smolensk – with more than half the army already gone, winter coming on, and the main Russian army yet to be met – some soldier figured (rightly, one might suppose) that defeat was assured by the conditions and the continual losses. Hence, that soldier's continuation on the march could not bring about victory but might well contribute to the casualty lists. Arguably, that soldier's desertion was better for France than his continuing on the march. If he deserted, did he then bear part of the causal responsibility for the eventual French defeat?

A manufacturing company may use several hundreds or thousands of workers to design, produce, and market its products. Most of them might individually be replaced without harm to the firm's output. Indeed, many of them might miss work without affecting the firm's output. Yet, if any great number of them failed to contribute, the firm would be less productive and might fail. What is the causal responsibility of any one of the workers for the firm's success (or failure)?

The problems of voters and of Napoleon's soldiers on the march to Moscow are variants of the more general class of collective action problems. In rational choice theory, the logic of collective action is about the conflict between a group's interest in providing x and the individual group member's incentives or interests. The concern is with incentives and their misfit, rather than with responsibility as in the voting example above. But all of these are instances of the far more general class of problems of strategic interaction in the production of outcomes. In such interaction, it makes little or no sense to say that you or I choose an outcome. We have interests in the potential outcomes. But what we choose is merely a strategy for getting to these. Hence, the common-sense moral language that links responsibility and choice or action is

---

[5]The French engineer, Charles Joseph Minard, portrays this debacle in a masterpiece of graphic representation. See Tufte 1983, pp. 40–41, 176.

partly out of place for choices of strategies. At the very least, it is complicated by the plural, complex causation of outcomes.

Collective action and organizational problems raise the same issues for individual moral responsibility. In either context, my particular action or choice may not be the cause of our outcome and therefore I am not responsible for that outcome in the simple commonsense meaning of the term. Indeed, it is a fallacy of composition to suppose the notion of responsibility generalizes from simple choice to interactive choice situations. For such problems of choice, deontological action theories are in need of further articulation. It seems likely that relevant articulation must rely heavily on consequentialist considerations. Hence, strategic interaction captures the problem of institutional design: Its moral assessment is inherently consequentialist (see further, Hardin 1988, pp. 68–70).

5.3.2   Practical Resolutions

How do we resolve assignments of responsibility in practice? This is a descriptive question about what we do, not what we ought to do. But an understanding of actual practices may inform our normative arguments, even if only by suggesting a range of possibilities. It is to this descriptive issue, as it arises in the law, that H.L.A. Hart and Tony Honoré address their concern in *Causation in the Law* (Hart and Honoré 1985, esp. chaps. 3 and 4). It is also to a descriptive question that contemporary economic analysis of the value of inputs in production is addressed.

In the law, a standard device is to focus on what was anomalous in the causal background of a result. Law commonly confounds actions and their effects as, for example, in the definition of murder as death brought about in certain ways with relevant intentions. Simple theories of direct causation may only poorly fit the actions that, taken together, bring about a particular death. I will take up more extensively the determinate nature of legal rules that may be arbitrary.

Business firms may commonly assess causal relations only at the design stage and then ignore the problem of individual-level causal responsibility, at least for most individuals, for what the firm creates or the profits it makes. For the individual level they focus instead on market allocations of prices for various causal inputs. They do not pay workers according to what the workers contribute causally but according to the market wages for such work. Those wages can change dramatically for demographic reasons of supply of workers having nothing to do with economic valuations of the firms' products.

In many contexts, proxy measures of inputs are used. For example, A did not act in certain ways, and is therefore held responsible for not helping to prevent some harm. Focusing on such proxy measures, particularly on kinds of actions, threatens to make our focus not causal but deontological, especially when we begin to focus on symbolic rather than efficacious action. But there may be good epistemological reasons for using proxy measures, as, for example, the test of alcohol concentration in the blood for a driver or an airline pilot. Stochastically, we may know there is a strong correlation between alcohol levels and incidence of accidents. Although we will not typically know that your high alcohol level means you will have an accident, we can still be sure that going after all drivers with high alcohol levels will reduce the rate of accidents.

In a variant of proxy measures of inputs, we may assign responsibility to someone – for example, in an organization – in order to create incentives for relevant action. We know that a lot of certain kinds of activity will produce the results we want and we wish to motivate such activity. We cannot assign shares of the responsibility for the final result to each activity or person, but we can enhance the prospect of achieving that result.

The striking fact is that all these resolutions of our problem are irrelevant for standard individual-level moral theory except in a contingent way. My following the incentives offered by my organization or reprimanding you for violating some proxy measure of output cannot be justified merely by the kinds of actions these are but must be justified with reference to consequences. To handle all of our individual actions within institutions in standard consequentialist moral theory we would be well served by a genuine capacity for assessing the composition of causes that would allow us to assign shares of responsibility for various outcomes. Proxy, pragmatic, and incentive devices are beside the point for such direct moral responsibility. And we surely have no ready moral analog of the economist's sly substitution of supply-and-demand price for causal contribution.

5.4 The Legal Model of Responsibility

Law is fundamentally unlike morality in the structure of its rules. In law we may conventionally select one of many possible rules for settling some class of issues. The rule need not be an a priori logical inference – it can be arbitrary. Often its main burden is to be determinate. All of this is possible in law because there are authoritative bodies to enforce application of legal rules, no matter that they may be arbitrary. Unless we turn moral restrictions into legal requirements, or we concede determination of morality to a religious authority, or we have a strong communal sense of unquestioned morals, there is no authoritative body to enforce an arbitrary moral rule. Note that legal, religious, and communitarian theories are typically command theories of the right, at least in part. The state, god, or the community commands rules, therefore it is right to follow those rules. If our morality is not under the duress of some authority's command, we will want our moral rules to be persuasively well grounded and not arbitrary.

Consider an arbitrary rule for assigning responsibility for harms that we might adopt in the law. If a corporation does harm, we might hold the corporation responsible for compensating the harmed and then let the organization work out how the burden is to be disaggregated down to the individual members of the corporation. This device might be fine as a matter of determinate law. But as a matter of morality, this device is afflicted with two problems. First, there is moral hazard – the Board and the chief executive officer, who work out the disaggregation, have a strong interest in the outcome.

Second, the device is afflicted with the problem of extracting resources from people who cannot be sensibly seen as morally responsible for the relevant harm. For example, a firm might do something whose harmful effect becomes legally clear only decades later, when virtually all individuals who might be considered causally responsible for the harm are gone. Johns-Manville was eventually held accountable for the harms that were inflicted on those who worked with its asbestos, as in the U.S. naval yards of World War II. Its liabilities bankrupted the firm, whose stockholders lost much of their investment. Suppose a small company's or church's retirement fund invested substantially in the stock shortly before news broke of its impending liability and the fund lost much of its retirees' reserves. That the system should work this way might be good for general productive efficiency or determinateness; or this way might be better than any alternative we think of because the alternatives require knowledge that is unavailable or too costly. The result is then right, but for large systemic reasons, not for reasons of the causal responsibility of the retirees for the asbestosis and mesothelioma caused by Johns-Manville's products.

Also consider a relatively abstract rule: Corporate responsibility for corporate harm should be disaggregated into personal responsibilities whose sum is equal to the corporate responsibility. Unfortunately, causal relations do not sum in this way. If we could disaggregate causally, the collective responsibility might be greater than, less than, or equal to individual responsibilities. Arbitrarily stipulating that they are equal may be a good legal rule. For one thing, it avoids the horrendous analytical problem of determining the full causal story and of parceling causal responsibility to individuals. And this may be a good moral reason for adopting the rule in the law. But, again, this means we have a systemic moral justification for setting corporate and individual responsibilities equal, not a reason of direct causal responsibility.

5.5 Institutional Purposes

How should we define the purpose or purposes of an institution? We could define the purpose narrowly or broadly. But the critical question is, as it is for organizational responsibility, one of composition. Who defines the purpose of institution X? Its current leaders? Its founders? Its entire membership, somehow determined? Can we discover an organization's purpose from an external vantage point with or without testimony from its members? And if we have such testimony, does it trump other claims we might make?

These are inherently difficult conceptual questions to which there are no easy answers. They are conceptually difficult the way the question of partial individual responsibility for a group or institutional action or result is difficult. There may be no way to braid the various contributions to an institution's purpose into a single, coherent strand. It is probably in the law that the problem of multiple determination of purpose has been most extensively addressed. Since it would be odd to speak of the intentions of the collection of people who were the relevant legislators, judges, and citizens, we can speak of the "meaning" of a law. The meaning of a law is how the law comes to be interpreted and understood and how it is filled out with tacit assumptions. Clearly, the focus of meaning is on the result of a long process, not merely the origin in, say, the many minds of a legislature. Such origin might be the more typical focus of an intentional account.

In assessing purposes of institutions we might do no better than to think of the organizational analog of legal meaning. We thereby escape the compositional problem of determining the purpose as an output of some complex process with many causal contributions. The result is a naturalistic, descriptive account of purpose rather than a developmental, intentional account. But if the account is descriptively accurate, it is hard to see what would be gained from a causal, intentional account. The latter might be of interest if our problem were to assess the rightness of actions of current organizational members by reference to what was intended for them. For example, some theorists of constitutional interpretation are concerned with what they call original intent. One might justify this concern by noting that constitutional constraints tend to lead to mutually beneficial stable expectations.[6] Such a justification

---

[6]Original-intent theorists also have deontological and purely intuitionist claims

would be far less compelling for many other institutions and organizations.

For many institutions and organizations we may have no difficulty in determining central purposes. Among the purposes of universities are education and the support of research. The purposes of police forces include the maintenance of order, of business firms the making of profits, of certain professional organizations the service of particular clienteles. As we expand the list of purposes for any of these organizations, we are apt to find less agreement. Moreover, we may often be convinced that some ostensibly other purpose is derivable from the central purposes. We may also suppose that some other purposes are themselves imposed from some larger context. For example, business firms might be constrained to further the larger social purpose of eliminating racial or sexual discrimination even if doing so might interfere with profitability.

Organizations often achieve their apparent purposes. Yet, it does not follow that we can assign individual causal responsibility for contributions to their collective products. What we might be able to do, instead, in some cases is determine what form an organization must take to accomplish its purpose and then hold officials responsible for fulfilling the specified duties of their offices. We would have only a relatively rough causal account of how the organization would achieve particular purposes. We would be unable in the cases of many office holders in the organization to show the causal relations between their particular actions and achieving the organization's purposes. The causal relations might often take the form of John Mackie's INUS conditions. One contributor to the grand result might be insufficient but necessary to a part of the organization that was unnecessary but sufficient to accomplish some task that helps achieve a purpose of the organization. Redundancy would be built into the system. We might not be able to factor any contributor out of the organization and find a resultant loss; yet we know that if we factor out enough contributors, the organization will fail.[7]

for the rightness of having today's citizens be governed according to the intentions of men from centuries earlier. I think none of these claims is compelling; only a consequentialist claim that addresses effects on present and future people can be compelling. One who finds a nonconsequentialist claim compelling might have difficulties with the question, "Why obey the law?" If that, too, is a matter of intuition, how do we decide empirically that this is the law?

[7] Iris Murdoch provides a reverse analog in *Black Prince*. Bradley Pearson is secretly at a vacation house where he has eloped with his beloved. He receives a telegram from Marloe asking him to telephone to learn of his sister's suicide. Such an event might seem to call for breaking off his elopement, although it was not yet consummated and might be fragile. Marloe should not have known how to find him, how-

In the law, there is an additional consideration that the law be fairly applied. This cannot be achieved through ad hoc devices of particular legal officeholders who override standard procedures. Could an organization which is not bound to the same degree by considerations of fairness more readily act from ad hoc assessments of the effectiveness of particular officeholders? Plausibly. For example, we might think the correct general purpose for a company in the market is to secure profits by securing sales. If an officeholder in a particular company happened to be an irritant to other officeholders, a supervisor might reasonably conclude that higher productivity would follow from dismissing the irritating colleague. Unless there were a larger social purpose that governed the company's personnel relations and that trumped the supervisor's discretion, it could be moral within the institution to allow such discretion. There might be a company rule not to allow such discretion to supervisors – perhaps on the belief that it could not be reliably put to use for the benefit of the company's goals. Then it would be immoral within the institution for the supervisor to act with such discretion. The supervisor might successfully appeal to higher authorities in the organization for authorization to act with such discretion, and then it would be moral within the organization. But to do so merely on her own belief in the fit of her action with the fundamental profit-making purpose of her firm would be immoral within the firm.

5.6 The Limits of Moral Design

Consider a near analog of institutional responsibility at the level of individual responsibility: stochastic problems of large-number or frequent interactions involving low levels of risks of large harms (for more extensive discussion, see Hardin 1989). The difficulties of handling such problems in standard ethical discourse have led philosophers to treat them as matters of "moral luck" (Nagel 1979; Williams 1981). For example, I may be one of thousands of drunk drivers on the road tonight, but I am unlucky enough to lose control of my car just where there happens, oddly, to be a pedestrian, whom I kill. Many others merely weaved out of lane, jumped a curb, or spun out of control and then recovered to drive on without harm to anyone. If my pedestrian had not been there, I might have been harmless. It is in part, therefore,

---

ever, and had figured it out from a letter from a real estate agent in Pearson's desk. "And if that terrible telephone call," Pearson reasons as he determines to stay the night, "had been so little determined, so casually caused, it made it seem that much less real, that much easier to obliterate from history" (Murdoch 1975, p. 326).

merely a matter of luck that I am held blameworthy while these other drivers are not.

An institution, such as the law, need not be bothered by the moral theorist's problem of moral luck. It can address such matters as drunk driving stochastically, counting the act of driving drunk as a crime. And it can choose to handle harms that occur according to an efficient rule, such as requiring drivers to have liability insurance to protect those with whom they have accidents, or according to a rule that sets up incentives to reduce the incidence of behavior that correlates with harm. Similarly, an organization that has rules for handling flammable or otherwise dangerous chemicals need not, when I violate those rules, defend the rules by claiming that I would have caused harm; it need only claim that, because following its rules has stochastic benefits, enforcing the rules has general benefits.

Such stochastic problems as drunk driving are morally serious not merely because of the actions involved but because of the plausible and likely consequences of the actions. However, any account of responsibility for such problems must focus not on actual results of action but on ex ante expectations of the results. For example, a drunk driver on a crowded superhighway in a city is culpable of a transgression, of an ex ante likelihood of harm to someone else. The same drunk driver on a secluded and abandoned military roadway in the desert or on a private racetrack may be much less culpable of such a transgression because there is so little ex ante chance of that driver's harming someone else. When we assign responsibility on ex ante suppositions, however, we may generally do so according to some proxy for the kinds of results we think likely to follow. You may be a better and safer driver while legally drunk than I am while legally sober. Or you may be much more careful in handling a jug of explosive chemical than I am even though you violate our organization's rules and I do not. For various informational and epistemological reasons, however, institutions may not be able to take the possibility of such considerations into account in a very fine way and we may satisfice on relevant calculations by simply resorting to a legal definition of drunkenness and culpability for drunk driving or a clear rule on safe procedures.

Perhaps an institutional authority could properly ask of the institution's officeholders, "What if everyone did that?" In private life, I might be able to answer this rule-utilitarian query that my action did not disrupt the more general achievement while it brought benefits of its own. I might plausibly be able to show that perfect compliance with some ostensible rule would be suboptimal, that occasional violation of the rule would produce a better outcome (Hardin 1988, pp. 65–68). One might suppose that if I have to answer an institutional query why I violated one of its rules, the very fact that my violation has been noticed in the institution suggests, prima facie, that it may have effects on the behavior of others in the institution through the example it presents. The institution's mobilization behind a particular rule of behavior, thereby standardizing it, might actually make it more likely to be optimal to adhere perfectly to the rule. But even if such an argument tended to be valid, so that there were a seeming difference between institutional and individual strictures, this difference would only entail a greater likelihood that the individual violation of institutional procedures or rules is genuinely counter to the purposes of the institution. On some occasions, the violation might still be justified even by the purposes of the institution.

Suppose my office requires certain actions from me to enable my institution to achieve its purpose. The requirement is causally deduced. Hence, there may be disagreement over how well the requirement fits the institution's purpose. Suppose I share my institution's purpose and genuinely wish to further it. But I conclude that what I am supposed to do, under the institution's rules, hinders rather than furthers that purpose. Have I done wrong if I therefore violate the institution's rules to help the institution? Within the institution I may have done wrong. If, however, my action is externally judged, just as the purpose of the institution itself must be externally judged, it may seem right. From that perspective I can conclude I have done right. Yet, my institution may rightly judge that I have done wrong. The difference turns merely on the differential assessments of causal facts. There may be understandable differences in epistemological capacities for organizations and individuals that lead them to reach different conclusions.

For an organization, unfortunately, we can commonly expect incoherency in the internal requirements on various office holders because there will be no fully worked out causal account of how the organization's structure and procedures achieve its purposes. And we can probably expect many of the requirements to be little more than conventional in the sense that no one could give a causal account of how the requirements contribute to the organization's purposes. Hence, the claim that the official requirements of an institution constitute the internal morality of the organization might be on shaky ground, at least for some requirements, although perhaps not for others.

But note that the assertion that a requirement is merely conventionally, and not causally, justified can be misleading. As in the argument above for institutions in general and for similar epistemological reasons, we can conclude that, in my life as a citizen under the law, it can be right for me to violate the law and nevertheless right for officials of the law to punish me for my violation (Hardin 1994). There is a perhaps urgent difference between the law and other kinds of institutions in this respect. Among the purposes of the law may be to achieve fairness and to reach finality. Hence, individual divergences by officers of the law may actually be causally harmful to its purposes. It might matter less which of various resolutions is reached than that the same resolution is reached for all like cases. Hence, although no one resolution may be clearly best, consistent application of any one of several might be better than inconsistent application of each of these in some fraction of cases. Insofar as similar concerns enter in the design of other institutions, the fact that a particular requirement is merely conventionally defined need not block its moral force within the institution. But there must be many instances in varied organizations in which there is not even this reason of precedent and fairness to moralize conventionally adopted rules for behavior.

5.7 Individual vs. Institutional Morality

A common response to institutions and their moral problems is to suppose that morality is only for individuals and that institutions are a problem, not a solution. In some moral traditions, this seems to be a relatively natural inference, although it is unlikely to be a hard logical inference. In other traditions, the move from individual-level to institutional-level theories seems to be incumbent on the theories. For example, utilitarianism was both institutional and personal from the beginning. Kantian theory has clear connections to institutional concerns already in Kant's own jurisprudence. And on a plausible reading, Aristotelian virtue theory requires functional derivation of personal virtues from the requisites for institutional roles. But much of what may be called commonsense ethics is virtually blind to institutions.

The novelist and philosopher Iris Murdoch judges people by their character, to which their actions give clues. She writes, "I daresay human wickedness is sometimes the product of a sort of conscious leeringly evil intent. . . . But more usually it is the product of a semi-deliberate inattention, a sort of swooning relationship to time" (Murdoch 1975, p. 189). Moreover, "The wicked regard time as discontinuous, the wicked dull their sense of natural causality. The good feel being as a total dense mesh of tiny interconnections" (Murdoch 1975, p. 125). Apparently, Murdoch supposes much of the world shares her views, at least instinctively, and she may be right. For example, Bradley Pearson, the protagonist of *Black Prince*, concludes in the end that he is "condemned for being a certain awful kind of person" rather than for a particular action (Murdoch 1975, p. 387).

One might suppose Murdoch merely asserts a definition when she associates wickedness with regarding time as discontinuous (which implies having a weak sense of personal identification) and having a dull sense of natural causality. But that would not be an interesting move. The extraordinary feature of Murdoch's view is that it makes morality a causal correlate of epistemology and sense of personal identification. Many of us dull "our sense of natural causality" because we do not have or believe in this view of the causal structure of the world, in which one's actions have explicit, determinate effects. The view of personal identity as "a total dense mesh of tiny interconnections" is also somewhat insular and archaic, although it may be widely held. In speaking of "being," Murdoch presumably means to imply not only identity but also identification with, or commitment to, one's self.[8] Both Murdoch's epistemology and her views of personal identification are reasonably up for debate independently of moral theory. It is plausible that one would conclude that, epistemologically and as a matter of personal identification, one should be as Murdoch describes the wicked person. How odd – we are plausibly wicked out of good sense.

We require large organizations for the achievement of many of our purposes, including moral purposes, including moral purposes that Murdoch would likely share. But such organizations inherently share the burden of the epistemology and identification of Murdoch's wicked. We are therefore damned to wickedness if we strive to achieve certain moral purposes. Murdoch's vision is consistent with Hannah Arendt's view of the amorality of institutions and the banality of evil. Large institutions break the sense of personal causal connection and they commonly produce a semideliberate inattention. These tendencies are, indeed, part of their great value. Institutions can bring things about despite the weakness of personal causal efficacy. And they achieve efficiency by dealing with problems in routinized aggregates rather than through deliberate, individualized attention.

As readers of Murdoch know, many of her central characters, if judged by what they do, are rotten – often merely because they are weak and self-obsessed and, in their self-obsession, they have what Murdoch calls "a swooning relationship" to time and much else. One of the greatest values of institutions is to block many kinds of rotten action. They may or may not succeed in elevating character, but they can often do well with the material they have. Given that institutions are necessary for our lives, we should wish to understand morality by design and its limits.

[8]Identity over a lifetime is a perverse notion no matter how widely held it may be. See further, Hardin 1988, pp. 191–98.

5.8   Omega School, Public School

Large organizations that have extensive experience dealing with problems tend to handle problems under two fairly distinct sets of rules:

1. Rules governing putative moral infractions that are not functionally related to the institution's purpose; and
2. Rules governing actions that harm the institution's capacity to fulfill its purpose.

It is the second category that is the focus of institutional morality. Indeed, for many organizations, it is the only category of concern, because these organizations have opted out of trying to regulate private behavior not clearly related to organizational success.

Because institutions must generally be concerned with legal as well as moral problems, these two categories will typically be more complex than this. The first category will commonly include legal infractions on matters not functionally related to the institution's purpose. The second category will include legal rules that blind the institution and hence become part of its purpose. For example, legal rules on nondiscrimination in hiring may govern central aspects of an organization so forcefully as to make nondiscrimination a part of the working purpose of the organization. Violation of these rules would be both an organizational and a legal matter. One might prefer to treat legal constraints as strictly external and not bring them into an institution's purpose or mission.

Smaller institutions are often less experienced in and burdened with handling problems of ethical violations within the institutions. They may therefore tend to run all these problems together as though they were one general class and to treat them in a somewhat ad hoc way, relying on seat-of-the-pants moral intuitions. Variance within and variance across such institutions is likely to be very large not merely because of differences in factual assessment of cases but because of idiosyncratic normative assessment.

Chief among the differences between less experienced and more experienced organizations is that the more experienced tend to ignore the first category of rules. They do not take moral infractions that do not fairly directly relate to the organization's tasks and achievements to be matters for institutional resolution. For example, if I lie to you about the positions of the chess pieces at the end of our lunch break yesterday in order to win the game when we set it back up today, that is not an organizational matter even though it happens in the organization and between members of the organization. Of course, there are some moral infractions that could take place entirely outside an institution and still be considered to have effect on organizational functioning. For example, many people think that pedophiles should not be entrusted with the care or teaching of children. Hence, the boundaries between the range of rules and (1) and (2) above may not be clear. Even then, however, the debate over where the boundary lies should be a debate about the causal implications of the proscribed behavior for the institution's purpose.

This is not to say that actions that are unrelated to relevant institutional purposes are beyond moral censure. Indeed, they need not even be beyond legal censure. For example, it might be fully reasonable that the law forbid and penalize driving beyond some speed, but it would be unreasonable if a member's legal guilt for speeding were taken as grounds for the organization's penalizing the member. One might reach this conclusion from Michael Walzer's claim that there are different spheres of justice and that they typically should not be mixed (Walzer 1983). But it follows simply enough from pragmatic and utilitarian concern with the division of labor and responsibility and from standard moral and legal concern with keeping sanctions fair by avoiding double jeopardy. It also follows for most organizations from the fact that investment in regulating matters unrelated to the functioning of an organization would interfere with its functioning.

What is wrong with running the two categories of rules together? In a philosophy department in which there was a perennial shortage of faculty to teach ethics, a colleague of mine once quipped to students that he could teach ethics but that his colleagues would not let him. Why not? Because he knew what is right and what is wrong. In fact his disqualification may afflict most of us. The trouble with one person's knowing what is right and wrong is that others know differently. You may think lying is a mortal sin worthy of banishment from our society; I may think it merely foolish in most cases. If organizations are to apply one knower's standards to cases this year and another knower's standards to cases next year, the result may be outrageous variance in the treatment of like cases. Seat-of-the-pants ethics is bad enough for parents to inflict on their children; it can be disastrous for organizations and broad institutions. This problem is exacerbated if the two categories of cases above are not kept separate, with organizational invocation reserved for the second category of functionally relevant actions.

Let us consider a comparative case of two institutions that display important features of institutional morality. We wish to highlight differences in degree of institutionalization and in the degree of separation of ordinary personal morality from institutionally functional morality. Consider an example of a small institution that has a large, more generally institutionalized counterpart. A private school, call it Omega,[9] that is not part of some larger organization of schools may make up all its procedures on its own. Its personnel may be clearly superb in some functions, such as teaching. But it does not readily follow that they will be good at moral regulation of students' behavior. Omega has few cases of problem behavior and understandably, therefore, it has very little available procedure for dealing with them. Two decades ago it had only administrative procedures. But it was caught by the drug revolution that permeated the school and wrecked many students' lives. In part, its problem was lack of knowledge at all of what was going on. The faculty were not even competent to discover the facts until the harm was widespread. Omega then made the use of drugs under certain circumstances – such as in the school and at events sanctioned by the school – subject to penalties in the school. Before the drug days, discipline problems at Omega were handled administratively by a couple of people. They were probably moralized and personalized in both bad and good ways and with a range of variance and, therefore, unfairness that depended on who the particular administrators were. Idiosyncratic, seat-of-the-pants morality may have intruded heavily into many decisions.[10]

After the drug disaster, Omega's experience with problems that seemed to interfere with the mission of the school grew more diverse. Its sense that it was not handling them uniformly and fairly and that it needed more discussion from diverse parties led to the establishment of a standing disciplinary committee that included students and faculty. That committee is to determine facts and to recommend sanctions. Perhaps out of fears the committee would not perform well, the administration reserved to itself the power to assign punishment, but in actual practice it came to respect the committee's recommendations.

Omega has a handbook that includes guidelines on behavior. The most important guideline is one which is almost undefinable. Students are to respect the Omega community and to adhere to the Omega spirit.

[9]The facts as reported here are somewhat stylized, but they are from an actual school, and they roughly fit a second school as well.

[10]Historically, seat-of-the-pants morality ruled many schools, even at the policy level. Plenipotentiary school principals have banned crewcuts for boys in some years and then long hair for boys in other years, banned ponytails for girls, banned and also required petticoats for girls, severely punished the use of even minor expletives, have required that shoes have laces, and so on in extremis. The long list of what individuals have seen fit to ban would be funny if the bans were not backed with sufficient power to harm young lives to no good purpose. One is reminded of the Texas fundamentalist preacher, possibly apocryphal, who ranted against teaching kids foreign languages, saying, "If English was good enough for Jesus, it's good enough for our children."

Failure to do so can result in substantial penalties, including expulsion. A school with far more experience might list the major things that have been found to violate the school's mission and thereby give students clearer guidelines for behavior. Omega often has to create its guidelines in the heat of considering actual cases. Of course, the Supreme Court and other appeals courts do likewise when the law seems ambiguous, but these courts are brought to bear on only a tiny fraction of all cases that arise in the law. Omega's creativity is brought to bear on many of its cases. There are categories of cases, such as plagiarism and cheating of other kinds, that occur frequently enough that there are clear and relatively definitive guidelines for them. But, given the creativity of students at Omega, including students who may very carefully try to determine whether their potential actions have ever been subject to school sanction, there is little surprise that a range of new behaviors is a constant challenge to the disciplinary system.

How does Omega handle the challenge of novel cases? First, some of the parties – perhaps many of them – no doubt apply seat-of-the-pants ethics to the cases, as though, with my philosophy colleague, they had access to true knowledge of what is objectively right or wrong. Seat-of-the-pants ethics in such a context is a variant of natural law. We determine what is right not by reading from the printed rules or law, but rather by inference from the supposed body of generalized natural law that some of us are privileged to know. Taking the stance of natural law leads Omega officials to ask "Should Omega condone behavior X?" A positive law theorist would insist that the proper question must be "Do the Omega guidelines prohibit behavior X?" If the answer to the latter question is a simple no, then Omega must adopt new guidelines before it can punish behavior X and it can only punish instances of it that follow adoption of the new guidelines. The natural lawyers at Omega might conclude that, since they believe it would be wrong for Omega to condone behavior X, that behavior is already prohibited and can be punished.

Second, some of the parties – perhaps including many of the first group – apply reasoning that is an amateurish but serious version of what lawyers use in assessing the fit of extant law to new cases, such as cases that arise out of new technology. For example, does a century-old law prohibiting the use of vehicles in the park prohibit the use of roller blades? Such reasoning at Omega should include attempts to fit the new case to the mission of the school. If previous guidelines were fitted to the mission of Omega, this consideration would be at least partially met. But if the previous cases have been resolved with large intrusions of seat-of-the-pants ethics, the body of rules or guidelines is apt to crumble into a hodgepodge of moralistic and functional elements. Analogical reasoning not heavily constrained by overarching concern with extant guidelines and with functional fit will be poor reasoning. Given the radical disagreements among school officials over proper behavior and what it is right for schools to do about their charges' morality, any argument for there being a credible natural law position on these matters seems implausible. Hence, it might seem that Omega must adhere closely to its specific guidelines in meting out punishments. But this may not be the whole story, as suggested below in the discussion of a violation of the "Omega spirit."

Omega is a school in a large city that has a huge public school system. That system has had enormous experience in dealing with putatively bad behaviors and it has been under constitutional, legal regulation much more extensive than what affects Omega. A particular school in that system – call it City School – benefits vicariously from the experience of the entire system. City School has to make its discipline open and somewhat formal. Indeed, to the extent that it has become directly regulated by law, it is very formal, with lawyers often involved at all stages on behalf of students accused of serious infractions that might lead to sanctions that would jeopardize their further education. Private schools often have quite closed procedures, closed by practice if not strictly by rules. One might say, as defenders of private school practices do, that private schools are more personal with their students. Alas, they can also be more draconian and more personalistic and moralistic in their official treatment of students. The moralism that could not stand up in a court case against City School could wreck the life of a student in Omega.

One might suppose personalism *must* cut both ways, that we must take the bitter with the sweet. But personalism could be structured to play only to the advantage of students, not to their detriment. For example, a school could treat an action that does not clearly fall under stated guidelines as an opportunity for the school community to learn something about how to behave in the future, rather than as an unfortunate opportunity to teach some student a lesson, in the sense to which this phrase has been degraded in the vernacular. Virtually any private school must think broad community teaching is true to its mission. Hence, it is a treatment that is arguably functionally required. At least it would have to be shown why such a policy should not trump the idosyncrasies of Omega's disciplinary proceedings.

In comparing Omega and City School we can see an analog of a fairly natural historical development in institutional morality. We move from justification from idiosyncratic, seat-of-the-pants morality to justification from functional fit with the educational mission of the school. The sheer number of occasions on which to discuss the problem of discipline induces a move to institutionalization. No doubt, there is also increasing bureaucratization, with its mixture of good and bad effects. Merely because of increased scale, personalization declines because the people (administrators, teachers, and others) in the disciplinary system have typically had less personal contact with the accused students. This must often lead to less judgment of the person and more strict reliance on judgment of the accused action. All of these changes together lead to a vision of *institutional* morality, in which individual actions are sanctioned only for their dysfunctional harm to the mission of the school. That mission, for both Omega and City School, is primarily educational, but it is also partly directly moral. Insofar as it is the latter, the argument here from institutional morality will not apply.

Even if we conclude that the City School disciplinary system is more procedurally just, we cannot conclude, merely therefore, that it is morally wrong of Omega to organize its disciplinary procedures as it does. After all, it faces the massive constraint of limited knowledge, the constraint of its very limited experience from its not very large, well-behaved student body. Good social scientists know that their understandings of particular things – practices, institutions, groups, cultures – are apt to be misleading. For example, accidental associations may be assigned casual significance. A standard way to escape this dilemma is to do comparative studies. But it does not take social science to comprehend the value of broadening the range of one's limited experiences by looking at the experiences of others. We do it daily, to choose restaurants and movies, to evaluate acquaintances, to come to a better understanding of our norms, and even to understand ourselves better. Still, systematic comparison of several schools, including City School, might well be beyond the competence of Omega and its staff. And if we were recommending where Omega should put its resources, we might well conclude that putting more resources into mastering or improving disciplinary procedures was a poor way to fulfill its mission. If so, then Omega is right not to invest in revision of the procedures.

Suppose Omega has done well so far but that it now faces an action by a student that is not directly or even analogically covered by its specific guidelines. It might nevertheless seem justified in arguing that the action violates the vague "Omega spirit." If the action does not seem to be a very great violation, Omega might invoke no sanction beyond serious discussion and it might add a new offense to its guidelines for future cases. But suppose the action is a major offense. It seems worse than, say, plagiarism or cheating or than abusive dealing with fellow students or teachers, but it is not even analogically related to these.

In the world of the law, if all the relevant judges are agreeable, there is no authority to block the use of severely stretched analogy to punish an action that seems not covered by statute or case law and that, therefore, should not be punished (at least not in the American legal system, in which punishment for an action before relevant law is created violates the prohibition of ex post facto law). We may rightly criticize a judge who allows such punishment even though we may not be able to prevent judges from doing so on occasion, perhaps especially when they are judging the person as much as the action.

Should Omega act like such an overreaching judge and deliberately, consciously punish what cannot be said to have been widely understood as a violation of its guidelines? Plausibly, yes. (But if so, it should probably temper its sanctions.) Omega can honorably attempt to act for the interests of its students, for its mission, even when this might violate what, in the law, is a compelling norm. The norm is compelling in the law for essentially pragmatic reasons: to block officials from abusing the law to attack certain people, such as blacks in the Jim Crow South, anarchists and leftists in the United States through much of the twentieth century, the homeless, and other people who supposedly do not "fit" by someone's standards. The mission of the law is to do justice; it is hard (though perhaps not impossible) to argue that doing procedural *injustice* is a good way to achieve procedural *justice*. The mission of Omega is to create a splendid atmosphere for education and character development. City School has had imposed upon it the legal requirement that it also do justice, even at potential cost to creating the best atmosphere for education. Eventually the law may also impose upon Omega to do justice in its disciplinary proceedings, and then Omega will be legally, and probably morally (Hardin 1994), bound to follow the norm against ex post facto laws or guidelines.[11] Or even before that, Omega may decide that it should include justice in disciplinary proceedings in its mission, even at the sometime cost of educational atmosphere.

A compelling reason for including a concern with justice to Omega's (or any school's) mission is the grotesque limits to which unregulated censure can go. A remarkably successful black student in a Miami high school gained admission to Harvard University in 1994. The student was then a graduation speaker at his high school. Following school custom, he had his speech approved by an administrator. He then added a brief passage encouraging his fellow black students to take education seriously. "America's true worst nightmare is someone young, black, and educated," he said, "for education is the key that unlocks the door

---

[11]One could phrase a stronger requirement that Omega include concern for *distributive* justice, but that could be an impossible burden if Omega is still to maintain its current educational mission.

of oppression." The administrator then wrote to Harvard to report the student's action. According to a Harvard admissions officer, such letters from school officials occasionally lead to the revocation of admission. The administrator may have reacted to the student's action merely as a violation of school policy, but he also characterized the speech as "of questionable taste."[12] It is striking in this case that a large fraction of citizens would strongly disagree with the administrator's seat-of-the-pants moral judgment of the content of the speech. Yet, the administrator's attempted punishment could have radically affected the student's further education and eventual career. The severity of the punishment of getting him barred from admission to Harvard is arguably grim and beyond the measure of anything of which the student might have been judged wrong under any actual rules or under any reading of a putative "natural law" principle. Such grim punishment cannot justly be left to the discretion of a particular individual's whim.

Finally, note that Omega has a distinctively complex moral problem in that it sees its mission in part as teaching or inculcating morality. It could not (indeed, would not) articulate a coherent or general morality, as some religious schools might do. But it does want to foster certain character traits in its students: in particular, a sense of respect for fellow students and teachers in the common enterprise of education and a strong sense of honesty in intellectual matters. The latter concern may heighten the degree to which the school sees plagiarism and other cheating as bad. They are functionally bad in the educational mission of the school and also bad for the kind of character the school wishes to develop in students. But these two concerns – character development and functional fit with the educational mission of the school – have independent weight. In this respect, Omega is different from many institutions. It is even different from City School to some degree, in that the content of morality in the mission of City School may be more minimal than that in Omega. In the multicultural city, City School and its larger school system could not politically succeed in teaching very much morality. In fact, the New York City schools are even prohibited from teaching tolerance, which is perhaps the most utterly minimal moral principle for life in that city. Omega can and does teach tolerance. Indeed, when its guidelines speak of respect, they largely mean tolerance, so that tolerance is at the core of the Omega spirit.

Clearly, part of the Omega spirit is to develop creativity and autonomy. The histories of individual creativity and autonomy are not exclusively but substantially histories of flouting authority. There is therefore

---

[12]*New York Times*, 31 July 1994, 1.19. The student's admission was not revoked and the administrator was reassigned to teaching after substantial public protest.

some tension in a charge to be creative and autonomous, as though these were a matter of following orders from an authority. This tension is more destructive in the so-called codes of honor of the military academies. These commonly seem directed at honor. But among the ways to honor are squealing on fellow cadets who violate the honor code and submitting to virtually absolute obeisance to authority. Honor is violated by its requirements. In this, the honor codes of the military academies are reminiscent of the brutal codes of honor in the duel, from which they may largely derive. The Omega board and administration must want much of the Omega spirit to be not a charge but an ideal or aspiration for its students. But that makes it an odd principle for enforcement. Where guidelines are poorly articulated, treating the Omega spirit as an overarching guideline may encourage administrative refuge in idiosyncratic, seat-of-the-pants ethics and the sometime corruption of natural law. That is, it encourages the violation of the understanding of institutional morality.

5.9 Concluding Remarks

In assessing the internal morality of an institution, our chief difficulty is compositional. We can, in our ordinary vocabulary, understand what we mean when we say that an individual is responsible for a certain action or that the individual acts morally or immorally. To say of a group or institution that it acts morally or immorally or is responsible is not completely contrary to sense, but it would be odd to think of an organization as an intentional being in the sense in which a person is an intentional being. The organization may be composed of intentional beings, but it is not one itself. Not least of the oddities of treating an organization as an intentional being would be in assigning moral responsibility and even punishment to the organization without having these be reductively applied to the individuals in the organization.

Despite the difficulty of assigning moral responsibility to an institution or organization without assigning it to individuals in the organization, organizations have capacities that transcend those of individuals. For example, organizations can have superior capacities to collect relevant information and theory for handling their tasks and radically superior capacities to mobilize resources to get things done. Organizational policies and actions may also often be much more coherent and consistent over time than individual "policies" and actions. If responsibility is typically associated with capacity, it seemingly makes sense to assign responsibility for outcomes to organizations that bring them about. But moral theories are not sensibly brought to bear on organizations and other institutions without reassessment of notions of responsibility.

In general, the internal morality of acting within an institution is not simply composed from the ordinary morality of individuals. It is artificially constructed to a large extent. The moral theory of institutions and of the behavior of institutional office holders must be derived from the purpose of the institutions. Complex, plural causation and the stochastic nature of many outcomes block the simple association of individual-level moral responsibility with causal responsibility. Hence, an uninstitutionalized act-utilitarian account or a deontological account based on individual-level action theory is largely irrelevant to institutions. We might conclude that institutions are therefore outside the realm of moral discourse. But that would be perverse. Without institutions we can achieve far too few of the moral purposes we have.

References
Bentley, Arthur. 1949. *The Process of Government.* Evanston, Ill.: Principia Press.

Dan-Cohen, Meir. 1986. *Rights, Persons, and Organizations: A Legal Theory for Bureaucratic Society.* Berkeley: University of California Press.

Fuller, Lon L. 1964. *The Morality of Law.* New Haven, Conn.: Yale University Press, 1969. Revised edition.

Hardin, Russell. 1982. *Collective Action.* Baltimore: Johns Hopkins University Press for Resources for the Future.

Hardin, Russell. 1988. *Morality within the Limits of Reason.* Chicago: University of Chicago Press.

Hardin, Russell. 1989. Ethics and stochastic processes. *Social Philosophy and Policy,* 7 (Autumn), 69–80.

Hardin, Russell. 1991. The artificial duties of contemporary professionals. *Social Service Review,* 64 (December), 528–41.

Hardin, Russell. 1994. My university's yacht: Morality and the rule of law. In Ian Shapiro, ed., NOMOS 26, *The Rule of Law.* New York: New York University Press.

Hart, H. L. A., and Tony Honoré. 1985. *Causation in the Law.* Oxford: Oxford University Press. 2nd ed. [1959].

Mill, John Stuart. 1872 [1843]. *A System of Logic, Ratiocinative and Inductive* (any standard eighth edition).

Murdoch, Iris. 1973. *Black Prince.* New York: Viking (Penguin reprint, 1975).

Nagel, Thomas. 1979. Moral luck. Pp. 24–38 in Nagel, *Mortal Questions.* Cambridge: Cambridge University Press.

Olson, Mancur, Jr. 1965. *The Logic of Collective Action.* Cambridge, Mass.: Harvard University Press.

Rawls, John. 1955. Two concepts of rules, *Philosophical Review,* 64, 3–32.

Rawls, John. 1971. *A Theory of Justice*. Cambridge, Mass.: Harvard University Press.

Scanlon, Thomas M. 1977. Liberty, contract, and contribution. In Gerald Dworkin, Gordon Bermant, and Peter G. Brown, eds., *Markets and Morals*. Washington, D.C.: Hemisphere; and New York: Wiley.

Tufte, Edward R. 1983. *The Visual Display of Quantitative Information*. Cheshire, Conn.: Graphics Press.

Walzer, Michael. 1983. *Spheres of Justice*. New York: Basic Books.

Williams, Bernard. 1981. Moral luck. Pp. 20–39 in Williams, *Moral Luck*. Cambridge: Cambridge University Press.

6

The Publicity Principle

DAVID LUBAN

IN A FAMOUS PASSAGE, Kant wrote: "Enlightenment is man's emergence from his self-incurred immaturity. Immaturity is the inability to use one's own understanding without the guidance of another." He added: "Have courage to use your own understanding!" (Kant 1784, p. 54). Though Kant himself was at pains to deny it, this injunction is an enormously subversive political ideal. The most characteristic demand of political leaders has invariably been that their subjects submit their own understanding to the guidance of authorities, either because the authorities are wiser or because an ordered society requires artificial unanimity.

Kant's injunction presumes that the understanding of ordinary citizens is up to the task of deliberating and reflecting on political affairs without the guidance of others; this assumption amounts to the Enlightenment's article of faith. It is profoundly controversial. Politicians often operate according to the self-serving assumption that ordinary citizens must be pacified with malarkey, for they cannot face hard truths. They believe, in the words of H. L. Mencken, that "bosh is the right medicine for boobs" (Mencken 1956, p. 43). This belief, prevalent in political debate and ubiquitous in political practice, is anathema to the Enlightenment's article of faith.

The Enlightenment thus rejects an older view of politics, going back to Plato, according to which government necessarily relies on noble lies – myths or deceptions designed to secure loyalty and love of country.

I delivered drafts of this chapter to seminars at the University of Wisconsin, the University of Maryland, Monash University, the Australian National University, New York University, the University of Iowa, and Wake Forest University. I am very grateful for the many helpful comments and criticisms I received from participants in those seminars.

154

Machiavelli, like Plato (though for rather different reasons), argued that lies and secrecy are essential instruments of successful government. A successful prince, Machiavelli says, must learn how *not* to be good; he must accept that lies, like betrayal and violence, are necessary tools of government. (A backhanded contemporary acknowledgment of this is an anecdote related by the late Louisiana Senator Russell Long. When Long was in secondary school, he approached his uncle Earl, then the governor of Louisiana, and said that he had been assigned to debate the question of whether one should use truth in politics. What should he say? Earl asked which side Russell had been assigned. When Russell replied that he was to debate the affirmative, Earl thought for a moment, then said, "Hell yes! In politics you use anything you can get your hands on.")

The present essay examines one strand of the debate between open and closed government – between the Enlightenment ideal and the arguments represented by Plato and Machiavelli. The examination itself will not move on so enormous a scale. Rather, my method will be to approach the central issues by examining a single principle of political morality that derives from the Enlightenment ideal.

In the second appendix to his essay "Perpetual Peace," Kant proposes the following "transcendental formula of public law":

All actions relating to the right of other human beings are wrong if their maxim is incompatible with publicity.[1]

The connection between this formula and the Enlightenment's article of faith is relatively straightforward. Publicity will enable citizens to submit "actions relating to the right of other human beings" – public policies, we may call them – to the scrutiny of their own understanding. If the Enlightenment's article of faith is correct, such public debate and

---

[1] "Alle auf das Recht anderer Menschen bezogene Handlungen, deren Maxime sich nicht mit der Publizität verträgt, sind unrecht" (Kant 1795c, p. 381). Normally I shall use the English editions of Beck and Reiss (Kant 1795b, a). But here I am unsatisfied with Beck's translation, which reads, "All actions relating to the right of other men are unjust if their maxim is not consistent with publicity" (Kant 1795b, p. 129). Beck's "not consistent" makes the disharmony between the maxim and publicity a matter of logical or practical contradiction. But Kant's "*sich nicht verträgt*" implies only incompatibility, not contradiction. As we shall see in section 6.2.3, it is an important interpretive question whether Kant thinks his publicity test requires a demonstration of practical contradiction or merely contingent incongruence. I want to avoid begging this question through the translation. Reiss does better: "All actions affecting the rights of other human beings are wrong if their maxim is not compatible with their being made public" (Kant 1795a, p. 126). But he pluralizes "*das Recht*"; as in English, however, talk of "right" is more general (and more ambiguous) than talk of "rights."

scrutiny are highly desirable, and the inability of policies to withstand publicity is suspicious. If, on the other hand, ordinary citizens' understanding cannot be trusted, then good government, and indeed justice itself, will require noble lies. In that case Kant's formula will be false.

Kant believed that his "transcendental formula of public law" – the *publicity principle*, as I shall call it – would provide an easy-to-use test for the moral rightness of political action, an "experiment of pure reason" that we perform by asking of any political action (roughly), "Could I still get away with this if my action and my reason for doing it were publicly known?" If the answer is no, then the action is wrong. John Rawls, the most eminent contemporary Kantian political philosopher, adopts this "publicity condition" as a "formal constraint on the concept of right," and employs it in his argument in *A Theory of Justice* (Rawls 1971, pp. 130, 133).

Kant's test does not imply a moral requirement that every political action actually be publicized.[2] It is a hypothetical publicity test: Kant speaks only of the "possibility" and "capacity" of a maxim's withstanding full public knowledge. His "experiment of pure reason" is a thought experiment.

It is quite possible, of course, that through thought alone we will be unable to answer the question of whether an action and its maxim could withstand publicity. Thus in many cases the thought experiment may yield no determinable result. Moreover, the test is purely negative: Kant is at some pains to emphasize that the bare fact that a maxim could withstand publicity does not by itself show that the maxim is right; the publicity principle says only that if the maxim could not withstand publicity it must be wrong.[3]

Yet even within these limitations the publicity principle is a remarkably powerful proposition of political morality, and indeed of individual morality as well.[4] As we shall see, on its face it rules out a variety of principles and policies, ranging from widely held views of the judicial process through the American Catholic Church's position on nuclear deterrence to utilitarian accounts of morality.

The publicity principle is not only a proposition of morality, moreover, but a principle of institutional design as well. Suppose that the

---

[2]The latter is the erroneous reading of Habermas, who glosses the test to demand that maxims of political action "were capable of, or indeed in need of, publicity" (Habermas 1989, p. 108).

[3]See Kant 1795c, pp. 381–82; Kant 1795a, p. 126; Kant 1795b, p. 130; likewise, Kant 1795c, pp. 384–85; Kant 1795a, p. 129; Kant 1795b, p. 133.

[4]Kant himself claims that his "transcendental formula" is both juridical and ethical, belonging to the doctrine of virtue as well as the doctrine of right. Kant 1795c, p. 381; Kant 1795a, p. 126; Kant 1795b, p. 129.

publicity principle were false; suppose, in other words, that on occasion just policies were incompatible with publicity. In that case, we would be forced to construct institutions capable of formulating and executing policies largely out of reach of public oversight, for fear that good government would be subverted by unwise or immoral public pressure. We would leave a good deal of latitude for official secrecy, and move very cautiously in constructing oversight and accountability institutions (and that fact might itself have to be kept confidential). If, on the other hand, the publicity principle is true, we would have an argument for augmenting public accountability and institutional openness: roughly, that the best way to make sure that officials formulate policies that *could* withstand publicity is by increasing the likelihood that policies *will* withstand publicity.

Kant's formula, however, leaves many questions unanswered. What is meant by "publicity"? What is it to be incompatible with publicity? Does the publicity principle mean to rule out all state secrets, as it at first glance appears to? Most important of all, of course, is whether the publicity principle is true. What is the connection between publicity and morality? Is it merely the intuition that anything one can't do openly has got to be wrong? I shall be arguing that the publicity principle is surprisingly difficult to defend; but, in the end, I shall offer a qualified and conditional defense (conditioned on the truth of some empirical conjectures that I am not in a position to defend but that strike me as more plausible than their denials).

6.1   The Publicity Principle in Action

My aim in this section is to exhibit the publicity principle in action – to show, by means of examples, that it is indeed a powerful tool for the moral criticism of public policy. What follows is an unorderly catalogue of views and arguments that are facially ruled out by the publicity principle – "facially," because subsequently we must see whether some of them may be rehabilitated. I choose examples from three arenas: the legal system, representing domestic issues; nuclear weapons policy, representing foreign policy and military issues; and moral theory.

6.1.1   Publicity and the Legal System

Should judges be candid about their reasons for deciding cases? Four Yale law professors, Charles Black, Alexander Bickel, Guido Calabresi, and Paul Gewirtz, have considered variations on an argument against judicial candor. For short, I shall call it the "Yale argument."

Calabresi frames the argument clearly in a discussion of whether judges ought to strike, limit, or otherwise undermine anachronistic laws that the legislature has not gotten around to repealing:

> [T]o admit this judicial power would be inevitably to admit its abuse; . . . we come closer to achieving the amount of judicial supervision we want by denying that it is permitted at all than we would by acknowledging what is going on and trying to control it by doctrine and language; . . . we decide better, in practice, by denying that it ever takes place at all. . . . [R]ecognition of the doctrine [of judicial revision of anachronistic laws] would have lawyers arguing its applicability where it should not apply. . . . (Calabresi 1982, pp. 174–75)

Charles Black argues similarly that a judge may want to insist on an absolute rule against torture while nevertheless permitting the torture of a terrorist who has hidden a hydrogen bomb set to go off in an hour and who will not otherwise reveal its location. The alternative to this judicial deception is admitting that the rule against torture may be balanced away, and that is too dangerous an admission. Analogously, he argues, for the late Supreme Court Justice Hugo Black's insistence that rights of free speech are absolute when Justice Black knew full well that they are not (Black 1961, discussed in Calabresi 1982, pp. 173–75). According to Charles Black, Justice Black was willing in his judicial practice to countenance the restriction of free speech rights. But he would not admit explicitly that free speech rights could be balanced away, for fear that if he did admit it lawyers would seize on his language to argue for restrictions in inappropriate cases.

The Yale argument likewise underlies Bickel's famous theory of the "passive virtues." The passive virtues consist in the judicious use of decision-dodging subterfuges by the Supreme Court to avoid placing its constitutional imprimatur on either side of certain politically divisive issues (Bickel 1962). According to Bickel, it would be catastrophic for the Court to admit that it wishes for political reasons to dodge constitutional issues, so instead the Court must appeal (disingenuously?) to technical doctrines of standing, ripeness, vagueness, abstention, and political questions which permit it to avoid reaching the merits of cases.

Gewirtz raises the Yale argument when he suggests that judges must often shape remedies with one eye directed toward the political resistance their actions will meet. The examples he has in mind are American federal court decisions ending school segregation, which the courts, fearful of white violence, coupled with remedies that ensured that segregation would persist for many years. The Yale argument points toward the conclusion that judges should deny that they are taking account of political resistance to their remedies, since to admit it would delegitimize the courts and create perverse incentives to lawlessness on the part of losing litigants (Gewirtz 1983, pp. 665–74).

I hasten to add that Calabresi and Gewirtz both reject the Yale argument, whereas Black and Bickel apparently accept it. But even Calabresi and Gewirtz reject it only on instrumental, cost-benefit grounds (weak ones at that, in my opinion). Gewirtz argues that "dishonesty always creates the risk of its detection, and, with detection, harm to the courts' stature that may exceed any losses that result from candidly admitting limited power."[5] Calabresi's argument is a more guarded version of Gewirtz's:

> [W]e are not comparing a certain harm-benefit with an uncertain one. We do not know the ultimate dangers of . . . use of subterfuges. . . . The burden must be on those who would argue for indirection. The choice must be for candor. (Calabresi 1982, p. 177)

The publicity principle, on the other hand, yields an immediate, and noninstrumental, argument against judicial subterfuge. If judges cannot openly state their real reasons for a decision, the publicity principle tells us that the decision is illegitimate. If Justice Black "was sometimes forced to twist the notion of free speech in order to square absolute protection with his opinion that certain speech-related activities could be regulated" (Calabresi 1982, p. 296 n. 11), he did wrong. Either he should have opposed regulating the speech-related activities in question, or, if he was convinced that the regulations were valid, he should have abandoned his professions of absolutism.

Interestingly enough, Judge Richard Posner has proposed a "publicity test" in the context of judicial decision-making. According to Posner, "a decision is principled if and only if the ground of decision can be stated truthfully in a form the judge could publicly avow without inviting virtually universal condemnation by professional opinion" (Posner 1985, p. 215). Posner is a leading federal appellate judge as well as one of America's most influential writers on jurisprudence, and his resurrection of Kant's idea underlines its centrality to the whole issue of judicial candor.

From the issue of judicial candor we may pass to the question of how transparent the legal system must in general be. Paraphrasing Thurmond Arnold with approval, Karl Llewellyn once wrote concerning the trial process:

> an impressive ceremonial has a value in making people *feel* that something is being done; this holds, whether the result is right or

[5]Gewirtz 1983, p. 671. I criticize this argument in Luban 1994, pp. 330–31.

wrong; and there is some value in an institution which makes men content with fate, whatever that fate may be. (Llewellyn 1940, p. 610)

In a different context, Charles Nesson has recently argued that some rules of evidence that seem irrational from a strictly scientific or epistemological point of view can nonetheless be justified because they are "ways to promote public acceptance of verdicts" (Nesson 1985, p. 1368). According to Nesson, "The aim of the factfinding process is not to generate mathematically 'probable' verdicts, but rather to generate acceptable ones; only an acceptable verdict will project the underlying legal rule to society and affirm the rule's behavioral norm [i.e., convince people that they should obey the rule]."[6]

Both Llewellyn and Nesson seem to be saying that public compliance and deference to legal rules are more important than the objective rightness or justness of those rules. This is a view of great antiquity; it assumes that order, compliance, and stability are more fundamental social values than justice. The problem, however, is that it is quite likely that people will willingly defer to legal rules only when they believe that those rules are just. (Studies of convict popfor example, have found that convicts, even those who freely acknowledge that they committed the crimes, will typically accept the legitimacy of their punishment only if they believe that they were fairly convicted.) Hence, people must be made to believe that legal institutions are genuine purveyors of justice whether or not that is so. Paradoxically, institutions of justice aim to stabilize society rather than to do justice. But if people believe that these institutions do not aim at justice, then they will not respect those institutions, and the institutions will break down – paradoxically, they will not stabilize society. Hence the view that institutions of justice exist to stabilize a society rather than to do justice must remain esoteric, and most people must instead be made to believe in the justice of these institutions.[7] Plato held some such theory and therefore proposed (in the *Laws* at 716a–b) that a public celebration of justice be promoted as a kind of official religion, even though a few philosophers understand that justice is less important than order and that the religion is false.[8] The religion of justice is a noble lie.

[6]Nesson 1985, p. 1359. Subsequently, however, it becomes clear that Nesson, unlike Llewellyn, is not defending acceptable-but-wrong verdicts. Rather, he is suggesting (a) that even a correct verdict will be acceptable only when it is taken to refer to the underlying event rather than the legal evidence, and (b) that a verdict may be acceptable-*and-right* even though its probability is not high. In my view, Nesson's actual argument is better than the less careful dicta quoted here.

[7]In this paragraph I am partly quoting Luban 1994, pp. 329–30. I elaborate on this argument on pp. 329–31.

[8]For a justification of this reading of Plato, see Luban 1994, pp. 321–29.

Llewellyn and Nesson seem to endorse this Platonic view that order is more important than justice and that the knowledge that order is more important than justice must be restricted to a few illuminati. Indeed, however, the Platonic view has wide acceptance among commentators on the judicial process. The often times repeated argument that overt judicial lawmaking is dangerous because it will make the general public lose respect for the judiciary (even though it is acknowledged that, realistically, judges cannot avoid lawmaking) makes sense only as a plea for judges to keep the political aspects of their craft esoteric.

It need hardly be said that all such views are inconsistent with the publicity principle. What would happen if everyone knew and accepted Llewellyn's point that a trial, accurate or inaccurate, is intended principally as a ceremonial to reconcile us to our fates? Then the ceremonial would no longer reconcile us to our fates. Similarly, if people generally knew that evidence laws were intended to make them accept verdicts rather than to keep the verdicts honest, verdicts would be less acceptable. If it were publicly known that institutions of justice exist for the sake of stability rather than justice, that knowledge would destabilize those institutions. None of these policies, it would seem, can withstand publicity. Thus, they all fail Kant's test.

Another example of a legal institution that facially fails the publicity principle arises from Meir Dan-Cohen's account of "acoustic separation" in the criminal law. By this Dan-Cohen means that some legal doctrines and rules are directed primarily at officials, and are not meant to be "overheard" by the general public – hence the term "acoustic separation." Dan-Cohen suggests that in many cases acoustic separation is a desirable feature of the law" (Dan-Cohen 1984). For example, proponents of a defense of duress point to "the unfairness of punishing a person for succumbing to pressures to which even his judges might have yielded" (Dan-Cohen 1984). If this argument is persuasive, the law ought to permit accused persons to defend themselves by pleading duress. However, if the availability of the defense is generally known, it invites obvious abuse. People will be less likely to resist pressures to commit crimes that they might in fact be perfectly capable of resisting. Similarly with many other defenses and mitigations in criminal law: they provide opportunities for judges to temper or mitigate a harsh response, and precisely for that reason it is better if they are not widely known, since general knowledge of their availability would weaken the deterrent effect of the law.

If the availability of such doctrines is transmitted only selectively, Dan-Cohen argues, we can have our cake and eat it too. The law can be merciful without losing its deterrent effects. "[T]he law's own violence and brutality may suggest a general rationale for selective transmission:

in some circumstances selective transmission can mitigate or serve as a substitute for the violent means that the law frequently employs" (Dan-Cohen 1984, p. 667).

As Dan-Cohen is acutely aware, however, acoustic separation seems antithetical to the publicity principle, which he understands to be an analytical component of the rule of law ideal as well as of political morality more generally. "Central to the rule of law is the requirement that the law be clearly stated and publicly proclaimed. The alarm likely to follow the realization that selective transmission may circumvent these requirements accordingly seems well founded" (Dan-Cohen 1984, p. 667). Violating the rule of law through selective transmission of legal doctrines contradicts the publicity principle.

6.1.2 Nuclear Deterrence and Publicity

Nations aim to possess nuclear weapons for a variety of reasons, but surely the most significant of these is to gain political advantage. Clausewitz defined war as the pursuit of politics by other means, and I will use the term *Clausewitzian theory* to refer to the view that nuclear weapons, like conventional weapons, may be used to gain political advantage.

Even at the dawn of the nuclear age, however, some military thinkers recognized that nuclear weapons are not simply more powerful versions of conventional force. In a famous 1946 book, nuclear strategist Bernard Brodie wrote: "Thus far the chief purpose of our military establishment has been to win wars. From now on its chief purpose must be to avert them. It can have almost no other useful purpose" (Brodie 1946, p. 76). I will use the term *pure deterrence theory* for the view that a nuclear arsenal exists for only one reason: to deter aggression in order to keep the nuclear peace. Most people consider an all-out use of nuclear weapons to be totally immoral. It is, in addition, irrational from a self-interested point of view, since an all-out nuclear attack may well precipitate nuclear winter. Even on a smaller scale nuclear war may be irrational from a self-interested point of view: if Israel, for example, used nuclear weapons on its Arab neighbors it would risk contaminating and poisoning its own population.

However, many people who are persuaded that nuclear warfare is immoral or irrational believe nevertheless that nuclear powers such as the United States must maintain the capacity for all-out use of nuclear weapons in order to deter other nuclear powers successfully. Indeed, especially if all-out use of nuclear weapons is totally immoral, one is morally required to prevent their use, and lacking anything like an effective Star Wars technology, deterrence – it is often argued – is the only way to keep the nuclear peace. Though *using* nuclear weapons is immoral or irrational, *having* nuclear weapons may be moral and rational. This is the rationale behind pure deterrence theory. In contrast with Clausewitzian theory, pure deterrence theory regards nuclear weapons as having to do not with political advantage, but with nuclear weapons and nothing else.

It is sometimes maintained that strategies based on "counterforce" – attacking only an adversary's military forces – and "flexible response" – focusing on less drastic responses than all-out nuclear war – make the arguments raised by pure deterrence theory against all-out use of nuclear weapons moot. This is incorrect. Even strategies that claim to abjure city-killing or all-out use must nevertheless maintain the capacity and will for these responses, because every strategy of nuclear deterrence demands the capacity to retaliate against any level of violence (including city-killing) with a level at least as great. Without the effective capability to launch all-out city-killing thermonuclear war, even strategies based on limited and "counterforce" responses unravel, since the high trump card remains in the adversary's hands.

Thus, pure deterrence theory remains central to the discussion of nuclear weapons policy. Pure deterrence theory demands that a nuclear power engage in bluff, deterring adversaries by threatening to retaliate, but in reality intending not to retaliate should deterrence fail. This is because according to pure deterrence theory nuclear weapons can be retained *only* to deter and *never* to be used. Adversaries must nevertheless believe, or at least suspect, that a nuclear power will launch a retaliatory second strike despite the power's commitment to pure deterrence. The nuclear power must credibly threaten the second strike, and the only way to make such a threat credible is to convince adversaries that the power in fact does not believe in pure deterrence theory – that is, that the power does not believe that all-out nuclear use is inevitably immoral or irrational.

This conclusion follows from the so-called paradox of deterrence, stated by Jonathan Schell as follows: "One cannot credibly deter a first strike with a second strike whose raison d'être dissolves the moment the first strike arrives. It follows that, as far as deterrence theory is concerned, there is no reason for either side not to launch a first strike" (Schell 1982, p. 202). Bluffing the adversary into believing that one does not believe in deterrence theory is the only way out.[9]

[9] The raison d'être for a second strike can dissolve in the face of an enemy first strike either for moral reasons (e.g., one believes that while it is morally acceptable to *threaten* a second strike, it is immoral to carry out the threat) or for prudential reasons (e.g., the second strike lowers one's own utility, for example by inducing nuclear winter). Thus, the paradox of deterrence may be viewed as either a moral

From this it follows that pure deterrence theory cannot survive the publicity principle. Pure deterrence theory requires from us a policy of constructing the capacity for the all-out second strike *but intending never to use it*. Each nuclear power is morally required to bluff the others, but clearly a bluff cannot withstand full publicity.

One might object that the publicity principle is intended for use only within a single community, so that the inability of a policy of nuclear bluff to withstand universal publicity, outside as well as within a single society, does not really run afoul of the publicity principle. Unfortunately, this does not matter. Even full publicity within a single nation of the policy of nuclear bluff is impossible, for the obvious reason that an entire nation cannot go off and huddle out of earshot of other nations.

6.1.3 Morality

My final two illustrations of the publicity principle in action are drawn from the arena of what might be called general morality. The first is an issue in political morality, while the second is drawn from moral theory.

A frequent accusation directed at politicians is that they are hypocrites, who profess a high standard of rectitude but compromise it repeatedly. The eminent political philosopher Judith Shklar has defended public hypocrisy on the part of politicians, which she believes is essential to a democratic political order. According to Shklar,

> representative democracy must, like any form of government, maintain its legitimacy by reinforcing the ideological values upon which it is based. . . . That means that those engaged in governing must assume at the very least two roles, one of pursuing policies and another of edifying the governed in order to legitimize these plans. . . . There is nevertheless a built-in tension; for the disparity between what is said and what is done remains great. . . . Without ancestor worship or divine provenance to rely on, modern liberal democracy has little but its moral promise to sustain it. That is why it generates . . . the interplay of hypocrisy and vocal antihypocrisy. (Shklar 1979, pp. 13–14)

Hence Shklar admires Benjamin Franklin, who defended hypocrisy as a requirement of democratic politics:

paradox or a paradox of rationality. On the first, see Kavka 1978; on the second, see Gauthier 1984, and responses to Gauthier in Kavka 1984, Lewis 1984, pp. 141–43, and Luban 1986.

He was a shrewd calculator who took it for granted that the politics of persuasion required hypocrisy. . . . Here is hypocrisy as a conscious act in response to a situation that demands it. Persuasion is not natural; it requires a great deal of effort, and in a man as superior to his fellows as Franklin was, it takes exactly what he described. . . . A democratic "social fabric" would "come undone" just as quickly as any other if everyone were always "wholly frank with everyone." (Shklar 1979, pp. 16–17)

Like the Platonic view of justice and legal institutions, Shklar's account endorses a double standard of behavior. A man like Franklin, who is "superior to his fellows," must engage in actions for reasons that he masks from his inferiors. Hypocritical action, however, cannot withstand the publicity principle: hypocrisy is the antithesis of publicity.[10]

In a sense, Shklar's argument translates Plato's concept of the "noble lie" into the political framework of modern democracy. But, like Plato's original notion, the argument concludes that some acts of political wisdom can never be publicized, and such a conclusion is inconsistent with the publicity principle.

Similar conclusions dog the moral theory of utilitarianism. A well-known problem with utilitarianism is that utility may best be served if people do not believe in utilitarianism. One way this can be so is that people may be happier if they do not believe in utilitarianism; in that case the utilitarian project of maximizing human happiness demands that people not believe in utilitarianism. As Bernard Williams writes,

Utilitarianism would do well then to acknowledge the evident fact that among the things that make people happy is not only making other people happy, but being taken up or involved in any of a vast range of projects. . . . Now none of these is itself the *pursuit of happiness*. . . . Happiness, rather, requires being involved in, or at least content with, something else. (Williams 1973, p. 112)

Peter Railton considers this to be an instance of the more general "paradox of hedonism," the fact that self-consciously pursuing happiness may actually make you less happy (Railton 1984, pp. 140–46).

Another way that utilitarian ends may better be served if few people believe in utilitarianism arises if, as seems likely, we are best motivated to do non-self-interested things such as utilitarianism may require of us if we believe in a different morality than utilitarianism – if, for example, we believe in Christian morality, or honor, or Cosmic Love. Williams has remarked that British colonial administrators in India, many of whom numbered themselves among the utilitarian faithful, decided

---

[10]I have criticized Shklar's argument in some detail in Luban 1982, pp. 1698–1703.

that the Indians would respond better to Hindu arguments than to utilitarian arguments, and therefore chose not to "convert" Hindus to the Benthamite creed. Such an elitist form of the theory has been termed "Government House utilitarianism" (Sen and Williams 1982, p. 16). In its Government House form, where the utilitarian elite inculcates antiutilitarian arguments to serve utilitarian ends, or teaches principles that are false from a utilitarian viewpoint while insisting that they are part of the Benthamite Gospel, it is clear that utilitarians embrace the use of the noble lie.

Nowhere is this clearer than in Sidgwick's famous exposition of utilitarianism. Sidgwick worries that the complex, exception-laden rules of utilitarianism might be misunderstood or abused by simple folk; he proposes that in that case the simple folk should be deceived. I quote his extraordinary argument at some length.

> Thus, on Utilitarian principles, it may be right to do and privately recommend . . . what it would not be right to advocate openly; it may be right to teach openly to one set of persons what it would be wrong to teach to others; it may be conceivably right to do, if it can be done with comparative secrecy, what it would be wrong to do in the face of the world. . . . These conclusions are all of a paradoxical character: there is no doubt that the moral consciousness of a plain man broadly repudiates the general notion of an esoteric morality, differing from that popularly taught; and it would be commonly agreed that an action which would be bad if done openly is not rendered good by secrecy. (Sidgwick 1966, pp. 489–90)

So far, Sidgwick is merely stating in more general terms an argument similar to Dan-Cohen's defense of "acoustic separation," including Dan-Cohen's acknowledgment that such a defense is fraught with paradox. But Sidgwick next adds a twist to the argument:

> We may observe, however, that there are strong utilitarian reasons for maintaining generally this latter common opinion. . . . Thus the Utilitarian conclusion, carefully stated, would seem to be this; that the opinion that secrecy may render an action right which would not otherwise be so should itself be kept comparatively secret; and similarly it seems expedient that the doctrine that esoteric morality is expedient should itself be kept esoteric. (Sidgwick 1966, p. 490)

The doctrine of acoustic separation must itself be acoustically segregated. From this, Sidgwick draws an explicitly political conclusion:

> Or if this concealment be difficult to maintain, it may be desirable that Common Sense should repudiate the doctrines which it is expedient to confine to an enlightened few. And thus, a Utilitarian may

reasonably desire, on Utilitarian principles, that some of his conclusions should be rejected by mankind generally; or even that the vulgar should keep aloof from his system as a whole. . . . (Sidgwick 1966, p. 490)

This is Sidgwick's final twist. Not only is it best if utilitarianism is not widely believed, but it is best if the very fact that belief in utilitarianism has been suppressed by the "enlightened few" is not widely believed. This is no longer Government House utilitarianism. It is conspiratorial utilitarianism.

A utilitarianism that cannot succeed if it is publicized violates the publicity principle; and Sidgwick's extraordinary metadoctrine that the "doctrine that esoteric morality is expedient should itself be kept esoteric" not only violates the principle but, by keeping that fact secret, violates it at two levels simultaneously.

Rawls employs a different antiutilitarian argument based on the publicity principle (Rawls 1971, pp. 180–83). According to Rawls, if utilitarianism were the public morality of a society, members of that society would understand that their interests would be sacrificed by public officials whenever doing so served the larger social good. Each of them would thereby come to understand that from a social point of view their interests have no intrinsic worth whatever – as H. L. A. Hart put the point, each counts for one because none count for anything (Hart 1979, p. 830). Inevitably, Rawls argues, this realization would undermine their self-respect, and in so doing, would undermine their respect for the interest of others. As the phenomenon of fratricidal underclass violence graphically illustrates, individuals to whom the larger society conveys the message that they have no intrinsic worth and that their interest can be traded away are scarcely likely to be inclined to respect the interests of others. In that case, however, where will public support for the principle of utility, which requires some citizens to sacrifice their own interests to further the interests of others, come from? A utilitarian public morality, publicly acknowledged, will undermine its own support. Hence, utilitarian public morality cannot be publicly acknowledged: it must remain esoteric. If the publicity principle is true, it follows that utilitarian public morality is unjust.

Notice that the conclusion that utilitarianism is inconsistent with the publicity principle requires only a few plausible empirical premises: that nonutilitarians are generally happier than utilitarians, that people are best motivated to altruism by nonutilitarian beliefs, that people are likely to reject the elitist implications of utilitarianism, that by denying the absolute worth of individuals the principle of utility weakens the psychological underpinnings for the other-regarding altruism that utilitarianism requires. If we accept these premises, we are forced to abandon either utilitarianism or the publicity principle.

6.2 Parsing the Publicity Principle

For the sake of convenience, I shall continue to discuss the publicity principle in Kant's formulation. In this section, I shall consider possible meanings of three of the key concepts in that formulation: "maxim," "publicity," and the notion of a maxim being "incompatible with" publicity. My purpose is not primarily philological: I am interested less in what Kant actually meant by these terms than in what meaning we should most reasonably ascribe to them.

6.2.1 Maxims

The principle tells us that actions affecting the right (or rights) of others are wrong if their "maxim" is incompatible with publicity. "Maxim" is a semitechnical term Kant introduced in his *Fundamental Principles of the Metaphysics of Morals*: "A *maxim* is the subjective principle of volition."[11] To talk about maxims is to focus attention on the subjective motivations of agents.

Restricting the publicity principle to maxims, as Kant does, has important consequences. The same action may result from more than one maxim; and some of those maxims may be less compatible with publicity than others. For example, hiring a white job applicant over a black job applicant may be done because the personnel officer reasonably believes that the former is qualified for the job and the latter is not; but it may also be done because the personnel officer is a racist. "Hire a qualified applicant rather than an unqualified applicant" is a maxim that could presumably withstand publicity, whereas "Hire a white applicant rather than a black applicant" is not.

By directing our attention away from actions toward their maxims, Kant means to focus our attention on the motives of political actors rather than on the nature of the actions they are performing. Since people's motives are often difficult for others to discover, Kant's restriction means that the publicity principle will be more useful as a principle of first-person deliberation by decision-makers than as a principle of third-person evaluation by observers. This way of reading it seems to

---

[11]Kant 1785/1949, p. 18n. Kant adds: "The objective principle (i.e., that which would also serve subjectively as a practical principle to all rational beings if reason had full power over the faculty of desire) is the practical *law*" (ibid.).

accord with Kant's own intentions: much of the argument of "Perpetual Peace" is a plea directed toward decision-makers.

Clearly, there are pluses and minuses to applying the publicity principle to the subjective motivations of decision-makers, rather than to the objective characteristics of their actions. On the plus side, Kant's strategy tells decision-makers that the bare fact that their actions may be publicly justifiable under *some* maxim is irrelevant if their actual maxim could not withstand the light of day. On the minus side, Kant's restriction may let decision-makers off the hook: since we are all capable of self-deception, decision-makers will undoubtedly persuade themselves that their subjective motivations are unimpeachable, even though it appears to others that they had acted for disreputable reasons. In such cases, it might do more good for the decision-maker to look at what he did, and not at the contents of his own soul.

Kant's focus on maxims, that is, on subjective *rules* of action, has another effect as well, and indeed helps clear up a puzzle about the publicity principle. The puzzle is the apparent incompatibility of the publicity principle with any secrecy whatever in public policy. Suppose, for example, that a government agency wishes to keep secret that weapons-grade plutonium is stored in Ravenna, Ohio. Obviously, if the action is described as "secretly storing weapons-grade plutonium in Ravenna, Ohio," it cannot survive the publicity test, for publicizing the action under this description reveals the very secret at issue.

The problem, of course, is that the description has too much particularity built into it. If instead the action is described simply as "secretly storing weapons-grade plutonium," it may well survive the publicity test, since most people would presumably agree that such a policy is desirable. By focusing the publicity test on maxims, that is, *general* rules of action, Kant invites us to deliberate at the level of policies, not at the level of specifics, which may indeed need to be kept secret.

6.2.2 Publicity

What exactly is the publicity that Kant invokes in his publicity principle? Let us consider three possibilities: publicity as general knowledge, publicity as mutual knowledge, and publicity as critical debate.

GENERAL KNOWLEDGE. X is public if everyone knows X. Of course, we should not mean *literally* everyone, since obviously there will be some people who don't follow the news or talk with others; or who are so geographically isolated that they do not find out much about the outside world. "Everyone" means *tout le monde*, "the general public," those who care about such things.

General knowledge is surely a necessary condition of publicity. It may not be enough to guarantee that an item is public in the politically relevant sense, however.

I have had experiences in which a colleague has approached me privately to tell me something quite significant – that he or she is getting a divorce, or has been offered a job elsewhere, for example. In each of these cases I assumed from the discreet way my colleague behaved that he or she had decided to confide in only a few people, and expected me to keep the information to myself – only to learn later that my colleague was in fact telling everyone. The knowledge of my colleague's predicament was *general*, in that everyone in the office knew about it. But, during the short period when we were all keeping it confidential from each other, it was not *public*. Our knowledge was more like parallel private knowledge.

This suggests that public knowledge is not merely general, but *mutual*.

MUTUAL KNOWLEDGE. X is public if everyone knows X and everyone knows that everyone knows X.

One could perhaps go further, and say that X is public if

- everyone knows X;
- everyone knows that everyone knows X;
- everyone knows that everyone knows that everyone knows X; etc.

Stephen Schiffer has introduced the term "mutual knowledge*" (read: "mutual knowledge star") to refer to the limit of this sequence: mutuality all the way up (Schiffer 1972, pp. 30–31; see also David Lewis's very similar notion of "common knowledge": Lewis 1969, p. 56). One could do worse than define publicity as Schiffer's mutual knowledge* though I suspect that soon enough the iterations become for all practical purposes identical to each other.

In practice, examples such as my anecdote about my overly secretive colleagues occur only in small organizations; thus, when we are talking about public policies or other societywide items of knowledge, general knowledge is invariably mutual knowledge as well. If I read about a federal policy in the newspaper, I know about the policy and I know that the rest of the public knows about it as well.

CRITICAL DEBATE. People may mutually know about something, however, without debating or discussing it; and we may think that the political significance of publicity lies in public debate rather than passive public awareness. This, I should note, is an idea stressed by Habermas in his influential study of the "public sphere" (Habermas 1989).

For Habermas, "the public" means "the critical-rational public," and much of Habermas's polemic against the contemporary mass media concerns the extent to which the media have become instruments of propaganda and pacification rather than of critical debate. Following Habermas, one might insist that publicity must mean not merely mutual knowledge, but rational public debate.

But a problem arises when this interpretation of publicity is coupled with Kant's claim that the publicity principle provides an easy test of the wrongness of maxims. How am I to determine whether a maxim is compatible with publicity if publicity is understood as rational public debate? How can I know a priori whether my maxim would be rejected by rational public debate? I could try to anticipate that debate in my own mind, and no doubt I should. But it is a mistake to think that debating the proposition in my own mind is anything over and above deliberating about it in the first place. At the end of my internal debate, I will arrive at what seems most reasonable to me, nothing more. In that case, the publicity principle has changed into the vacuous injunction not to follow maxims that, after full deliberation, seem wrong to the agent. This is hardly "an experiment of pure reason."

The problem is that the more content we pack into the notion of publicity, the more difficult it becomes to use the publicity principle as an independent test of maxims: all our questions about the wrongness of the maxim will simply translate themselves into equally perplexing questions about whether the maxim is compatible with some fancy notion of publicity. Perhaps the publicity principle is true only if the concept of publicity means something like critical-rational debate; in that case, however, the truth of the principle is purchased at the cost of its usefulness as a test.

Let me cast this caveat in slightly more general terms. Kant asserts not only that the publicity principle is true, but also that it provides an easy-to-use test of public policies. Much of the interest of the publicity principle rests in the prospect that Kant was right on both counts. In the examples I presented earlier, the test seemed easy to apply, and therein lay the fascination.

That being so, we must guide our interpretation of the publicity test by two hermeneutic principles: interpret it in the most plausible way, but also in the way most likely to preserve its usefulness – not merely *salve veritate*, but *salve utilitas* as well. Perhaps it is impossible to do both, but that should be our conclusion of last resort.

For this reason, I think that we should settle on mutual knowledge as our preferred interpretation of publicity. Mutual knowledge no doubt implies mutual discussion, but it does not imply full-fledged rational debate. Interpreting publicity as mutual knowledge offers the best chance, I think, of salvaging Kant's claim that the publicity principle provides a useful test of the wrongness of public policies.

6.2.3 Incompatibility

Lastly, we must ask what it means to say that a maxim is incompatible with publicity, or cannot withstand publicity. Here, as with the concept of publicity itself, there are several possibilities: a maxim is incompatible with publicity if it is *self-frustrating, arousing necessary and general opposition, unpopular,* or *politically suicidal.* Of these possibilities, Kant explicitly discusses the first two, but the latter two are, as we shall see, plausible interpretations of what incompatibility might mean.

SELF-FRUSTRATING. Kant says that his test will rule out "a maxim which I may not *declare openly* without thereby frustrating my own intention" (Kant 1795a, p. 126). One of his examples illustrates what he has in mind. He asks whether a state may make a promise to another, reserving the right to break the promise "when its own welfare is at stake" (Kant 1795a, pp. 127–28). Kant answers that

> if the ruler of a state were to let it be known that this was his maxim, everyone else would naturally flee from him, or unite with others in order to resist his pretensions; which proves that such a system of politics, for all its cunning, would defeat its own purpose if it operated on a public footing, so that the above maxim must be wrong. (Kant 1795a, p. 128)

Most, or perhaps all, of the policies discussed earlier fail the publicity principle because they would be self-frustrating if publicized. But it may be helpful to distinguish various ways publicity might make them self-frustrating.

First, a policy might be *performatively inconsistent* if the agent makes it public. If I announce that I am about to leave the house secretly, the fact of announcement – the performance – contradicts the content of the announcement. A policy by the CIA director to provide misleading intelligence to the president in order to influence the president's conduct of foreign affairs would be performatively inconsistent if the director made it public. (Note that if someone else makes it public there is no performative inconsistency, although the policy will fail.) In the nuclear deterrence case, maintaining a policy of nuclear bluff – that is, threatening to retaliate to a first strike but intending not to retaliate if deterrence fails – would enwrap one in performative inconsistency if it were announced. One might likewise argue that Sidgwick was involved in a performative inconsistency by the very fact that he published his defense of esoteric morality.

Second, publicizing a policy might set in motion a chain of events leading to its defeat. This is, strictly speaking, the pure case of publicity making a policy *self-defeating*. Kant's example illustrates this case. So does a Llewellyn/Nesson-like policy of tailoring legal procedure to reconcile us to trial results rather than to produce justice, for we saw that publicizing such a policy would do the opposite of reconciling us to trial results.

Third, publicizing a policy might set in motion a chain of events leading not to the policy's own defeat, but to the defeat of some other important, usually related, policy. In that case we may say that publicizing the policy is *collaterally self-defeating* (it leads not to the policy's own defeat, but to the defeat of some collateral policy). The various examples of judicial candor illustrate this form of self-frustration. Take, for example, Calabresi's argument about judicial sunsetting of anachronistic laws. His point is that if this judicial power were formally acknowledged in legal doctrine, the result might be abuse of the power. He is not arguing that doctrinal acknowledgment of the power would lead to the loss of that very power. Thus, he is not arguing that publicizing the power would be self-defeating. Rather, Calabresi holds only that publicizing the power would lead to other bad effects on the legal system – thus, that publicizing the power would be collaterally self-defeating.

Similarly, Bickel's theory of the passive virtues proposes that the Supreme Court manipulate doctrine in order to duck constitutional questions. The Supreme Court could hardly announce publicly that that is what it is doing. ("We deny standing to the appellant, not because she really lacks standing, but because we don't want to reach the constitutional question"? – Hardly!) But that is not because announcing it publicly would compel the Court to decide the constitutional question it was trying to avoid. Rather, it is because announcing it publicly would create an immense scandal. Thus, publicizing that one is using the passive virtues is collaterally self-defeating rather than directly self-defeating.

One special case of collaterally self-defeating policies deserves special mention. In some of our examples, publicizing a policy would be collaterally self-defeating because it would set up *perverse incentives*. In Dan-Cohen's "acoustic separation" argument, the reason that publicizing the defenses of duress, necessity, and provocation would be self-frustrating is that public knowledge of the defenses might induce people to give in to pressure, or respond to provocations, that they might otherwise have resisted. Knowledge of the defenses changes the structure of incentives in the society for the worse, and that is why publicizing them would be collaterally self-defeating.

Other examples of perverse incentives are easy to come by. Late in 1991, the newly formed Russian Republic decided to remove price controls on many goods. But economists expressed concern about publicizing the date of the price rise (it was January 2, 1992), because suppliers might withhold needed goods from the market until the announced date in order to take advantage of decontrol. Thus, publicizing the date might create perverse incentives, leading to the collateral self-defeat of the policy of decontrolling prices. Similar concerns arise whenever governments decide on a currency devaluation.

NECESSARY AND GENERAL OPPOSITION. Kant writes that "a maxim . . . which I cannot *publicly acknowledge* without thereby inevitably arousing the resistance of everyone to my plans, can only have stirred up this necessary and general (hence a priori foreseeable) opposition against me because it is itself unjust . . ." (Kant 1795a, p. 126). Though the argument here seems somewhat question begging – isn't the injustice of such maxims precisely what he is trying to establish? – the passage suggests an interpretation of what it means for a maxim to be incompatible with publicity. It is incompatible with publicity if it "inevitably arouses the resistance of everyone," "stirs up necessary and general (hence a priori foreseeable opposition)," and thus "is itself unjust." A policy is incompatible with publicity, that is, if it is intrinsically loathsome – something akin to genocide.

This interpretation is eminently plausible, but it raises doubts parallel to our earlier doubts about the critical debate interpretation of publicity: if the test of incompatibility is a priori foreseeable opposition, intrinsic loathsomeness, then the injustice of the maxim will be as it were written on its face, and one would hardly need to apply the publicity principle to determine that it is unjust. That is, the publicity principle adds nothing over and above the direct contemplation of the maxim itself, and thus it is useless as an independent test of maxims.

UNPOPULAR. If it is nearly impossible to know whether opposition is necessary and general, perhaps the test should be that maxims are incompatible with publicity whenever one can foresee that they will be extremely unpopular. This, however, is not an acceptable interpretation of the publicity principle, for it would then say that any action that, if publicized, is unpopular is therefore wrong. Clearly, under this interpretation we would have a principle of demagoguery, not morality.

Recent American politics illustrates this point perfectly – unfortunately. The clearest example concerns taxes. American voters insist on an undiminished delivery of governmental services and entitlements, but mercilessly punish any politician (such as Walter Mondale in the 1984 presidential election) who announces publicly that they must be paid for through tax hikes. (The attitude of the electorate has been caricatured by some observers as "It's unfair to make the taxpayers pay for it – let the government pay for it!") Given the demand for services and entitlements, tax increases are surely not wrong – but they could not pass the publicity test if it is interpreted as a popularity contest.[12]

There is one way, however, in which interpreting incompatibility as unpopularity makes sense. If we interpret publicity as critical debate, then the publicity principle could be read along the following lines:

> All actions affecting the rights of others are wrong if, after a critical-rational public debate, their maxim is generally unpopular.

This formula is very close to Habermas's theory of communicative ethics, and is also in the neighborhood of Dewey's social philosophy. For reasons we have already examined, it is not going to be useful as an independent test of public policies; but it is certainly a serious contender for the palm of truth.

POLITICALLY SUICIDAL. Our last interpretation of incompatibility emerges quite naturally from pursuing the issue from the standpoint of *Realpolitik*. For the politician, the question of whether a maxim can withstand publicity will be heard as a question of what the political fallout of publicity would be. Does it mean angry letters from the voters? Does it mean not being reelected? Does it mean being impeached? Does it mean being forced to resign? Does it mean armed resistance? Does it mean the fall of the government, execution, assassination? From the politician's point of view, a maxim is incompatible with publicity only if publicizing it would be politically suicidal, precipitating the loss of power. Richard Nixon discovered that his policies of endorsing political dirty tricks were incompatible with publicity, because he was forced from office.

We must reject this interpretation, for the simple reason that what is politically suicidal typically depends on how tough a politician is prepared to be. Machiavelli makes the point dramatically: a short dip into *The Prince* yields a nonstop tale of butcheries, strangulations, and atrocities used successfully by princes to secure their power. Agathocles the Sicilian and Machiavelli's contemporary Oliverotto di Fermo both be-

---

[12]Kant himself explicitly rejects the unpopularity interpretation of incompatibility. Kant 1793, p. 79.

came rulers by gathering together the leading citizens of their cities and then treacherously ordering their soldiers to murder them all (Machiavelli 1532, chap. 8). Presumably, rulers willing to engage in such tactics would not resign from office simply because word got out that they had authorized the Watergate burglaries. Thus, a policy of burglarizing one's political opponents is compatible with publicity if one is willing to behave like Oliverotto.

This shows that the political suicide interpretation of incompatibility cannot be right. For it implies that the more ruthless a government is, and the more it is willing to hang onto power by injustice and violence, the more "compatible" its policies are with publicity. Political homicide is the tried and true alternative to political suicide. In short, the more unjust the government, the less likely its actions are to fail the publicity test.

To summarize, the political suicide interpretation of incompatibility must be abandoned. The unpopularity interpretation is quite unattractive, unless it means unpopularity after critical-rational debate, in which case the publicity test is unusable. If unpopularity means *inevitable* unpopularity, it is no different from the necessary and general opposition interpretation. Thus, only the first two interpretations of incompatibility survive. Kant himself accepted the disjunction of the two:

> For a maxim which I may not declare openly without thereby frustrating my own intention, . . . or which I cannot publicly acknowledge without thereby inevitably arousing the resistance of everyone to my plans . . . is itself unjust and thus constitutes a threat to everyone. (Kant 1795a, p. 126)

Maxims are unjust if publicizing them results either in self-frustration or inevitable opposition. However, we have seen that the "inevitable opposition" interpretation cannot be applied as a self-standing test by decision-makers. Thus, we should interpret the notion of incompatibility in the publicity principle along the lines of the self-frustration interpretation (on any of the various modes of self-frustration).

6.3   Kant's Arguments for the Publicity Principle

In the first four paragraphs of the second appendix to "Perpetual Peace" Kant unveils the publicity principle amid a dense clot of arguments, argument fragments, and hints of arguments for its truth. Kant is seldom easy on his readers, and these passages are perhaps more gnomic than is usual even for Kant. Gnomic or not, his arguments form the natural starting point for our inquiry into whether the principle is true: they remain, I believe, the most plausible arguments for the publicity principle.

6.3.1 The Public Law Argument

Start with the opening paragraph of the "Perpetual Peace" appendix (I insert bracketed numbers for ease of reference):

> [1] If, in considering public law [Recht] as legal scholars usually conceive of it, I abstract from all its matter (as determined by the various empirically given relationships of men within a state, or of states with one another), I am left with the form of publicity [Publizität], which every legal claim [Rechtsanspruch] potentially possesses, since [2] without it there can be no justice (which can only be conceived of as publicly knowable) and therefore no right [Recht], which can be conferred only by justice.
>   [3] Every legal claim must have this capacity for publicity. . . . [13]

Consider clause [1]. The argument seems to be that the only thing all public laws have in common is that they are public, hence publicity must be their formal attribute.

Kant draws this conclusion about public law "as legal scholars usually conceive of it." The traditional Roman concept of public law, as found on the first page of the *Digest of Justinian*, was thoroughly familiar to Kant. However, in this sense of public law, Kant's argument amounts to little more than a play on words, for "public law" does not mean "law that is public." It means "law that concerns relations between state and citizen (rather than between citizen and citizen)." Roman lawyers labeled such law "public" not because it is publicly promulgated, but because it concerns matters of public interest. Kant writes as though the publicity of public law follows from the very meaning of the term, but

---

[13]Kant 1795a, p. 125 (my emendation to the translation, based partly on Kant 1795b). Following Beck (Kant 1795b, p. 129), I have translated "*Recht*" at one point as "law" and at another as "right." The word occurs twice in the same sentence, the first time in the phrase "*öffentliches Recht*," which I believe must be translated "public law" rather than (as in Reiss) "public right," in order to retain Kant's focus elsewhere in "Perpetual Peace" on the role of law in international relations. This being so, it is of course taking considerable liberty with the text to translate the second occurrence of "*Recht*" in the same sentence as "right," as Beck and I do. However, the second occurrence cannot possibly be translated as "law," for then Kant's use of the verb "*erteilen*" (to confer or award) makes no sense: while justice can confer rightness on a claim to legality, it cannot confer law on it. It seems clear that Kant is exploiting the double sense of "*Recht*": he is arguing that only justice can confer moral rightness to positive law.

it does not, any more than the fact that lawyers place contract doctrine in the category of private law implies that contract law is secret.

Nor does the argument get much further if we read "public law" in Kant's own idiosyncratic sense of law "that need[s] to be promulgated generally in order to bring about a lawful condition [*rechtlicher Zustand*]" – Kant's definition of public law (Kant 1787, p. 123).[14] For then the argument amounts to little more than a tautology. Law that must be promulgated generally shares the attribute of publicness. So what? How do we know that all, or even any, law must be promulgated generally? We need some such claim to get to the desired conclusion in passage [3], which tells us that *every* legal claim must be capable of publicity, not just that legal claims requiring publicity must be capable of publicity.

6.3.2 The Rule of Law Argument

On the other hand, many contemporary writers accept the proposition that every legal claim must be capable of publicity, because they regard public promulgation of laws as a defining condition of the rule of law.[15] This suggests that, in its legal applications at any rate, the publicity principle may be a corollary of the rule of law ideal.

In that case, however, the argument for the publicity principle is only as strong as the argument for the rule of law ideal – and indeed, only as strong as the argument for the publicity of law within that ideal. It is far from plain, however, that the rule of law ideal should not sometimes give way. If a progressive South African government, stymied by conservative opposition, found itself politically unable to end apartheid, a secret proclamation directing officials not to enforce apartheid laws might improve justice in South Africa. As we shall see, plausible counterexamples to the publicity principle typically represent situations in which we are tempted to compromise the rule of law ideal in favor of other values.

Nor is it wholly obvious that the publicity of law is essential to the rule of law ideal. Consider first that, although law in contemporary liberal democracies is publicly promulgated, all this really means is that it is available in official publications that lawyers know how to find. In daily life, very few people actually know what the law is on any given subject. Only to those able to secure professional legal advice, therefore,

---

[14]The phrase "bring about a lawful condition [rechtlicher Zustand]" means, I take it, something like "establish the rule of law." (I have altered Gregor's translation of *rechtlicher*.)

[15]These include Fuller 1964, Rawls 1971, pp. 235–43, and Raz 1977.

is the law public in fact rather than fiction. Consider next that professional legal advice is so costly that it is available to only a tiny fraction of the population. Consider finally that this state of affairs is the consequence of deliberate public policies: Every liberal democracy has elected to distribute legal services primarily through market mechanisms, subsidizing legal aid only at negligible levels; and no liberal democracy permits nonlawyers to offer legal advice except in certain highly specialized circumstances – a state-mandated professional oligopoly of lawyers that serves chiefly to keep the cost of legal services high.[16] In effect, Dan-Cohen's acoustic separation principle is enforced worldwide through the simple expedient of pricing legal knowledge beyond the means of most citizens. More than any other form of government, liberal democracies are characterized by their principled commitment to the rule of law, but they pay only lip-service to the publicity of law. The only reasonable conclusion to draw is this: either no nation in the world has come anywhere near establishing the rule of law, or else the publicity of law is not an essential part of the rule of law ideal.

6.3.3 The Public Justice Argument

Next consider sentence [2] from the opening paragraph of the "Perpetual Peace" appendix: "Without it [i.e., publicity] there can be no justice (which can only be conceived of as publicly knowable) and therefore no right, which can be conferred only by justice." Here Kant appears to be arguing not from the public character of law, but rather from the public character of justice "which can only be conceived of as publicly knowable." Rawls, who assumes the publicity principle as a constraint on any construction of the concept of justice, evidently has this argument for the principle in mind.

Unfortunately, the argument seems at once question begging and incomplete. Question begging, because through most of human history justice has been conceived of as not publicly knowable, as an esoteric science revealed to the Chosen Few – the divinely sanctioned prophets, the philosophical souls. Some of the most sophisticated philosophy of the Middle Ages held that principles of justice contain an ineliminable kernel of revelation. Even some philosophers (Averröes is an example) who believed that the principles of justice can be discovered through natural reason held as well that only a very few individuals are up to

---

[16]See Rhode 1981. Rhode argues that standard bar arguments in favor of restricting legal practice to licensed lawyers rest on empirical premises that available data contradict.

the inquiry, and thus that the mass of mankind must be steered clear of the philosophically correct methods of scriptural interpretation. (This view is evidently a precursor of Sidgwick's theory of esoteric morality.) Contemporary philosophers who derive principles of justice from technical arguments in game theory or axiomatic bargaining theory may likewise agree that knowledge of justice is only for the mathematically trained few. In either form – revelation or restricted reason – proponents of esoteric justice argue that a profound inegalitarianism marks humanity. Principles of justice are only for the few.

The public justice argument is incomplete because even if justice must be regarded as publicly knowable, and laws must accord with the publicly knowable principles of justice, it scarcely follows that the laws cannot be secret. Perhaps, among the publicly knowable principles of justice, we find a principle permitting officials to act on policies that could not withstand publicity when discretion seems the better part of valor. Particularly when we consider the defects, vileness, and propensity for self-dealing that seems to characterize human nature and political life, the case for secrecy and dissembling in public policy can seem overwhelming, and not the least out of accord with publicly knowable principles of justice.

6.3.4 Universalizability

Rawls remarks that "[p]ublicity is clearly implied in Kant's notion of the moral law" (Rawls 1971, p. 133n). The moral law, of course, is the categorical imperative, "Act only on that maxim whereby you can at the same time will that it should become a universal law" (Kant 1985/ 1949, p.38). If Rawls is right, the moral law may provide an argument for the publicity principle distinct from the rule of law and public justice arguments.

Kant conceived of morality on a legal model, and identifying morality as a kind of law is perhaps the single most characteristic feature of his moral philosophy. The categorical imperative says, "Act only on that maxim whereby you can at the same time will that it should become a universal *law*," not "Act only on that maxim whereby you can at the same time will that it should become a universal *practice* (or *custom*)." The point is plainer still when we turn to Kant's reformulation of the categorical imperative in the language of the "kingdom of ends": "A rational being must always regard himself as giving laws either as member or as sovereign in a kingdom of ends . . ." (Kant 1785, p. 50). Kant states explicitly that "[b]y a 'kingdom' I understand the union of different rational beings in a system by common laws" (Kant 1785, p. 50).

The test Kant intends in the categorical imperative is thus whether one could *legislate* one's maxim, not merely generalize it.

Now perhaps one can enact secret legislation even in the kingdom of ends. But it would be unthinkably bizarre to attribute such a view to Kant. Remember that Kant defines public law as law that must be made public to establish a lawful condition (i.e., to be efficacious as law). He also, however, argued that all positive law, including the traditionally private law departments of tort, property, and contract, is "public" in this special sense.[17] Kant's philosophy of law is built around the requirement that law operates publicly. On his legalistic understanding of morality, the categorical imperative includes not just universalizability, but publicity (what we earlier called mutual knowledge*) as well: "willing that my maxim should become universal law" means "willing that my maxim should become universal *and publicly known* law." This yields a simple and natural derivation of the publicity principle from the categorical imperative. If I could not publicize my maxim, I surely could not "will that it would become a universal law," for that should be tantamount to willing that it be made public. Hence, any maxim that cannot pass the publicity test will be equally incapable of passing the test of the categorical imperative. The maxim will therefore be wrong, just as the publicity principle says.

Without entering into the interpretive question of whether Kant intended to relate the publicity principle to the moral law – I regard the textual evidence as too ambiguous for a clear answer – let us note that Kant never so much as mentions the categorical imperative in his discussion of the publicity principle. Why? I think that the most plausible answer is that Kant did not distinguish between the universalizability and publicity components of the moral law, but instead simply combined them in the single complex he termed "uni-

---

[17]In the introduction to Kant 1787/1991, Kant explains that the distinction between private and public law is simply another name for the distinction between natural law – law in the pre-social-contract state of nature – and civil (*bürgerliche*) law, in other words positive law. "The highest division of natural Right [*Naturrecht*] cannot be the division (sometimes made) into *natural* and *social* Right; it must instead be the division into natural and *civil* Right, the former of which is called *private Right* and the latter *public Right*. For a *state of nature* is not opposed to a social but to a civil condition, since there can certainly be society in a state of nature, but not *civil* society (which secures what is mine or yours by public laws). This is why Right in a state of nature is called private Right: of which the first is termed private law, the second public law. For the natural condition is not counterposed to the social, but rather to the civil: since in the state of nature society can indeed exist, but not civil society (which secures the 'mine' and the 'thine' through public statutes); thus law is called private law in the former" (Kant 1787/1991, p. 67).

versal law" (cf. Rawls 1971, p. 133). If Kant was not prone to partition the categorical imperative into universalizability and publicity components, then any moral argument he might fashion for the publicity principle would derive the principle from the categorical imperative *taken as a whole*. But Kant would be very unlikely to find that an appealing derivation, for it is blatantly circular. The publicity principle, remember, is preeminently a test of the moral wrongness of (public) laws. To test such laws by means of the categorical imperative amounts to asserting that a (public) law is morally wrong if one could not will it as a universal law, or as a piece of legislation in the kingdom of ends. That is singularly uninformative, and Kant would hardly trouble his readers with an argument that boils down to the proposition that a piece of legislation is unacceptable if it is unacceptable. Clearly, he would prefer to regard the publicity principle as an *independent* test of the morality of public laws. It is small wonder that under such circumstances Kant did not mention the categorical imperative in his arguments for the publicity principle.

This point, however, highlights a deep problem in the entire effort to argue for the publicity principle on the basis of Kantian morality. We have seen that Kant built publicity into the categorical imperative because at bottom he conceived of morality itself on the model of public law (in Kant's sense of law that must be made public). It will hardly do to argue that law incapable of publicity is immoral, if the basis of the reasoning is simply that morality has been defined as a kind of public law. In that case, law turns out to be like morality only because morality has been modeled on law.

We may put the point in a different way. Obviously, anything that violates the publicity requirement thereby violates the publicity requirement *and* universalizability, that is, violates the categorical imperative. But universalizability does no work in this argument. Any property could be substituted for "universalizability" without affecting the derivation.

This is important because philosophers in the Kantian tradition have focused their interest and attention on universalizability, rather than on publicity or the quasi-legal character of morality. And this is for good reason: the universalizability requirement, far more than the publicity requirement, expresses the moral demand of impartiality and the conception of the underlying moral equality of all rational beings – ideas that are surely the principal attractions of Kantian ethics. To learn that universalizability plays no essential role whatever in the derivation of the publicity principle from the moral law surely removes most of the interest and importance of that derivation.

6.4. The Case against the Publicity Principle

In the end, I don't believe that Kant himself makes a persuasive case for the publicity principle. Indeed, I shall suggest that *no* a priori argument for the publicity principle is likely to work. To see this more clearly, I now want to turn to the case against the publicity principle, which I present through a series of counter examples: policies that fail the publicity principle but that nevertheless seem on the whole the right thing to do. I group them into four categories: examples of *mercy*, examples of *sunsetting*, examples of *Victorian compromise*, and examples of *shielding the righteous*.

6.4.1 Examples of Mercy

1. When I was in graduate school, one of my fellow students was caught shoplifting from the university bookstore. The store detectives took him into the back room and, to his great relief, told him that they would let him go that day – but (they sternly added), if they caught him twice more they would press charges.

Whether the bookstore's policy of pressing charges only on the third offense was a wise one is of course open to debate. It was, at any rate, a merciful one, and probably saved the store unnecessary fuss, so that it may have been an efficient policy as well. Plainly, however, it was a policy that was incompatible with publicity – and the store detectives were literal-minded dunderheads.

2. At a more sophisticated level, Dan-Cohen's examples of acoustic separation in the criminal law are also counter examples to the publicity principle based on mercy. Devices whereby knowledge of certain defenses and mitigations is restricted only to officials – judges, let us say – allows us to retain the deterrent effect of criminal law while at the same time permitting judges to show mercy to defendants who have succumbed to forgivable and all-too-human impulses. As in the preceding case, publicizing merciful policies creates perverse incentives for the unscrupulous to take advantage of them.

3. One such device is particularly instructive. Nothing prevents a criminal jury from acquitting a defendant who is plainly guilty as charged, guilty beyond a reasonable doubt; and because of the ban on double jeopardy, the jury's decision to acquit cannot be appealed. Juries thus possess the power to nullify the criminal law. Theorists typically applaud this power of jury nullification, suggesting that it is a device whereby the community's evolving sense of justice, expressed by a representative group of ordinary citizens, can temper excessive harshness

or anachronism in the law.[18] An example of tempering harshness would be acquitting an elderly, devoted husband who has mercy-killed his beloved but severely Alzheimer's afflicted wife; an example of tempering anachronism would be acquitting individuals (heterosexual as well as homosexual) indicted under nineteenth century anti fellatio statutes.[19]

Yet even those who applaud the power of jury nullification may well object to a judge or attorney explicitly pointing out to the jury that it possesses the power. Some American jurisdictions forbid lawyers from explicitly asking a jury to nullify, and judges will typically instruct the jury that if it is convinced that the state has proven its case, it *must* convict – leaving it for the jurors to figure out on their own that if they choose to ignore those instructions the sky will not fall and the defendant will go free.[20] Though the argument is never put in entirely frank terms, the thought seems to be this: permitting lawyers or judges to call the nullification power to the jury's attention might confuse jurors, making them believe that their assigned task is not to find facts and match them to law, but rather to decide whether or not they think the law is fair. The distinction between *leaving nullification to the jury's spontaneous act of conscience* and *inviting the jury to decide on the basis of conscience rather than law* is crucial but subtle, so subtle (it is feared) that to call the power to the jury's attention at all is to invite its abuse in cases when nullification is inappropriate. Nullification cannot survive publicity.

---

[18]For a sophisticated treatment of jury nullification and similar issues, see Kadish and Kadish 1973.

[19]Heterosexual cases are surprisingly common; they typically rise in the aftermath of a prosecution for rape, in which both parties agree that an act of fellatio took place, but in which the man insists it was consensual while the woman charges coercion. If the judge or jury is persuaded that the complainant had consented, the man will often find himself acquitted of rape but indicted for oral sodomy.

[20]Thus, in the well-known trial of "subway vigilante" Bernhard Goetz, who had shot four black youths who approached him in a New York subway asking for money, Goetz's lawyers made a back-handed appeal for jury nullification. When Goetz was convicted of a weapons charge, he appealed because the judge had instructed the jury that, "if it found that the People had proved each of the elements of the crime beyond a reasonable doubt, it 'must' find the defendant guilty." Denying the appeal, the New York Court of Appeals said: "The jury's function is to apply the legal definition of the crime to the evidence and to convict if it is satisfied that each element has been established beyond a reasonable doubt. While there is nothing to prevent a jury from acquitting although finding that the prosecution has proven its case, this so-called 'mercy-dispensing power' is not a legally sanctioned function of the jury and should not be encouraged by the court." *People v. Goetz*, 532 N.E.2.d 1273 (1988).

6.4.2 Examples of Sunsetting

1. Consider again the 1992 Russian price decontrol. An old price regime was about to sunset; but to inform people when it would sunset invites them to withhold needed goods from the market. A good policy can be disastrous if it is publicized.

Other examples of the same type are easy to come by. Governments never announce the date of intended currency devaluations; and, in the United States, skeptics about the efficacy of gun control rightly warned that a ban on assault rifles would lead to an enormous run on gun stores before the date the legislation took effect. (Yet in this case it was impossible to keep the date secret.)

2. More abstractly, theorists of the Prisoner's Dilemma have long argued that a supergame consisting of several consecutive Prisoner's Dilemma games between the same players would lead to the same outcome as a single play – mutual defection – if the players know exactly how many games are in the supergame. Suppose, for example, that the players are told that they will play ten repetitions of the Prisoner's Dilemma. After game 9, they have only one game to play, and so they will both defect. Knowing that mutual defection is certain in game 10, after game 8 they will in effect have only a single uncertain-outcome game left to play, namely game 9. Thus, they will defect in game 9. In the end, the dominoes collapse in series and they will defect in all the games. In order to allow stable cooperation to emerge in Prisoner's Dilemma supergames, it is therefore necessary to conceal from the players how many times they will be facing one another. Only in that case will the possibility of being rewarded for cooperation and punished for defection in subsequent plays affect the players' calculations and allow them to cooperate rationally. As in the previous examples, knowing when a situation is going to sunset may alter one's behavior for the worse.

3. During the 1960s and 1970s the Chinese government wished to experiment for a limited time with a variety of different institutional arrangements on agricultural communes. They soon discovered, however, that residents of the communes would change their behavior in the waning months of the experiment in order to prepare for the return to preexperiment arrangements, thereby queering the experiments. Consequently, the government began instituting experiments without announcing that they would sunset after two or three years.[21]

---

[21]I owe this example to Stephen Holmes, who attributed it to Jon Elster.

6.4.3   Examples of Victorian Compromise

"Victorian compromise" is Lawrence Friedman's term for the typical Victorian manner of handling sexual impropriety: so long as you don't rub my nose in it, I will tolerate your escapades.[22] If you force me to acknowledge that I know what you're up to, you will likewise force me to stop tolerating your vices. The pattern is a familiar one: it is the way many parents deal with their teen-agers' sex lives (the teen-agers understand without being told in so many words that they can sleep with their boy- or girlfriend so long as they enable their parents to continue pretending that they don't know what is going on).

It is also a pattern in politics, however. During the Cold War, both Americans and Soviets repeatedly violated each others' air space with spy planes. Both governments knew about the violations but understood that if the public knew, the government would be forced to respond with some form of hostility. So great were the dangers that both governments developed unspoken policies of tolerating the spy planes, provided that the other government did nothing to publicize its flights.

6.4.4   Examples of Shielding the Righteous

Another episode from the career of Russell Long: on one occasion, Long hoped to extract a hefty campaign contribution from a wealthy businessman. As quid pro quo for the contribution, Long offered to attach to pending tax legislation a provision from which the businessman would profit handsomely. The businessman balked at the size of the proposed contribution, however, and asked Long what he would get if he contributed a much smaller amount. Long answered: "Good government."

It is not exactly news that special interests and good government are often at odds, nor that politicians frequently owe their jobs to the former rather than the latter. That raises an important question of institutional design: suppose that politicians actually would prefer good government to policies designed principally for the benefit of predatory special interests (there is no reason beyond facile cynicism to suppose otherwise). Suppose further, however, that politicians are no more likely than anyone else to engage in kamikaze behavior, and that voting publicly for good government and against special interests is kamikaze be-

---

[22]Friedman 1985, p. 585 (defining the Victorian compromise as "a certain toleration for vice, or at least a resigned acceptance, so long as it [remains] in an underground state").

havior. The conclusion that follows would seem to be this: we need institutions designed to permit politicians to do the right thing away from the scrutiny of special interests. U.S. Senator Robert Packwood explains:

> Common Cause [an American political reform organization] has everything upside down when they advocate "sunshine" laws. When we're in the sunshine, as soon as we vote, every trade association in the country gets out their mailgrams and their phone calls in twelve hours, and complains about the members' votes. But when we're in the back room, the senators can vote their conscience. They vote for what they think is the good of the country. Then they can go out to the lobbyists and say: "God, I fought for you. I did everything I could. But Packwood just wouldn't give in, you know. It's so damn horrible."[23]

Along the same lines, Richard Neely has argued persuasively that workable democratic political systems must evolve sophisticated mechanisms for privately killing, rather than publicly defeating, bad legislation. For if legislation could be halted only by public vote, legislators "would either be required to vote for every predatory bill which comes up or anger so many powerful interest groups that their political life expectancy would be about as long as that of an artillery forward observer" (Neely 1981, p. 56). These bill-killing mechanisms include intricate committee systems, calendar and agenda manipulations, and bicameralism, which permits "the experienced manipulator's stock in trade . . . guaranteeing that the bill will pass both houses in different forms – thus never becoming law."[24]

Assuming that these arguments have merit, it follows that the politics of the back room, which seems plainly contrary to the publicity principle, is nevertheless indispensable in a workable democracy. At the same time, of course, the example is double-edged, and indeed reveals the basic tension underlying the publicity principle: Packwood's hypothetical acts of public-spirited virtue are possible only behind closed doors, but so was Long's effort to extort a contribution in return for special interest legislation. Backroom politics protects the virtuous and the vicious alike from public exposure.

[23]Quoted in Birnbaum and Murray 1987, p. 260.

[24]Neely 1981, p. 60. He adds: "In Norway the constitution establishes a unicameral legislature, but the pernicious qualities of such an institution are so widely known that the Norwegian unicameral legislature has divided *itself* into two separate houses, which by internal rules must each independently pass a given piece of legislation" (Neely 1981, p. 59).

6.5   A Defense of the Publicity Principle: A First Step

A hard-line defense of the publicity principle would reject the counterexamples. One might argue, for example, that the Chinese agricultural experiments really were immoral, precisely because they were so manipulative that they would fail if their conditions were publicized. One might reject backroom politics on the grounds that the sleazy transactions probably outnumber the public-spirited ones, or even that the gain in openness is worth some loss in public weal. One might observe that *in fact* telling players the number of Prisoner's Dilemmas they are about to play in a long series does not lead them to defect on every play, and thus that the game theorist's domino theory lacks descriptive bite; one might likewise doubt that publicizing the availability of criminal defenses such as duress or necessity would actually make any difference in the crime rate.

I think that this hard-line defense is unpromising, because I doubt that all of the counterexamples can be conjured away. Together, I believe these and similar counterexamples we might construct show that the publicity principle cannot be accepted *in an unqualified form* as a "formal constraint on the concept of right," let alone a "transcendental formula of public law." I shall argue, however, that the counterexamples themselves suggest a qualification of the principle that makes it much more plausible. I shall then offer an argument that, if not a complete defense of the qualified publicity principle, at least amounts to a sketch of how that defense might run.

The most persuasive of our counterexamples seem to be of two sorts. Consider:

1.   The Russian price decontrol example. Suppose that I were a Russian farmer who knew a bit of game theory. I might think to myself:

> Hmmm! Price decontrols are for the good of the entire country, for in the medium to long run they will entice us farmers to bring more of our goods to market and alleviate scarcity. If the date of decontrol is announced publicly, however, then it will behoove each of us farmers to withhold our goods from the market until that date, even though our country risks collapse as food supplies dwindle in a harsh December. Too bad for the country. Furthermore, we risk flooding the market come Decontrol Date, driving prices down and annihilating our own profits from the price decontrol. Too bad for us. On the other hand, my individual strategy of withholding my crop until D-Date clearly dominates the strategy of sending the crop to market now, and so does the withholding strategy for all the other farmers. If the government announces D-Date, then it will plunk us farmers

into a multiperson Prisoner Dilemma, in which the only rational strategy is to withhold the crops and ruin the country.

If, on the other hand, the government keeps D-Date a secret until the last possible moment, none of us will have a rational motivation for withholding our crops (which may, after all, simply rot if we gamble on a prompt decontrol). For the good of the country, I hope that the government keeps D-Date under wraps.

In this case, the farmer has an *autopaternalistic* motive for wishing the government would keep Decontrol Date under wraps: he wants the government to remove a source of temptation (in this case, *rational* temptation) by concealing an important policy.[25]

2. The graduate student shoplifter. Here the analysis is slightly different. We want the store detective to conceal the policy of charging shoplifters only on the third offense, but not (necessarily) to remove *ourselves* from the temptation to steal, as in an autopaternalism case. We may have no such temptation. Here I am not worried about you or me. I am worried about the Wicked Ones. I'm O.K., you're O.K. – but what do we do about them? In this as in other examples of mercy, the problem is that if merciful policies are publicized they will provide perverse incentives to the wicked, who can't be acoustically separated from the rest of us. The case is not much different, in fact, from our motivation for wishing our government would keep secret the location of weapons-grade plutonium: though *we* have no temptation to steal weapons-grade plutonium, we fear that the world contains plenty of people who do.

In both cases, the key to reconciling secrecy with the publicity principle lies in realizing that the publicity principle can be used to test second-order as well as first-order maxims: the maxims "Government may adopt policies that violate the publicity principle when that is the only way to prevent us from self-destructive behavior" and "Government may adopt policies that violate the publicity principle when that is the only way to forestall perverse incentives to the wicked" may themselves pass the publicity test. If the reasons for keeping a first-order policy secret can themselves be justified in a public manner, then the second-order policy of keeping the first-order policy secret is fully compatible with the publicity principle.

We may worry that this strategy will initiate a slippery slope permitting government secrecy any time government officials think they have a good reason for it. If second-order appeals to the publicity principle are acceptable, why not third- or even higher-order appeals? And if such

---

[25]On the topic of autopaternalism, the principal source is Elster 1979.

higher-order appeals are valid, the publicity principle has become so weak and attenuated that it is hardly worth defending.

Consider, for example, the Iran-Contra affair. The U.S. Congress permits various government agencies to engage in covert operations, provided that congressional committees are secretly informed of them and are able to oversee them. The American public seems to accept the legitimacy of such covert actions, and thus the policy of secrecy coupled with independent oversight seems to pass the second-order publicity test.

However, members of the Reagan administration involved in the Iran-Contra activities concealed them from congressional oversight as well as from the rest of the world – and, obviously, kept secret the fact that they had unilaterally determined to conceal the operation from Congress. In the aftermath of the scandal, several Iran-Contra figures explained that CIA Director William Casey ordered Oliver North to lie to Congress because he did not trust Congress to keep the matter confidential (though it seems likely that this was merely an excuse, and that in fact Casey wished to conceal the operation from Congress because he anticipated opposition and outrage).

In effect, this explanation amounts to a *third*-order use of the publicity principle: the Iran-Contra figures believed that the (third-order) policy of keeping secret the (second-order) decision to conceal from Congress information about a (first-order) covert operation could be publicly justified by their concerns about congressional leaks. But – one worries – if this explanation is a legitimate appeal to the publicity principle, it is hard to see how the publicity principle constrains any kind of governmental secrecy or concealment at all.

I reply that while third- and higher-order appeals to the publicity principle represent coherent logical possibilities,[26] they will almost never succeed in practice (and the Iran-Contra defense of lying to Congress in fact persuaded no one except right-wing fundamentalists who needed no persuasion). Thus the threat higher-order appeals seem to pose to the publicity principle is purely notional.

There is, after all, an enormous difference between second-order appeals to publicity and third- or higher-order appeals. The idea that policies of secrecy might be publicly acceptable on autopaternalistic or perverse-incentive-avoiding grounds seems straightforward and plausible. But the idea that a policy of concealing public justifications for

---

[26]Except that on logical grounds an adherent to the publicity principle could not accept the Ω-principle that allows all policies and higher-order policies of secrecy to be kept secret, including the Ω-principle itself. For the Ω- principle could not pass the publicity test.

policies of secrecy might itself be publicly justifiable has no real-world plausibility at all. Such a policy amounts to permitting officials not merely to make secret decisions, but to conceal the very fact that they have awarded this permission to themselves. Decisions to keep secrets are thereby removed from oversight by publicly established mechanisms of checks and balances. It is hard to imagine why someone who approved of such a policy would accept the publicity principle in the first place.

Higher-order appeals to the publicity principle will almost never succeed, whereas second-order appeals may succeed in a variety of circumstances. The task, of course, is to determine what those circumstances are. I have been arguing that autopaternalistic violations of publicity – permitting government to keep policies secret in order to avoid landing us in situations (such as prisoner's dilemmas) where we anticipate we will behave self-destructively – are among those policies that will pass the publicity test at the second level. And so do violations of publicity designed to forestall perverse incentives to the wicked.

It is worth reflecting on *why* these examples violate the publicity principle at the first level but not at the second. In both cases, publicizing a maxim turns out to be self-frustrating, *but not for reasons that seem to have anything to do with the morality of the maxim.* That, precisely, is why policies of secrecy in these cases can pass the publicity test at the second level.[27]

The publicity principle thus seems to work as a test of morality only in the following circumstance: not merely is publicizing a maxim self-frustrating, but moral phenomena play a causal role in the chain of events leading to self-frustration. The arguments and examples we have looked at reveal two causal patterns that fit this description.

1.   If the maxim is publicized, public *disapproval* plays a causal role in its self-frustration. Llewellyn's and Nesson's arguments that institutions of justice should strive for public acceptance rather than authentic justice would fail if publicized because the public disapproves of institutions of justice that do not strive for justice. In Kant's treaty example, a nation that announced that it would violate treaties whenever it was in its interests to do so would fail to achieve useful treaties because other nations would *mistrust* it. (At some cost in precision, I am here regarding mistrust as a form of moral disapproval.)

2.   If the maxim is publicized, public *corruption* plays a causal role in

---

[27]I came to appreciate this point thanks to the forceful objections that Peter Singer raised to an earlier version of my argument. Singer asked why the bare fact that a maxim would be self-frustrating if it were publicized should count as a moral objection to it, and made me see that I had no answer to the question.

its self-frustration. Here I have in mind Rawls's argument against utilitarianism. If the utilitarian maxim became generally known, citizens would become demoralized – they would lose self-respect, leading in turn to the loss of respect for others that utilitarianism requires of its adherents. It is not necessarily true that the public would disapprove of utilitarianism: demoralized individuals are just as likely to blame themselves rather than the policy that has demoralized them. But a recognizably moral phenomenon – public corruption – plays a causal role in the self-frustration of utilitarian public morality.

Is there any formulation of the publicity principle that captures both these patterns? Let me suggest a feature they share. In both cases, public disapproval as well as public corruption, publicizing a maxim undercuts the legitimacy of the public institutions proposing to adopt the maxim. I mean the term "legitimacy" to refer to the institution's capacity to garner empirical support based on its constituents' moral commitment to it (or, in foreign relations, to garner its interlocutors' respect). Let us, then, reformulate the publicity principle as follows:

> All actions relating to the right of other human beings are wrong if publicizing their maxim would lead to self-frustration by undercutting the legitimacy of the public institutions authorizing those actions.

6.6 A Defense of the Publicity Principle: Second Step

This reformulation helps pare away counter-examples, but offers no affirmative case for the publicity principle. To my mind, the most persuasive affirmative argument for the publicity principle derives from considerations of popular sovereignty: an action or policy that cannot withstand publicity is one that cannot garner popular consent, and that is why the action is wrong.

But this argument raises the obvious question of what is so compelling about popular sovereignty. It seems clear that some issues are really better left to the experts, not the people – the Wise, not the Many. Those in public authority may be better informed, more intelligent, more moral, or wiser than the common denominator represented by the citizenry; and in those cases, Plato may have been right to insist that the virtuous ruler should do the right thing and then placate the ruled with noble lies. (Consider, once again, the case of a progressive South African government confronting an intransigently racist white electorate.)

I am persuaded that no a priori argument can dispose of this possibility. My response is rather to reformulate the question, translating it out of the realm of a priori philosophical argument and into the realm of historical and political experience. Suppose we grant to Plato and Machiavelli the point on which both insist – that the Many are often wrong (ill-informed, incompetent, prejudiced) about the crucial issues of public life. Suppose we grant as well that some people, the Wise, may be right where the rest of us are steeped in error – indeed, not only *may* be right, but at countless moments in human history *have* been right in the face of popular error and thoughtlessness.

It simply does not follow that governments should be permitted to make policy in secret, placating the Many with noble lies. That conclusion would follow only if the Wise happen to coincide with those who occupy positions of official authority.

To put it another way, the empirical validity of the publicity principle turns not on whether the Many are ignorant or wrong-headed, but on whether their leaders are less ignorant or less wrong-headed. No doubt the Wise are few; and the leaders are few; but it hardly follows that the leaders are wise. Before we reject the publicity principle because the leaders know best, we must have reason to believe that the leaders know better. And to find that out, we must look carefully at the variety of mechanisms by which decision-making elites are actually selected. If actual selection mechanisms choose randomly between the Many and the Wise, or affirmatively disfavor the Wise, then the foolishness of the Many is irrelevant: the Few in official positions have no reason to suppose that their policy brainstorms are any less foolish. It would be absurd to insist that officials should disregard the publicity principle merely because the Many view matters through a glass darkly. The officials may view matters through the same leaded glass.

These observations do not, of course, offer a defense of the publicity principle. Rather, they offer (in the most general terms, at that) a research program for assessing whether and when the publicity principle is defensible. How well do various selection mechanisms succeed in empowering the Wise? – political party systems, democratic elections, civil service examinations (such as the 2,000-year-long Imperial Chinese system), nepotism and hereditary officeholding, palace intrigue, the business/government revolving door, grooming through *hautes écoles*, . . . In those systems that succeed in selecting the Wise, the publicity principle is false; in those that offer only random or worse chances of selecting the Wise, the principle is true (in a sense that I shall explain shortly). Plainly, this is a difficult research program to execute or even to formulate operationally. How one defines "the Wise" may itself beg crucial questions.[28]

---

[28]One might object that the inquiry not only begs crucial questions, but contains

Is this all that can be said? Must we end with an evanescent question? I think not. Though I am insisting that the justification (or lack of justification) of the publicity principle turns on empirical inquiry, there is no reason not to offer an educated guess about what that inquiry will reveal. Let me sketch an argument in support of the conjecture that in most if not all selection systems the publicity principle is true.

It is important to realize that the character of those who seek and attain office in a political system depends in large measure on the moral expectations attached to the offices. Commentators on recent trends in American politics have worried that the voting public demands a level of personal rectitude, or even asceticism, that may be inconsistent with the extroverted vitality and "fire in the belly" needed for national office. Court watchers have groaned that intellectual achievements may disqualify candidates for the Supreme Court; numerous organizations have argued that current ethics-in-government laws discourage capable individuals from accepting appointment to government offices.

These are examples of a more general point: the "moral job descriptions" of leadership posts serve in effect as recruitment devices for those posts; they serve also as filtering devices on the kind of person who survives on the job. A moral principle vesting dictatorial powers in an office may attract mainly megalomaniacs; a moral principle licensing unfettered political ruthlessness may guarantee that only the ruthless survive in politics; a moral principle permitting noble lies may attract mainly liars, and not necessarily noble ones.

One possibility we cannot rule out is that a principle of political morality that could be exercised wisely by the right individuals will tend to recruit and retain precisely the wrong individuals, that is, individuals who are incapable of exercising it wisely. I wish to suggest that precisely this is the most likely result if we reject the publicity principle and adopt instead a principle permitting noble lies – a principle in which government officials are licensed or encouraged to deceive the Many for the Many's own good. That principle makes sense if we can count on the superior wisdom and virtue of officials; but it seems much more plausible that those who would be attracted to public office by the unfet-

---

an in-built circularity, since political wisdom surely includes the ability to gain and retain political power in a given selection system. I reject this latter proposition, however. Our inquiry, remember, is whether existing selection mechanisms will pick officials who can make better (wiser, more virtuous) policy than the hoi polloi – indeed, policy so much better that its rationale must be concealed from the hoi polloi. There is absolutely no reason to presume that wisdom in this sense includes, or even correlates with, the ability to gain and retain political office. That, in fact, is what the inquiry is all about.

tered discretion to deceive are precisely those who are neither wiser nor more virtuous than the rest of us.

Viewed in this light, the publicity principle should be accepted as a *principle of rational skepticism* on the part of officials.[29] Suppose, that is, that I am an official contemplating a certain policy. Suppose in addition that I believe that my policy would violate the publicity principle: if it were publicized, widespread public disapproval would undermine my legitimacy and frustrate my pursuit of cherished political goals. My first impulse is to conceal my policy, because I think that I know better than the wider public.

At this point, rational skepticism should lead me to reflect on how I came to occupy the office I now possess. Is it really because I'm such a smart cookie? Or is it that I knew somebody who knew somebody? Perhaps I made it on my own; but – the voice of rational skepticism reminds me – the skills that I used to make it on my own were maneuvering skills in turf wars coupled with opportunism. (In politics you use anything you can get your hands on.) In my nasty little corner of the bureaucratic world, wisdom and virtue may well be counteradaptive traits; if so, the fact that I outmaneuvered the Wise doesn't show that I am wise. Quite the contrary. So even if the Many are neither wise nor virtuous, the smart money says that I am one of them rather than one of the Platonic Few. Rational skepticism – the smart money – says that if publicizing my maxim would undercut my legitimacy, it is probably because my maxim is wrong.

One might object that supporters of noble lies need not assume that policymakers are wiser or more virtuous than the public at large. They need assume only that policymakers who have devoted long, patient hours to learning the intricacies of a complex issue know a lot more about it than the man or woman on the street. The relevant distinction is neither wisdom nor virtue, but accumulated experience and time on the learning curve. A former U.S. official who had worked on the sea treaty told me that it took him three years on the job to really understand the issues. Why, then assume that *vox populi* represents *vox Dei*? If the public must be deceived for its own good, that is simply because the public is ill informed, not that it is less wise or virtuous than the policymaker.

My reply to this objection is that there is a crucial difference between being sufficiently knowledgeable to set policy about complex issues and being sufficiently knowledgeable to render intelligent consent to it.

---

[29]I owe this formulation to Michael Smith, whose astute but sympathetic criticisms of an earlier version of my argument improved it greatly.

What takes three years to learn may take only three minutes to explain. In fifteen years of law teaching, I have never encountered a legal or public policy issue that couldn't be explained to a bright twelve-year-old in half an hour. That is not to say that the twelve-year-old would decide the issue intelligently, but it is to say that she would accurately understand why the issue is in dispute and what the chief arguments are on all sides. By supporting deception, opponents of the publicity principle assume not only that the public is less informed than policymakers, but that the public is for practical purposes ineducable. That, I think, really does amount to a presumption that policymakers are wiser and better than their fellows. Rational skepticism should lead us to doubt this presumption. If a policy would excite across-the-board moral condemnation, the reasonable conclusion is that, even if the public doesn't know best, it probably knows better.

In that case, the publicity principle – like the Enlightenment ideal of popular sovereignty that it represents – would be justified by a version of Winston Churchill's bromide about democracy: it is the worst form of government we can imagine, except for all the others.

References

Bickel, Alexander. 1962. *The Least Dangerous Branch: The Supreme Court at the Bar of Politics*. New Haven, Conn.: Yale University Press.

Birnbaum, Jeffrey H., and Alan S. Murray. 1987. *Showdown at Gucci Gulch*. New York: Random House.

Black, Charles. 1961. Mr. Justice Black, the Supreme Court, and the Bill of Rights. *Harper's Magazine* 63 (Feb. 1961).

Brodie, Bernard. 1946. Implications for military policy. Pp. 70–107 in B. Brodie, ed., *The Absolute Weapon*. New York: Harcourt, Brace.

Calabresi, Guido. 1982. *A Common Law for the Age of Statutes*. Cambridge, Mass.: Harvard University Press.

Dan-Cohen, Meir. 1984. Decision rules and conduct rules: on acoustic separation in criminal law. *Harvard Law Review* 97: 625–77.

Elster, Jon. 1979. *Ulysses and the Sirens: Studies in Rationality and Irrationality*. Cambridge: Cambridge University Press.

Friedman, Lawrence M. 1985. *A History of American Law*. 2nd ed. New York: Simon and Schuster.

Fuller, Lon. 1964. *The Morality of Law*. 2nd ed. New Haven, Conn.: Yale University Press.

Gauthier, David. 1984. Deterrence, maximization, and rationality. Pp. 101–22 in Douglas MacLean, ed., *The Security Gamble: Deterrence Dilemmas in the Nuclear Age*. Totowa, N.J.: Rowman & Littlefield. Reprinted in *Ethics*, 94 (1984), 474–95.

Gewirtz, Paul. 1983. Remedies and resistance. *Yale Law Journal* 92: 585–681.

Habermas, Jürgen. 1989. *The Structural Transformation of the Public Sphere:*

An Inquiry into a Category of Bourgeois Society, trans. Thomas Burger and Frederick Lawrence. Cambridge, Mass.: MIT Press; originally published 1962.

Hart, H. L. A. 1979. Between utility and rights. *Columbia Law Review* 79: 828–46.

Kadish, Mortimer R., and Sanford H. Kadish. 1973. *Discretion to Disobey.* Stanford, Calif.: Stanford University Press.

Kant, Immanuel. 1784. An answer to the question: "What is Enlightenment?" Pp. 54–60 in Hans Reiss, ed., *Kant: Political Writings,* trans. H. B. Nisbet. 2nd ed. Cambridge: Cambridge University Press, 1991.

Kant, Immanuel. 1785. *Fundamental Principles of the Metaphysics of Morals,* trans. Thomas K. Abbott. Indianapolis, Ind.: Bobbs-Merrill, 1949.

Kant, Immanuel. 1787. *Metaphysical First Principles of the Doctrine of Right.* Pp. 35–161 in *The Metaphysics of Morals,* trans. Mary Gregor. Cambridge: Cambridge University Press, 1991.

Kant, Immanuel. 1793. On the common saying: "That may be true in theory, but it does not apply in practice." Pp. 61–92 in Hans Reiss, ed., *Kant: Political Writings,* trans. H. B. Nisbet. 2nd ed. Cambridge: Cambridge University Press, 1991.

Kant, Immanuel. 1795a. Perpetual peace. Pp. 93–130 in Hans Reiss, ed., *Kant: Political Writings,* trans. H. B. Nisbet. 2nd ed. Cambridge: Cambridge University Press, 1991.

Kant, Immanuel. 1795b. Perpetual peace. Pp. 85–135 in Lewis White Beck, ed., *Kant: On History.* Indianapolis: Bobbs-Merrill, 1957.

Kant, Immanuel. 1795c. Zum ewigen Frieden. Vol. 8, Pp. 341–86 in *Kants Werke.* Berlin: Prussische Akademie Ausgabe, 1923.

Kavka, Gregory S. 1978. Some paradoxes of deterrence. *Journal of Philosophy* 75: 285–302.

Kavka, Gregory S. 1984. Deterrent intentions and retaliatory actions. Pp. 155–59 in Douglas MacLean, ed., *The Security Gamble: Deterrence Dilemmas in the Nuclear Age.* Totowa, N.J.: Rowman & Littlefield.

Lewis, David K. 1969. *Convention: A Philosophical Study.* Cambridge, Mass.: Harvard University Press.

Lewis, David K. 1984. Devil's bargains and the real world. Pp. 141–54 in Douglas MacLean, ed., *The Security Gamble: Deterrence Dilemmas in the Nuclear Age.* Totowa, N.J.: Rowman & Littlefield.

Llewellyn, Karl. 1940. On reading and using the newer jurisprudence. *Columbia Law Review* 40: 581–614.

Luban, David. 1982. The twice-told tale of Mr. Fixit: reflections on the Brandeis/Frankfurter connection. *Yale Law Journal* 91: 1678–707.

Luban, David. 1986. The paradox of deterrence revived. *Philosophical Studies* 50: 129–41.

Luban, David. 1994. *Legal Modernism.* Ann Arbor, Mich.: University of Michigan Press.

Machiavelli, Niccolò. 1532. *The Prince*. Many editions.

Mencken, H. L. 1956. *A Carnival of Buncombe,* ed. Malcolm Moos. Baltimore: Johns Hopkins University Press.

Neely, Richard. 1981. *How Courts Govern America.* New Haven, Conn.: Yale University Press.

Nesson, Charles. 1985. The evidence or the event? On judicial proof and the acceptability of verdicts. *Harvard Law Review* 98: 1357–92.

New York. Court of Appeals. 1988. *People v. Goetz.* 532 N.E.2d 1273.

Posner, Richard A. 1985. *The Federal Courts: Crisis and Reform.* Cambridge, Mass.: Harvard University Press.

Railton, Peter. 1984. Alienation, consequentialism, and the demands of morality. *Philosophy & Public Affairs* 13: 134–71.

Rawls, John. 1971. *A Theory of Justice.* Cambridge, Mass.: Harvard University Press.

Raz, Joseph. 1977. The rule of law and its virtue. *Law Quarterly Review* 93: 195–211.

Rhode, Deborah L. 1981. Policing the professional monopoly: a constitutional and empirical analysis of unauthorized practice prohibitions. *Stanford Law Review* 34: 1–112.

Schell, Jonathan. 1982. *The Fate of the Earth.* New York: Alfred A. Knopf.

Schiffer, Stephen R. 1972. *Meaning.* Oxford: Clarendon Press.

Sen, Amartya K., and Bernard Williams. 1982. Introduction. Pp. 1–21 in Sen and Williams, eds., *Utilitarianism and Beyond.* Cambridge: Cambridge University Press.

Shklar, Judith. 1979. Let us not be hypocritical. *Daedalus* 108 (3): 1–25.

Sidgwick, Henry. 1966. *The Methods of Ethics.* 7th ed. New York: Dover.

Williams, Bernard. 1973. A critique of utilitarianism. Pp. 75–150 in J. J. C. Smart and B. Williams, *Utilitarianism: For and Against.* Cambridge: Cambridge University Press.

7

Designing Institutions in East European Transitions

CLAUS OFFE

THIS CHAPTER is divided in two main sections. The first section serves conceptual purposes. I lay out a dualist concept of institutions and contrast it to related concepts such as organization, norm, ritual, and convention. How do we recognize an institution, in the proper sociological sense, if we see it? The second part looks at institutions in a longitudinal perspective. What happens to them over time, how can we explain what happens, and how can we conceivably intentionally determine what happens to institutions and, as a consequence, to those living in or under these institutions?

"Institution" is a key conceptual tool in the social sciences. Sociology, political science, economics, but also the disciplines of history, anthropology, and law can hardly work without it. Moreover, the creation of institutions, or the building of new and "better" social, political, and economic institutions is generally considered to be the central practical problem that societies confront as they emerge from their thoroughly discredited past, such as postauthoritarian and, in particular, postcommunist societies.

7.1 The Dual Nature of Institutions

Let me start with the proposition, widely shared in the sociological but not so in the economic literature on the subject, that institutions embody normative intuitions or principles of those who live in or under the institutions in question. The relationship between institutions and social norms is, however, not unilateral, but reciprocal and cyclical. Social actors generate, support, and enact institutions, and these institutions, in turn, generate social agents capable of observing social norms. Institutions establish standards, both normative and cognitive, as to

199

what is to be held to be normal, what must be expected, what can be relied upon, which rights and duties are attached to which positions, and what makes sense in the community or social domain for which an institution is valid. Institutions accomplish a socializing function in that they serve as examples and reminders of how people "ought to" behave and relate to each other,[1] and what they legitimately can expect from each other. Institutions play a "preceptorial" role, as Lindblom (1977) has called it. Thus, good citizens make good institutions, and good institutions are "good" to the extent they generate and cultivate good citizens or the "better selves" of citizens, who at least get "used to" and "feel at home" in those institutions, develop a sense of loyalty, and come to adopt the cognitive expectations and moral intuitions from which the institutions themselves derive. The "preceptorial" or "hegemonic" function that (successful) institutions perform is most importantly a negative one: they encourage the self-imposition, on the part of social actors, of behavioral disciplines that curb "opportunistic" modes of action. At the same time institutions provide actors with socially validated standards as to what preferences and goals are licensed and can be expected to meet with approval. The presence or absence of both of these operative feedback loops – discipline and license – is the first test by which we can determine whether a given social arrangement is an institution or not.

There is also a second test concerning the quality of institutions: institutions must not just perform the task of what we might term "congruent socialization," but they must also *function* properly, i.e., accomplish the task or mission set for them, or be compatible with the supply of resources they depend upon and must hence extract from their environment. It is exactly in order for an institution to be able to accomplish its (more or less specified and defined) imagined function or mission that the predominant concern with this outcome must be bracketed or suspended. A well-functioning institution unburdens actors from purposive and strategic considerations, as an institutionally prescribed course of action can be trusted to yield beneficial or at least tolerable outcomes. Thus institutions allow for instrumental concerns being displaced by a healthy dose of ritualism and conservatism. Once established and widely supported, institutions, as it were, fly by themselves due to the invisible operation of an autopilot. That is to say, they

---

[1]From Aristotle on, and not ending with Rousseau, many political theorists have believed that institutions, such as the law, the constitution, or, for that matter, the socialist collective farm, are capable of "perfecting" human beings, e.g., by turning "ordinary" citizens or workers into "good citizens" or workers.

function satisfactorily as a supraintentional framework of appropriate action.

It is easy to see that the two criteria of institutions that I have distinguished are not synonymous. Even if institutions (such as the business firm, the university, the hospital, the military, the church, parliamentary government, marriage, the profession, or social security) do generate the most solid support and loyalty of those who belong to them (as well as of outside observers), they may still fail in successfully coping with the problems they are supposed to cope with, or in extracting the resources needed for the implementation of their function. And conversely, even manifest failure does not necessarily undermine the moral support that an institution enjoys, as such failure may positively lead to an attitude of doctrinaire overidentification on the part of actors with the rules, values, and routines embodied in the institution that fails. Furthermore, an institution may be reasonably successful in performing its functions and extracting its resources, while remaining weak and virtually nominal as far as its operative capacity for generating normative guidance and the security of cognitive expectations is concerned.[2]

Thus both dimensions are conceptually necessary as criteria of the existence and viability of institutions, internal socialization and external effectiveness, or the consolidation of beliefs, on the one hand, and the implementation of goals or the control over resources, on the other. These dimensions do obviously somehow correspond to famous pairs of concepts such as Weber's "ideas" versus "interests," Lockwood's (1964) "social integration" versus "systems integration," Lipset's (1981, pp. 64–70) legitimacy and effectiveness or Habermas's (1981) "life world" versus "system." Using a simpler language, we might also say that an institution in the strict sense of the concept (as opposed to institutional ruins, or degenerate or deficient version of it) does survive the dual test of "making sense" and "being fit" for its mission.

Institutions in this sense can be located somewhere in between *social norms* and norm-oriented action, on the one hand, and purposive rational or *strategic action*, on the other. Or rather, they contain and combine elements of both of these modes of action, doing things "the right way" and "getting things done." March and Olsen (1989, p. 23f.) refer to the same dualism when locating action and the rules that govern it on a time axis. They suggest that institutionalized action combines

---

[2]The new "institution" of the European Union may serve as an illustration of this case of a "deficient" institution – particularly if seen in contrast to the solid institution of the (West) European nation state, which seems to be much richer in terms of its quality as a source of standards of "appropriateness."

backward looking ("obligatory") and forward looking ("anticipatory") motivational forces, the first being informed by some "logic of appropriateness" and the second by instrumental or strategic rationality ("logic of consequentiality," p. 160). Particular instances of institutionalized action may differ as to the relative weight of these two motivational components as well as the reflective awareness of the actors, but neither of the two is, by definition, completely absent. Closely related, if not identical instances of this sociological dualism are represented by distinctions and pairs of concepts such as rules versus decisions, status versus contract, or necessity versus preference, order versus choice, boundaries versus contingency. Institutions are "bridges," or synthetic arrangements which allow for the coincidence of such apparent opposites. To illustrate this synthesis, we can think of the institution of private property, which is the *status* right to make *contracts* according to preferences. Similarly, the institution of money generates an enormous range of choices that is contingent exactly on the fact that the range of these choices and the value of the currency remains *exempt* from contingent choices.

Institutions, in a word, inculcate duties and generate outcomes. In order to generate the outcomes, they must rely on cognitive and moral resources which in their turn, however, are not to be created by administrative fiat. *"There is no administrative production of meaning"* (Habermas 1975, p. 70; emphasis in original). Consequently, whoever wishes to advocate, design, construct, change, or criticize institutions will have to bear in mind this dualism and the inherent limits of potential control over meaning.

There are two competing approaches in the social sciences which both fail to appreciate this dualism of institutions. On the one hand, "culturalists" and some sociological and philosophical "institutionalists" fail in that they advocate and explain certain institutions solely in terms of the social norms and values that institutions embody and manage to spread in their social domain, while ignoring the systemic "fit" between the institution and its environment.[3] On the other extreme, utilitarians notoriously also fail to conceptualize institutions in a balanced way, as they place one-sided emphasis upon the instrumental aspect of institutions. They advocate or defend institutions (such as the market, property rights, or the business firm) in terms of their efficiency-

---

[3]"The propensity to social change arising from the functional incompatibility between an institutional order and its material base has been ignored by normative functionalists because of their concentration on the moral aspects of social integration" (Lockwood 1964, p. 256).

enhancing and hence utility-maximizing effect, and they even explain the presence of certain institutions in given societies in terms of their evolutionary superiority, e.g., as to their capacity of economizing on transaction costs.[4] Methodologically similar is the structure of some Marxist arguments, as they conceptualize at least some institutions as the direct and intended outcome of ruling-class strategies to achieve exploitative distributional outcomes.

What the utilitarian, evolutionist, and Marxist approaches amount to is a denial of the crucial conceptual difference between an "institution" and an "organization." The latter, but not the former, can and do actually subordinate (in accordance with Weber's notion of "purposive rationality") "duties" to (expected) "outcomes." In organizations "duties," or authoritatively prescribed and enforced roles and rules, are assigned so as to achieve optimal outcomes. To an extent, it is thus entirely a matter of the formal authority of the boss over the employee which task the latter will have to perform this afternoon. But only to an extent, because the duty assigned affects the role of the employee, not the employee as a person; and it is more or less narrowly constrained by numerous institutional rules, e.g., the employee's status rights associated with the work contract and his citizen rights, that limit the range of duties the boss is actually entitled to assign. It is only the non-contingent institutional framework of status rights that creates the space for organizational decision-making and purposive action.

The difference between an organization and an institution can be summed up in three points. (1) Organizational duties are dyadic, while institutional rules are triadic, i.e., established and enforced by "third parties" who are not part of the institutionalized interaction. (2) "Duties" are subordinate to intended outcomes in organizations, but stand at least on the same logical plane in institutions. (3) Organizational duties are much more restricted in their scope, validity, and impact upon the person involved; they are restricted to the range of discretion that institutions (such as property rights, marriage, political parties, the business firm) grant the agents in their domain for the pursuit of their purposes.

To illustrate, the university as an institution does not allow you to concoct the data base of your research or to plagiarize the work of other scientists (although that can be highly purposive-rational!), but a given university as an organization encapsulated in the institution permits

---

[4]"The bulk of the literature appearing under the label of 'New Institutional Economics' seems to rest on the assumption that institutional change occurs primarily in an efficiency enhancing form" (Grosser 1993, p. 21).

certain incumbents of certain offices to change the curriculum, if only according to certain noncontingent rules.[5]

The "triadic" or "embedded" nature of institutions bears elaboration. Institutions depend for their viability and survival upon the knowledge and at least tacit consent of "third parties" that are not directly involved in the particular interaction the institution regulates. "Working rules"[6] must be common knowledge and must be monitored and enforced. Common knowledge implies that every participant knows the rules, knows that others know the rules, and knows that others also know that the participant knows the rules" (Ostrom 1992, p. 20). Institutions – in sharp distinction to conventions,[7] which are strictly self-enforcing – are social arrangements which are designed to settle potential conflict. For that, they need to be endorsed by "third parties." If they are endorsed in this way, the phenomenon of second-order expectations (or "expected expectations," in Luhmann's parlance) emerges: what those involved in an institutional interaction can and cannot expect from each other is itself expected by third parties or outside observers. As they allocate privileges, licenses, and duties to actors, institutions – in contrast to unquestioning habits, routines and traditions – establish an order that is always potentially contested and hence needs to be tolerated, supported, and enforced by external actors. In enforcing institutions, third actors will normally invoke rudimentary theories, sometimes derived from a formal institutional charter, supplying arguments as to why an institutionalized status order is to be held valid and hence deserves to be adhered to.

This potential for conflict – and hence the need for external enforcement and strong justificatory "theories" – is particularly evident in the case of those institutions that deal with the jurisdiction over the production and distribution of core values such as health, peace, power, knowledge, truth, love, prosperity, mobility, aesthetic beauty, security (both military and social), friendship, justice, jobs, salvation, punish-

---

[5]Meyer and Rowan (as reprinted in Powell and DiMaggio 1991) have provided a powerful argument to the effect that the balance between internally assigned duties and rules extracted from the institutional environment of the organization, or between organizational and institutional functions, is actually shifting toward the latter, as organizations, partly for their lack of utility-maximizing algorithms of their own, come increasingly to rely on institutionalized rules they adopt from their environment. To the extent this hypothesis is valid, the utilitarian view of institutions is further discredited.

[6]"Working rules" is a synonym for the term "institution" introduced by J. R. Commons (1934).

[7]Standard examples are the convention to drive on either the right-hand or left-hand side of the street, or the distribution of characters on the typewriter keyboard.

ment, education, and the like. The relationship between the shape and distribution of procedural rules, restraints, resources, and licenses, on the one hand, and these reference values, on the other, can be found in implicit theories, ideologies, and justifications institutions cultivate about themselves which are often enshrined in an institutional "charter." It ultimately depends on the quality, i.e., the compelling power, or immunity to critique, of these theories whether or not a particular institution will manage to suspend open conflict over the licenses, privileges, and rules of which its status order consists.

Other institutions are less directly and less obviously related to such core values, but they still help to establish rules in the absence of which friction would occur. Many of these institutions regulate the social use of space and/or time, as is the case with parks, market squares, vacation trips, carnival, bank holidays, birthday parties, sports stadia, political party conventions, bars, music halls, and many others. They have in common that they evoke and legitimate certain themes, routines, and orientations and thus facilitate the interaction (or economize on the transaction costs) of those involved, and restrict this interaction to a particular range of themes, practices, entitlements, and premises. The strength of these thematic, spatial, status related, and temporal demarcation rules becomes evident in the sentiments of comicality, embarrassment, shame, and protest that are aroused if the "wrong" persons do the "wrong" things at "inappropriate" places or times. It is only to the extent that these demarcation rules are firmly established and recognized that a social and thematic "space" (or, in the arts, a "genre") is created within which innovation, elaboration, variation, etc., of styles and practices can occur.

Such complex codes concerning who is supposed to do what, when, and where, and in what relation to what reference values, help to relieve all members of society from decision loads and conflicts – provided that these codes are known and serve to shape attention and cognitive expectations beyond the group of people directly involved in the institutionally patterned activity. In this sense, institutions can be compared to an exoskeleton of social life. If – and only to the extent that – such demarcation rules are common knowledge, institutions perform the function of "saving energy" – the energy and costs, that is, that would otherwise have to go into the cognitive assessment and moral evaluation of what is going on and how "I" should relate to what "everyone else" is doing. Institutions unburden action because they relieve us from much of the need to generate ad hoc judgments. The experience of conditions of lack of institutional rules (or lack of knowledge about existing rules) shows that enormous amounts of cognitive as well as moral efforts are required to evaluate the appropriateness of our own behavior unless institutionalized status rights, routines, rules, and demarcation lines assist us in making our judgment.[8]

Because of their "energy-saving" features, institutions are not just constraining, but also enabling, and much beyond their function of economizing in transaction costs that is highlighted by economists. They are commonly known frameworks of regulation that help us to develop the "right" understanding of situations and to anticipate what is likely or unlikely to happen. Moreover, the constraint is often only marginal, as institutions can be employed for a variety of purposes, without any of them being prescribed as the all-dominant one, like in an organization. It is this commonly shared knowledge about demarcation rules and the expectations based upon this knowledge that provides institutions with a measure of counterfactual validity and stability. It is important to distinguish between institutions proper and individual cases, instances or realizations of the rules that make up the institution. If an organization fails, it fails and is no longer there. If an institution fails in a particular instance (a marriage, a political party, a state), that does not by itself affect the institutional pattern of which it has been an embodiment.

Such stability of institutions, and the functions performed due to their stability, come at a price. This price is rigidity. On the one side, institutions such as the market, the university, the party system, general elections, or the business firm make an almost unlimited range of choices available which can be selected by combining and recombining the resources and interactions possible within them, thus allowing for the maximization of utilities or the refinement of styles and tastes. On the other side, this option-generating arrangement itself must be relatively immune from choice.

There seems to be a correspondence between the range of choice

---

[8]This "unburdening" effect (*Entlastungseffekt*), as it has been called by the German philosophical anthropologist Arnold Gehlen, becomes evident if we have to relate to a situation in which we cannot rely upon the assistance of institutions. One could think of a situation when a serious traffic accident has occurred and the police and ambulance do not come for some reason. Similarly, we can think of a distributional conflict the solution of which cannot be provided by an institution because the nature of the conflict is so new that no institution for processing it has yet been installed. This is the single most important theme in German domestic politics right now. Whereas the usual distributional conflict between labor and capital is quite solidly institutionalized, the new distribution conflict between the former West and East German Länder is still to be resolved not only in substantive, but also in procedural and institutional terms. Until it is, the political system as a whole is suffering from an extraordinary cognitive and moral burden of determining legitimate and acceptable ad hoc solutions of this distributional conflict.

made available within an institutional arrangement and the "requisite rigidity" of the arrangement itself. To reiterate, the institution of money can mediate, as it does, innumerable transactions only because none of the participants in these transactions can intentionally affect the value of money, or its quality of being a universally acceptable measure of value and means of exchange in economic transaction. Similarly, democracy as a preference aggregating machinery can only work under a framework of rights that is protected by independent courts and at least relatively immune from democratic contingencies; for it would evidently be the end of democracy if majorities had, for instance, the right to decide that minorities are no longer entitled to vote or organize. In both of these and many other cases, the uncertainty of outcomes is matched by the certainty of procedures, rules, and parameters. One key problem of East and Central European transitions from communism is exactly that there is too little of this kind of "requisite rigidity," as the regime which could enforce such rigidity has broken down, and therefore too little scope for reasoned choice, as every actor has reasons to expect that institutional parameters of action (such as the enforceability of rights, the value of money, or civic nonviolence) cannot be relied upon, as every such parameter is subject to sudden change. The action that takes place is not under institutions, but about institutions: it is all discretion, and no rules governing and constraining discretion.

7.2 Modes of Institutional Stability and Change

In this section I want to review the ways in which institutions do – or do not – change. As it will turn out, "design" is a rare and unlikely mode of change, and even less likely is it that the activity of "designing" is recognized, acknowledged, and remembered as such. The modes that affect the continuity of institutions are discussed under the headings of "stability," "founding," "breakdown," and "critique."

7.2.1 Stability as a Process

Institutions are not "natural," but man-made. At the same time, they have a naturelike longevity. The first thing we associate with them is stability. Hegel has captured the dual aspect of institutions (of being doubtlessly man-made, but of being at the same time also naturelike and often as impossible to change as the law of gravity) by the term "second nature." A popular, though, I submit, deeply misleading mechanical metaphor for the stability of institutions is the notion of "inertia." To account for the stability of institutions, it is much more helpful to rely on biological rather than mechanical analogies, and to compare institutions to "identical reproduction" rather than "inertia." Such biological metaphor highlights the fact that identical reproduction is a process rather than a steady state, and that the "identicalness" of the reproduction of a species is well compatible with virtually unlimited variations of individual specimens, depending upon the complexity of the genetic pool of the species. Identical reproduction is, however, itself not unlimited, but indeed continuously precarious. All social life is affected by "dual contingency," i.e., the openness of the answers to two questions. First, is rule A or rule B to be adopted? Second, whatever rule is in force, should I comply with it or defect? Because of this dual contingency, any identical reproduction can come to an end at a point where either some external phenomenon stops it (cf. the "dying out" of the dinosaurs) or where it stops through mutation and selection.

A less metaphorical understanding of the stability of institutions is "path dependency." My interpretation of this rather powerful explanatory intuition is this. Path dependency is a mechanism of identical reproduction of institutions due to either or both of the two features mentioned above. Not only are institutions man-made, but also men institution-made – they are socialized by the educational or "hidden curriculum" effect of institutions into the values, norms, and rules embodied in them, and as a consequence they know, expect and anticipate that institutions can be relied upon and reckoned with (almost like the objects of nature). This curriculum, incidentally, must not be so "hidden." Institutions generate vested interest in their own preservation, sometimes to the extent that the endogenous rise of effective preferences for an alternative arrangement becomes virtually inconceivable. Just think of the likelihood that within simple majority, "winner-takes-all" electoral systems a coalition emerges that favors proportional representation, whereas a transition in the opposite direction appears much more likely. Second, as long as institutions function properly and continue to generate tolerable levels of outcome, there is no perceived need to think about, and even less to try to implement the potentially costly process of innovating institutions or of introducing institutional alterations. On the other hand, proponents of institutions are always in danger of "promising too much," thereby inadvertently encouraging the quest for institutional reform. In short, the stability of institutions is based upon a social process of identical reproduction that is driven by an institution's socialization effect and its functional viability.

Furthermore, some institutions become stable by reflectively providing for their own stability by institutionalizing what has been called "ultrastability." This happens in either of two ways. The first concerns the degrees of freedom that they leave to individual behavior and choice. Institutions provide just a framework within which purposive choice remains possible. They must be distinguished from rituals where such choice is maximally reduced. The more liberal the regime that institutions impose upon agents, the less vulnerable they will probably become to disloyalty or attempted institutional innovation[9] – at least up to a point, at which "excessive" liberalism will begin to negatively affect the socialization, or preference forming, effect upon which the continuity of institutions normally depends. Also, institutions protect themselves, as it were, from being strained not only through their "framework" character, but also through the possibility they provide to actors to switch to other institutional codes in case their behavior can no longer be accommodated within the rules of one institution.

The other stability-enforcing mechanism that some institutions provide for consists in institutional rules for changing (lower-order!) institutional rules. Thus institutions defined by statutory law can be altered according to constitutional rules governing the legislative process, and even most constitutions contain procedural rules (such as articles 79–81 of the German Basic Law) which specify which parts of the respective constitution can (or conversely cannot) be changed in which way.[10] Both of these allowances – built-in scope for discretion on behavior (including the switch to "neighboring" institutional patterns) and built-in scope for discretion on part of the institutional rules themselves – help to (and are explicitly designed to) preserve institutional stability through provisions for flexibility in the face of changing circumstances and preferences. In these cases, institutions are designed to redesign themselves – and through this two-tiered structure to escape the need to be explicitly designed anew.

Within such two-tiered arrangements, very much scope can be opened for reform and revision of institutions. As long as some features of the institution remain in place, others may be exchanged. In this way, social order can be renegotiated by the agents which are institutionally charged with the license and mandate to do so. The most radical case of institutionally regulated institutional change is *"transicion pactada"* or "round table talks," as they have occurred in the Spanish and East European transitions from authoritarianism. In such cases, actors which are charged with political functions within the old regime coopt and admit other actors with no such previous function in order

---

[9]"Defensive liberalization" is the apt term that Batt (1991, p. 387) employs to describe the desperate last-minute maneuvers of Czechoslovak and East German leaders to benefit from this self-stabilization mechanism in late 1989.

[10] The institutional doctrine of papal infallibility and ultimate authority is another case in point, to which Roman Catholicism owes much of its ultrastability, whereas the recent Fujimori coup in Peru is not, as presidential authority to suspend the constitution is not provided for by the constitution of that country.

to negotiate new rules and new issues. The implication of such cooptation of new actors in regime transitions may be, as it has been, for
instance, in Poland 1989 or in East Germany 1990, that the presence of
the old, formerly monopolistic actors serves just as a temporary face-
saving device without any substantive significance. The least radical and
most routine case is when both institutional actors and institutional
rules remain unchanged and just new substantive issues are admitted
to the agenda.

7.2.2   The "Founding" of Institutions: The Problems of "Hyperrationality" and "Mental Residues"

Diametrically opposed to stability, identical reproduction, path dependency, and ultrastability are those rare cases in which institutions
are actually created at a certain point in time and then succeed to actually perform as institutions vis-à-vis both their constituents and their
resource environment, rather than remaining short-lived blueprints imposed upon agents or simply new names for – or new actors in – old
institutions.

The rare conditions that can give rise to the conscious and intentional
design of institutions – as opposed to the mere design of designs or
names or facades – are partly well known, at least as far as political
institutions are concerned. First, the existing institutions that are to be
replaced[11] by the newly designed institutions must be both thoroughly
discredited (i.e., have failed to perform a congruent socializing function)
and, perhaps partly as a consequence of that loss of credit, must also
have lost their ability to cope with functional problems in their environment. Thus economic crises and wars, as well as the thorough loss
of legitimacy of the regime that has to take responsibility for these
events, will typically give rise to intentionally attempted institutional
innovations. To say this is just paraphrasing Lenin's definition of a rev-
olutionary situation as a condition in which the rulers cannot continue
to rule and the ruled resist the continuation of the rulers' rule.

But a further condition must also be present in order for this situation
to transform itself into one of newly designed and created institutions,
as opposed to mere breakdown and chaos. This second condition is the
presence of a model of the new institutional order that is typically not
invented on the spot, but "imported" and suitably adapted from more

---

[11]The unique feature and facilitating condition of the American Revolution – and
all the institutions it created, such as federalism – is probably that it did not really
have to replace anything, as the new order to be erected was to be built on a terrain
that was both physically and institutionally "empty space," and as the location of
the "old regime" was geographically distant.

or less remote points in time or space. Institutional designs are typically copies, and they are frequently advocated as such.

For an illustration of this point, let me dwell for a moment on the German case of the post–World War II rebuilding of political and economic institutions in both East and West Germany. The first condition of total military defeat plus total moral discrediting of the Nazi regime was certainly fulfilled. But the second condition for institutional reconstruction was also there, namely the ready availability of a positive reference model. As far as West Germany was concerned, the reference model was a combined replica of the "better past" of the Weimar Republic and its democratic institutions plus certain features of the Anglo-Saxon democracies, which were adopted in order to immunize the second German republic from the dangers to which the first had fallen victim. Moreover, the implementation and enforcement mechanism of the new institutions created was "imported"[12] as well, consisting as it did in the occupation forces of the Western allies. The same applies of course to the very different process of institution building that unfolded in East Germany after 1945 and in which the "invented tradition" of the Weimar Communist Left played the same role as did the adopted institutional models of Social Democratic and Christian political forces of Weimar and their institutional legacies in West Germany.

During the process of institutional transformation that started after 1989 in East Central European societies, the visible presence of nuclei of an oppositional political culture capable of entering into relations of compromise and competition with the authorities of the old regime turned out to be a decisive determinant in the process of institution building. Unsurprisingly, these nuclei could best unfold in the two largest societies in the region, namely Poland and Hungary – societies which, partly due to their geostrategic location, could afford the comparatively greatest measure of independence from Soviet control, the strongest sense of national identity, as well as a comparatively long history of economic and political reform initiatives that in both cases dates back to the late seventies. Much weaker and more encapsulated centers of oppositional culture were to be found in the cases of the German Democratic Republic and the Czech and Slovak Socialist Republic, while they were virtually missing in the two remaining cases, Bulgaria and, most definitely, Rumania. Ideas such as pluralism, antiauthoritarianism, human and workers' rights, and self-organization within a civil society, as well as the persons (such as Jacek Kuron in Poland), circles and move-

---

[12] Cf. Rousseau's recommendation that the Legislator should be a foreigner, as he is less likely than any domestic agent to take partisan views in the process of law making and institution building.

ments that were publicly credited with the quality of being trustworthy proponents of those ideas in Hungary and Poland, turned out to be powerful resources in the process of institution building, as they represented, at the round tables, in the media, and elsewhere the moral infrastructure and normative meaning of the order to be built. To be sure, even in these two most fortunate cases of institution founding, competing models of social integration and collective identity, namely nationalist, religious, and traditionalist ones, were by no means absent. They also came to play their role in the process of institutional reform. But what the Polish and Hungarian cases seem to demonstrate is the importance of a preexisting mental and cultural capital as a source of social integration and the most promising starting point of a bottom-up process of institution founding. "Appropriateness" to what was widely, if controversially, perceived to symbolize the respective history and aspirations of the Hungarian and Polish nation was clearly the dominant criterion of institution building in these two cases.

In contrast, the East German and Czech experience, but also, in a much more erratic fashion, the Bulgarian and Rumanian experience, was that of attempted institution building along a logic of "consequentiality," i.e., a logic of imitating, importing, and transplanting, in the name of some presumed "interest of society," economic and political institutions that have "worked elsewhere," irrespective of whether they meet with ideas, traditions, and mentalities that prevail in these societies. Bypassing the level of social integration and concentrating instead, in a hyperrationalist top-down perspective, on the crafting of new institutions that supposedly would establish a new mode of system integration is, however, an enterprise that easily becomes vulnerable to the unreconstructed mental and moral dispositions inherited from the old regimes. As a result, the newly founded institutions are in place, but they fail to perform in anticipated ways and thus become subject to ever more hectic cycles of renewed institutional engineering and concomitant efforts to "reeducate" people so as to make them fit for their roles in the new institutions.

The designing of new institutions occurs through the replication of old or spatially distant ones. Before designers can start their job, they will typically seek inspiration and legitimacy in a construed model of the past of their own society. This past is often schematically subdivided into a rejected, though immediate "dark" past and a more distant but celebrated "golden" past. Nineteenth-century European *risorgimento* nationalism and the institutions created by it, most importantly the nation state, is a case in point. Others are looking around for foreign models to be replicated.[13] Sometimes it is rather easy to distil a workable

---

[13]Cf. the statement by former Polish Finance Minister L. Balcerowicz (quoted in

synthesis of models that are being found in the "golden" past and the "golden" West, but sometimes the respective models imported from the "past" and the "West" are diametrically opposed to each other, as it appears to be the case in much of present-day East Central Europe, at least outside the relatively fortunate cases of Poland, Hungary, and perhaps the Czech Republic.

Needless to say, what actually happens in the process of institution building is often a far cry from the mere replication of rules that have been in operation at other places or times. What interests me in this imaginary transplantation of institutions across time and space is not whether such transfer has actually taken place, but the function played by the presentation of the activity of designing and building institutions as an activity that mainly consists in imitating institutions. It looks as if the designers of institutions shy away from accepting responsibility in public for what they are really doing, and that they tend to hide instead behind the often rather fictive notion of imitation or transplantation. And even if the imitation (say of the institutional rules governing political parties, academic research, private property, or central banks) were to result in a flawless replica of some successful model, it still remains an open question whether the new institutions turn out to operate the same way and with the same results as the "original" – given the fact that only the latter, but not the former, is supported by a congruent "spirit" and the collective recollection of the process in which this "spirit" or "ethos" has been transformed into a set of institutional rules. At any rate, constructivist approaches to institutional innovation must cope with the thorny problem that is strangely reminiscent of the well-known quandary of "creating socialist men": The "spirit of capitalism," in striking contrast to Weberian notions of "elective affinities," etc., must be installed after the institutions of capitalism are already in place (and without the benefit of its supportive transcendent motivations!).

Imitation, both across national as well as sectoral boundaries, is a powerful device of institutional innovation. The rhetoric of "learning from others" or "learning from successful examples" is employed in order to play down the differences that may exist between sectors and countries, to create a deceptive clarity about some evidently and easily acceptable superior solution, to mobilize support, and to disguise the creative alterations that the supposed "imitation" is likely to involve. Transsectoral imitation follows the suggestive analogy that what has worked in one sector is bound to work in other sectors as well. In this way, the German social security system (which is based on man-

Neuber 1992, p. 20): "Poland is too poor to experiment. We will therefore follow working models."

datory income-graduated contributions plus interclass parity plus self-government of public corporations) has spread through continuous imitation from health to old age to unemployment to (right now) care for the elderly in the course of more than 110 years.

If I am right in generalizing that institution designers, whatever their creative contribution, tend to be reluctant to confess to their author-ship, this tendency might follow from an important intuition on their part. This intuition can be captured in the following way: it does not help the viability and operative success of newly designed institutions if they are perceived by others as actually being newly designed. The designer, if seen as such, will unavoidably come under the suspicion of trying to impose his partisan interest or normative point of view upon the broader community, and that suspicion alone, unjustified though it may be in some cases, may invalidate the recognition and respect of the new institution and prevent it from unfolding its socializing function. It is as if the man-made and hence contingent nature of institutional change must be denied and artificially "forgotten." Otherwise, the example of the designer will invite others to attempt a different design, the consequence being an overload of contingency, complexity, and uncertainty which contradicts the essence of what we mean by an institution.

This skepticism about the "designing" of institutions is of course most explicitly argued in conservative political and economic philosophies, such as the Hayekian critique of "constructivism" or Oakshott's critique of political rationalism.[14] The very activity of institution building, if visible as such, could thus easily end up in the hyperrationality trap (Elster) of "willing what cannot be willed." It cannot be willed because if it is seen as being willed, rather than "inherited" or "replicated," it will be more controversial and less binding than if it is seen as a legacy or imitation. Conversely, if newly designed institutions can be depicted as being not so new after all, but rooted in some respectable past, that may add to their obligatory and preference-forming power flowing from that past, as the trust in their capacity for performing the functions that they are supposed to perform can be strengthened by the pretense that they are just replicas of demonstrably successful models imported from elsewhere.

This intuition is also reflected in the discourse that institutions cultivate about their own history and origin. In the rare cases where individual persons are credited with the design and creation of institutions,

---

[14] The object of Oakshott's critique is that "the consciously planned and deliberately executed is being considered (for that reason) better than what has grown up and established itself unselfconsciously over a period of time" (1962, p. 26).

these authors are also attributed charismatic and extraordinary qualities: they are depicted as heroes, prophets, saints, founding fathers, pi-
oneers, great statesmen (Napoleon, Bismarck, Lenin), or "classical"
thinkers who have been active at exceptional junctures of history. But
more often, reflective discourses about the origin of institutions seem
to avoid the notion of intentional creation. Instead, they rely on subjectless categories by describing the coming-into-being of institutions
as driven by "tradition," a creeping process of experimentation and imitation. In this perspective, institutions just "evolve," "develop,"
"emerge," are "discovered," or "spread," or their coming into existence
is thought of as the process of a "vitalistic" emanation of a subjectless
idée directrice (Hauriou 1925), all of which is to obscure their origin in
intentional action of concrete individuals and groups.

At any rate, too much "tinkering" with institutions, an excessive effort to design and redesign them in order to make them turbulence-
proof and fit for their mission, as well as other visible indications of
"designer activism" (David Stark), will almost certainly have the unintended effect of both undermining trust and committing the authors of
such innovations to ever more and ever hastier readjustments. Too
rapid and too comprehensive institutional reforms may easily overtax
the support of those affected by them, or it will frustrate the expectation
generated by the reform process itself that rapid transformation also
means rapid success. This is the paradox of "designer capitalism" (Stark
1992), or capitalism by decree, that we see unfolding in East Central
Europe and the former Soviet Union. The paradox is compounded if
this discretionary design of new economic institutions coincides with
the introduction of democracy by decree and the redefinition of territorial states by decree (Offe 1991). If anything, the success and the survival capacity of the newly built institutions is likely to depend more
on people's trust, compliance, and patience in enduring the transition
costs involved than in the quality of the design of these institutions
themselves. The paradox is also exacerbated if it is generally (and probably rightly) understood that the institutional choices that are now being made are of the greatest significance for the future power and
economic positions of virtually all kinds of actors,[15] and that therefore

[15]The crux of the situation is the coincidence of high levels of transparency and
salience. Whatever institution choice is made (concerning, for instance, the mode of
privatization or electoral law), there is no "veil of ignorance" that would allow us to
decide these questions on their own merits rather than in the light of immediate
consequences that are easily anticipated. For instance, whatever the merits of early
elections versus late elections, proportional representation versus pure majority, local
government autonomy versus centralization, private versus public television, or presidentialism versus parliamentary government, it is evident in most cases which al-

hardly anyone can be expected nor trusted to make these choices in a fair, nonpartisan, and disinterested way. Nor can anyone among the actors who see themselves as potentially negatively affected by newly designed institutions be expected to keep silent in the process, given the vastly expanded opportunities for raising their voices through the means of the newly established democratic process.[16]

The paradox would thus seem to boil down to the painful contradiction that exactly at the moment when the rapid introduction of new political and economic institutions is most urgently needed, there is, for systematic reasons, no one who could possibly be entrusted with the responsibility to design them – and neither is there some external agent who could effectively impose them from the outside[17] nor a widely accepted model in some "better past" of post-Communist societies that could be revived.

As the leaders of post-Communist societies emphasize again and again, they "have no time" to argue about principles. The urgency of the economic condition forces them to adopt an instrumental and outcome-oriented perspective. However, if from this perspective they select Western institutional models (political parties, social policies, a banking system, local self-government, or whatever), they actually copy something that is different from the original. For no Western political, economic, or social institution has been invented for the purpose of extricating an entire group of societies from the conditions of state socialism and its ruins. The original of the institutions that are now being copied has rather come into being for other or at least additional reasons[18] than the functions it has eventually turned out to perform, these

ternative will benefit whom. Whoever advocates either of these and many other alternatives will almost automatically be suspected, whatever his arguments are, of doing so in the service of one particular interest.

[16]A conclusion from the observation that democracy might stand in the way of the designing market and property institutions – a conclusion that appears as consistent in its logic as it is cynical in its consequences – is that "capitalism" must take precedence over "democracy" if the "healthy" path of institutional innovation, such as it has been chosen in South Korea and Chile, is to be accomplished. Cf. for this argument Schwarz (1992).

[17]Such an external agent would have to have, in order to effectively impose an institutional design, either unquestioned intellectual authority and expertise or be in a position of unchallenged political, economic, or even military power. Neither the members of various international advisory commissions that have become active in East European countries nor the IMF can lay claim to either of these qualities.

[18]The locus classicus of this argument is of course Max Weber's demonstration in his Protestant Ethic that the "spirit of capitalism" was not inculcated for the sake of gain, but for the sake of spiritual salvation, and that its "real" functions were as much

reasons being the rights, traditions, and principles embodied in these institutions – "political" arguments, not steering calculi, as Albert Hirschman (1977) has argued. The identities and arguments on which institutions were originally based in the West have helped to shape the political and economic culture on which institutions depend for the sake of performing their functions. The "copying" of institutions approach tries to bypass, or at any rate shorten, this period of gestation and slow maturation. While certainly being anti-Stalinist in substance, this instrumental approach to institution building comes often close to being Stalinist in method. That is not to suggest that institution designers in post-Communist societies could actually afford to wait. They rarely can, given the pressing economic needs and the lack of legitimate political authority in their countries. It is only to suggest that "copied" and transplanted institutions that lack the moral and cultural infrastructure on which the "original" can rely are likely to yield very different and often counterintentional results, in which case ever more hectic and short-breathed further designs (with all the familiar pathologies of overshooting, stop-and-go cycles, short-lived governing elites, and an oscillation on the mass level between extreme forms of political expressivism and an apathetic disdain for politics) must be expected as a consequence.

Hyperrationality is just one of two weaknesses inherent in the idea of institutional design. The other weakness has to do with the fact that in the modern world "designed" institutions are almost always "successor" institutions. They are not built on a *tabula rasa*. Successor institutions are affected by the long arm of their predecessors. These predecessors may have failed in one or both of the two senses in which institutions may fail, failure of socialization and preference formation or failure of performing their function. But there may still be traces and remnants of the old institutional arrangement in the presence of which the new institutions cannot function properly. In spite of the fact that state socialist institutions have clearly failed to generate socialist preferences (to say nothing about "socialist man"), they have, as a rule, generated a state of mind, a set of expectations and assumptions that now often turn out to be inimical to the growth of democratic capitalist and civil institutions. This state of mind, regardless of whether it has

by-products as its intended functions were failures. A parallel argument, this time not concerning salvation but concerning peace, order, and freedom, was made by Albert Hirschman (1977, p. 130), who argues that the case for capitalism in the seventeenth and eighteenth centuries was made not for the sake of material prosperity, but for the political "virtue of imposing restraints on princely caprice, arbitrary government, and adventurous foreign policies."

been cultivated by the last fifty years of experience of state socialist institutions or the cultural and political inheritance of the last five hundred years of precarious and often failed modernization processes, is described by many authors (e.g., Morawski, Schöpflin, Sztompka) as a combination of apathy, depletion of communal bonds, passivity, unwillingness to accept responsibility, atomization, lack of respect for formal rules, "short-termism," and a pervasive "grab and run attitude" toward economic gain (Neuber 1992, p. 10). Furthermore, economic attitudes are shaped by zero-sum-assumptions as well as the expectation that success must be, as a rule, due to patronage, corruption, and cooptation, not effort.

Such elements of the cultural infrastructure on which institutions must rely are not only time consuming to consolidate (as Dahrendorf and many others have argued), but equally time consuming to abolish. This infrastructure can perhaps fruitfully be compared to a computer software, with the formal rules, jurisdictions, and licenses of the institution itself being the hardware. But in the case of institutions, unlike that of computers, the software on which they depend for their operation is not easily exchanged and replaced, as it is generated by the hardware itself in the process in which people "get used to" and "make sense of" or "cope with" the institutions, thus adopting a set of standards, obligations, and expectations that in Weber's terminology is referred to as the "spirit" (*Geist*) of institutions. This includes, in addition to moral commitments, familiarity with the institutions, codes of appropriate conduct, a reasonable measure of trust in their proper functioning, and the like.

Let me illustrate this point by distinguishing three variants of the operational meaning of "equality." In a liberal polity, it emphasizes equality before the law: no one should be denied the rights that everyone else enjoys. In a more social democratic version it shades into a distributive meaning that also looks at, in addition to rights, material conditions or outcomes. More specifically, it is a *downward-looking* notion of equality akin to Rawls's difference principle which highlights the moral intuition that those below "us" should be granted priority in having their condition improved. What seems to prevail in post-Communist societies, however, is an *upward-looking* variant of distributive concerns, which is itself derived from the political culture of the old regime. What this semantic of "equality" boils down to is the envy-driven notion that "they" are evidently richer than "we," and the state should therefore prevent them from getting ahead even further – the *authoritarian* conclusion. But the same semantic can also give rise to an ultra*libertarian* reasoning: unless the state does so, "we" are entitled to use every means available (including illegal means) to get ahead as well.[19] At the very least, the tolerance for distributional inequalities and resulting "privilege" is extremely limited.

"Designed" institutions suffer from a dual handicap: They have an architect and they are successors. Two conclusions can be drawn from the discussion of this dual liability from which the activity of "founding" institutions suffers, hyperrationality and the long arm of the past. As far as the first of these liabilities is concerned, the ideal situation for the "founding" of institutions seems to be one in which no explicit *engineering* is called for, but where there is a rich vegetation of inherited institutional patterns which already enjoy the allegiance of relevant actors – an allegiance that can be further cultivated by an activity that has been described as "institutional *gardening*." But as far as the second of these liabilities is concerned, namely the "long arm of the past," it is just the opposite conclusion that must be drawn: the more the situation conforms to a notion of *tabula rasa*, and the more the old routines are explicitly deprived of their validity, the more readily and easily will the newly designed set of institutions win the loyalty of constituents and unfold its ultimately beneficial functions. Would-be institution designers certainly cannot have it both ways.

7.2.3 Challenges, Breakdowns, and Survival Responses

The breakdown of institutions can occur in response to any of three challenges. First, they may fail to inculcate the *norms and preferences* that condition the loyalty of members. In this case, institutions stop to "make sense" to members and to be "taken seriously" by them or by the wider social domain for which an institution claims validity, and consequently the institution loses support and recognition. Scandals and cases of corruption in which representative agents of an institution become seen as betraying core values are particularly powerful causes of the sudden loss of an institution's credibility. The same effect can be caused by slow cultural changes, which are often referred to as "secularization" in the case of religious institutions.

Second, institutions may decay because *alternatives* emerge which allow for the satisfaction of those needs and the fulfillment of those functions over which the institution used to hold a monopoly. An example is the institution of the dues collector in trade unions and other working-class organizations who would visit members at home, provide information, social control, and advice, and also would symbolize the faithful, committed and loyal example of a "good" union member and

---

[19]Needless to say, both the authoritarian and the libertarian conclusion will give rise to what Rose (1992) has aptly termed an "uncivil economy."

of working-class values in general. This institution has disappeared a long time ago, as the payment of dues (as many other payments) is increasingly processed through bank accounts without the use of cash. The same applies to the institution of the local athletics club as it is being marginalized through commercial fitness centers, on the one hand, and events of professional spectator sports, on the other. The rise of new opportunities must be distinguished from the rise of opportunity costs. The institutions of downtown vegetable markets or, for that matter, parks or even department stores, have become questionable, given the boom in central city real estate prices and transportation problems, as well as the availability of the alternative of large peripheral shopping malls and recreation areas.

Third, institutions may break down because of their manifest failure in performing the functions with which they are charged. For instance, the state is an institution whose existence is contingent upon its capacity to protect and control territorial borders, and marriage is an institution that prescribes the exclusion of third persons from sexual and other interactions. Failure to perform these functions will thus lead to the breakdown of particular instances of institutions (i.e., particular states and marriages), as opposed to the institution itself. A case of the latter is the disappearance of guilds which regulated all aspects of particular trades in medieval European cities (including the personnel admitted, the quantity, quality and price of the goods produced, conditions of sale, codes of conduct, etc.). Other cases of defunct institutions are those regulating political prerogatives of the nobility or, perhaps (and hopefully) at some point soon, the Italian Mafia. The tipping point at which the incidence of empirical acts of defection begins to undermine the quasi-counterfactual validity of the institutional pattern itself is hard to determine ex ante and is likely to vary from institution to institution.

It is worth stressing that the three types of causes that I have specified may lead to the breakdown of an institution, but that such breakdown is by no means a necessary consequence of the presence of one or even all of these causes. In cases it is not, institutions adopt survival strategies which are themselves a major mode of institutional change, as captured by the Lampedusa principle: "If things are to stay as they are, everything must change." Instances of such survival strategies are goal displacement (e.g., the NATO adopting new missions in the field of academic research and environmental protection), change of constituencies (churches and religious sects targeting young people), or change of institutional means (as in the case of extreme acts of violence that occurred on the Square of Heavenly Peace in Peking on June 4th, 1989).

But these survival strategies might be seriously self-defeating in their outcome, which I think can be shown to have been the case with the breakdown of the Communist regime in the Soviet Union and the other CMEA-countries. Why has communism failed? Although we are still far from understanding the causes and consequences of this momentous breakdown, I submit that explanations of the breakdown itself can be grouped in several broad categories.

Two of them suffer from the slight embarrassment that, at least ideally, today's explanatory hypotheses should have been the basis of yesterday's predictions, and that hardly anyone predicted what now must be explained. This embarrassment can be dealt with by claiming that the breakdown of Communist regimes was caused by external forces (such as hostile military, economic, political, or communication strategies of Western countries) and that it had little or nothing to do with institutional structures of the regime itself. This is clearly an unpromising approach as it begs the question why the institutional structures of the regimes themselves were so weak and vulnerable as to become incapable of dealing with these externally generated challenges which after all were by no means unanticipated. Second, we might argue that the breakdown was ultimately caused by a single person (the only conceivable candidate being Mikhail Gorbachev) or a small group of his followers. In spite of considerable evidence that is available in support of this reading of history, it ultimately must fail because it, too, ignores the question of which institutional arrangements and rules made this kind of person(s), as well as their rise to top positions of power, at all possible.

Again, we are back to an institutional approach, of which two variants are available. One starts with institutional failures of social integration, the other with failures of system integration. Let us consider them in turn.

The first type of explanation claims that the failure of state socialism is due to the failure of its institutions to generate congruent motivations, or at least to check incongruent ones. A famous battle cry of nineteenth-century Italian *risorgimento* nationalism was Massimo d'Azeglio's *dictum* that "As we have now made Italy, let's now proceed to make Italians." In other words, a condition of stability of the new regime is seen in its ability to inculcate a sense of loyalty, faithfulness, and obligation toward the rules of the institutional regime. Similarly, "the feasibility of socialism must rest on the assumption that socialization of the means of production causes individuals to adopt socialist preferences" (Przeworski 1991, p. 116). If it can be shown that there is a systematic and incurable incapacity of state socialist institutions to generate congruent motivations among its strategic core agents such as planners, managers, workers, and households, all of which will impair the necessary level of cooperation and may even breed cynicism as a prevailing outcome of endogenous preference formation. Furthermore, the undemocratic and repressive means by which socialist institutions try to compensate for this deficiency will usually add to the problem rather than alleviate it. If all of this can be shown to be true for systematic reasons, this pathology of social integration is the key to explaining the system's breakdown.

The alternative, though by no means incompatible, explanation is that state socialism has failed, for equally systematic reasons, on the level of system integration. It simply does not function sufficiently well as an economic system, partly because it lacks an equivalent for the market's capacity for the smooth, continuous, and, most importantly, anonymous elimination of inefficient combinations of the factors of production. A related view of socialism's systemic failure focuses on the problem of coordination. The model case of this kind of failure occurs when it is simply not possible to deliver the right spare part at the right time to the place where it is needed, exactly because no economic sanction is attached to failure to deliver. Generally speaking, the state socialist system of planning, allocation, and distribution that abdicates the principle of "profit maximization" has been blamed for its consistent failure to minimize losses. There was simply no legal, economic, intellectual, or political mechanism to declare and render elements of the system obsolete. In spite of its pathetic claim to being based upon "scientific" knowledge, the system, lacking as it does appropriate devices of accounting and self-monitoring, simply does not accumulate enough knowledge about itself in order to cope with and correct its own inherent wastefulness.

As long as institutions suffer from just one of these complementary deficiencies, the respective other one may well be able to make up for this limited failure. For instance, if output failures are met with a strong sense of loyalty, hope, patience, heroism, and optimistic expectations, breakdown may well be avoided or postponed. (Cuba of the sixties may be an example of this extreme.) Conversely, if output is booming, loyalty may appear to a large extent dispensable. It is difficult to speculate about marginal rates of substitution between social and system integration. At any rate, the two complementary solutions of appealing to people's endurance under conditions of severe shortage and of buying a measure of self-interested loyalty by delivering an abundance of goods are each likely to fail at some point, at which the latent imbalance of the two functions of institutions becomes manifest.

In order to avoid either of these two emergencies as well as their cumulative interaction, the Gorbachev reforms of the mid-eighties seem to have relied on a reformist way out that he and his supporters believed was compatible with the overall institutional structure of the Soviet empire. He introduced, under vague labels such as "perestroika" and "glasnost," supposedly marginal institutional alterations and alternatives which, however, in actuality turned out to be veritable explosives. Instead of instigating new optimism, trust, and loyalty, he seems to have caused panic in the economic and political elites at home and among the Soviet Union's allies abroad. And instead of improving the mode of coordination of the Soviet political economy, the reforms created ever greater turbulence and stagnation, exacerbated by the implied admission that the system is suffering from serious faults. We thus see that not only breakdown can provoke survival strategies, but miscalculated though well-intentioned rescue operations can accelerate breakdown. Under some conditions, the greatest damage one can inflict upon an institutional system is an attempted large-scale repair operation performed in public.

7.2.4 Critique

I have argued before that institutions depend on the meaning that is accorded to them by the actors. They must not only be known to exist, but "make sense" to actors and even oblige them. Such obligation flows from implicit theories by which the proponents of an institutional order defend it and try to cope with challenges. If this justificatory effort succeeds, a sense of loyalty is generated that will lead actors to ignore some of their own conflicting interests and submit to the obligations stipulated.

Asking the right persons the right questions in public can be a powerful device to expose the weakness of those implicit theories. Why, for instance, should the office of the priest, bishop, etc., be the monopoly of the male gender in the Roman Catholic church? Why should German nationality (which is a precondition of the civil service status of Beamte) be a prerequisite for becoming a mailman and cop? Critique can undermine the bindingness of obligations and ultimately demolish the social and moral infrastructure of institutions and trigger their breakdown. This is most easily accomplished in the case that institutions are defended by reference to empirical arguments alone, such as the claim that "everyone else" is actually complying with the institutional order or that it has "always" been honored. Such empirical claims by themselves, apart from being probably wrong in any particular instance, cannot possibly serve as the foundation of any bindingness, apart from the case of conventions, which by definition are self-enforcing and have little if any potential for conflict. Other, more demanding arguments in defense of particular institutions invoke moral obligations, widely shared values, or consequences that are generally held to be desirable.

All of these claims, if questioned, must be backed up with rather elaborate and explicit theories, and the validity of these theories can again be tested and questioned by critique.

Such critique corresponds to one of the three varieties of institutional breakdown that I have just discussed. It can either (a) try to challenge the normative premises that the institution invokes, or it can (b) try to demonstrate that these normative premises, if valid, might also be implemented by alternative institutional patterns, or that (c) the consequences claimed in support of a particular institutional pattern are not, on balance, as unquestionably desirable as it is claimed in defense of an institution (or, if evidently desirable, are not actually achieved by its operation).

Let me illustrate each of these three modes of critique with an example from the field of social policy. First, most pension systems have the feature that benefits are earnings-graduated, which is usually justified in terms of an equitable reward. If we can demonstrate, however, that most pensioners from the upper income categories derive additional old-age income from sources other than pensions, namely from savings and other assets they have been able to build out of their relatively high market income, equivalence in terms of pensions becomes a less compelling normative premise, because it virtually amounts to doubling the reward for the well-to-do income categories. Second, instead of paying unemployment benefits to jobless people, the supply of labor and hence unemployment might be reduced by the alternative of large-scale anticyclical programs of mandatory continuing education and other statutory leaves from regular employed work, with the balance of budgetary costs and labor productivity being perhaps even demonstrably better than is the case with regular unemployment insurance. Third, and concerning consequences, if it could be demonstrated that there is a zero correlation between marginal increases of the total health budget and marginal improvements of independently measured subjective or objective indicators of health, the conclusion is warranted that either what (the budgetary increments of) the institutions of the health system serve is not actually "health" or the health they do serve is not unequivocally worth serving.

To be sure, such critical counterarguments against the claims of institutions to validity and loyalty are themselves contingent upon whether they "make sense" to those to whom they are addressed. At the very least, however, they are likely to put some learning pressure upon the institutional complex in question. As a consequence of this pressure, they may instigate some search for survival strategies on the part of the institutional elites which are being challenged by the critic.

By stimulating this search, and by subjecting its outcomes to reiterated critical scrutiny, we are, on this indirect way, probably as close as we can possibly come to the hyperrational ideal – and strangely mysterious practice – of "designing" institutions.

References

Batt, Judy. 1991. The end of communist rule in east-central Europe: a four country comparison. *Government and Opposition*, 26 (3), 368–90.

Berger, Johannes. 1992. Der Konsensbedarf der Wirtschaft. Pp. 151–96 in H.-J. Giegel, ed., *Kommunikation und Konsens in modernen Gesellschaften*. Frankfurt a.M.: Suhrkamp.

Bromley, David W. 1989. *Economic Interests and Institutions: The Conceptual Foundations of Public Policy*. Oxford: Basil Blackwell.

Commons, John R. 1934. *Institutional Economics*. New York: Macmillan.

Dahrendorf, Ralf. 1990. *Reflections on the Revolution in Eastern Europe*. London: Chatto and Windus.

DiMaggio, Paul J., and Walter W. Powell, eds. 1991. *The New Institutionalism in Organizational Analysis*. Chicago: University of Chicago Press.

Grosser, Joachim. 1993. Efficiency and power as stimuli of institutional change. Pp. 21 ff. in H. Wagener, ed., *On the Theory and Policy of Systemic Change*. Heidelberg: Physica.

Habermas, Jürgen. 1975. *Legitimation Crisis*. Boston: Beacon.

Habermas, Jürgen. 1981. *Theorie des kommunikativen Handelns*. 2 vols. Frankfurt: Suhrkamp.

Hauriou, Maurice. 1925. Théorie de l'institution et de la fondation: Essai de vitalisme social. *Cahiers de la Nouvelle Journée* #4: 1–45.

Hirschman, Albert O. 1977. *The Passions and the Interests: Political Arguments for Capitalism before Its Triumph*. Princeton, N.J.: Princeton University Press.

Korpi, Walter. 1991. Institutions and the cost of power: a rational choice approach to the emergence and change of welfare state institutions in the western countries. Mimeo., Swedish Institute for Social Research, Stockholm University.

Lindblom, Charles E. 1977. *Politics and Markets*. New York: Basic Books.

Lipset, Seymour M. 1981. *Political Man: The Social Bases of Politics*, expanded edition. Baltimore: Johns Hopkins University Press.

Lockwood, David. 1964. Social Integration and System Integration. Pp. 244–57 in G. Zollschan and W. Hirsch, eds., *Explorations in Social Change*. Boston: Houghton Mifflin.

March, James G., and Johan P. Olsen. 1989. *Rediscovering Institutions: The Organizational Basis of Politics*. New York: Free Press.

Meyer, John W., and Brian Rowan. 1991. Institutionalized organizations: formal structure as myth and ceremony. Pp. 41–62 in P. J. DiMaggio and W. W. Powell, eds, *The New Institutionalism in Organizational Analysis*. Chicago: University of Chicago Press.

Morawski, Witold. 1992. Economic change and civil society in Poland. In P. G. Lewis, ed., *Democracy and Civil Society in Eastern Europe*. London: Macmillan.

Neuber, Axel. 1992. Toward a political economy of transition in eastern Europe. Mimeo., Harvard University.

Oakshott, Michael. 1962. *Rationalism in Politics and Other Essays*. Indianapolis, Ind.: Liberty Press.

Offe, Claus. 1991. Capitalism by democratic design? Democratic theory facing the triple transition in east central Europe. *Social Research*, 58 (4), 865–92.

Ostrom, Elinor. 1992. *Crafting Institutions for Self-governing Irrigation Systems*. San Francisco, Calif.: CS-Press.

Pickel, Andreas. 1992. Jump-starting a market economy: a critique of the radical strategy for economic reform in light of the East German experience. *Studies in Comparative Communism*, 25 (2), 177–91.

Przeworski, Adam. 1991. *Democracy and the Market*. Cambridge: Cambridge University Press.

Rose, Richard. 1992. Toward a civil economy. *Journal of Democracy*, 3 (2), 13–26.

Schöpflin, George. 1991. Post-communism: constructing new democracies in central Europe. *International Affairs*, 67 (2), 235–50

Schwarz, Gerhard. 1992. Marktwirtschaftliche Reform und Demokratie– eine Hassliebe? *Ordo*, 42, 3–28.

Stark, David. 1992. Path dependence and privatization strategies in East Central Europe. *East European Politics and Societies*, 6 (1), 17–54.

Sztompka, Piotr. 1991. The intangibles and imponderables of the transition to democracy. *Studies in Comparative Communism*, 24 (3), 295–311.

8

Political Deals in Institutional Settings

KENNETH A. SHEPSLE

SO MUCH OF REAL POLITICS involves making deals: power lunches and gentlemen's agreements; horse trades, vote swaps, and log rolls; and, at a more formal level, contracts and coalitions. All of these have at their core the notion of aligning expectations about mutual obligations and, ultimately, about the outcomes to be secured by the aligning parties. The deal is also a fundamental concept in theoretical studies of politics. In this respect, at least, theory and practice share the same foundation. In this brief essay I offer some theoretical elaboration of this concept and apply it to one of the central deals made in parliamentary democracies – the making of governments.

To begin, I offer what I believe to be the standard way in which the deal enters most theoretical analyses. Although abstract and something of a caricature, it captures most of what people mean by the concept. It also flags two potential deficiencies in standard usage – feasibility and enforceability. I take these topics up in succeeding sections of the chapter. I then suggest how the analysis affects the way we think about government formation in parliamentary democracies. A conclusion follows.

8.1 Deals in Theoretical Analysis

In conventional approaches to deal-making, of which the game-theoretic literature on bargaining is the most explicit (e.g., Osborne and

This essay grows out of a major research project on government formation in parliamentary democracies with Michael Laver of Trinity College, Dublin (Laver and Shepsle 1996). It has received the generous support of the U.S. National Science Foundation. In what follows neither collaborator nor benefactor is implicated.

227

Rubinstein 1990), agents of a potential deal come to a deal-making situation with endowments, opportunities, beliefs, and preferences. The deal-making situation transforms participant inputs into a result through what we might think of as the deal-making technology.

Endowments are those resources that, at least in some states of the world, affect outcomes. Thus, a change in an agent's endowment will, in some circumstances, alter the outcome that would otherwise have been produced absent the change. In a parliamentary government formation setting, for example, a change in a party's weight (the proportion of parliamentary seats it controls) may affect the composition of the government that actually forms.

Opportunities are occasions in which an agent may deploy its endowment. In many parliamentary democracies, for example, the party with the largest weight is typically asked by the head of state to attempt to form a government, thus giving it first-mover agenda power. Likewise, each party offered a portfolio in a new government is given the chance to veto the deal, since it may simply refuse to participate in the proposed government. And, of course, all parliamentary parties have the opportunity to throw their weight around in investiture and confidence votes. Proposal power, veto power, and vote power are agent endowments that the deal-making technology provides opportunities to deploy.

Preferences are, well, preferences. They characterize agent evaluations of outcomes and, given a deal-making technology and knowledge of how agent endowments and opportunities affect outcomes, they permit agents to reason and act strategically. In most theories of parliamentary government formation, agent preferences are broadly classified as office-directed or policy-directed, depending upon whether perks of office or directions of public policy are uppermost among agent objectives.

The *deal-making technology*, as I have been using the notion in the preceding discussion, subsumes a game form – a set of rules and an order of moves according to which agent inputs are transformed into outcomes. Once we specify agent endowments and preferences, we have an extensive form game.

Although the deal-making technology transforms agent inputs into a result, and I assume that agents are fully informed about how this works, what the result means for agents is a more complicated matter. It depends upon agent *beliefs* about what will transpire when agent endowments are deployed in a particular fashion. Politics is not chemistry, where two parts hydrogen plus one part oxygen necessarily yields one molecule of water. In politics we want to take account, since political agents surely do, of the prospect of slips 'twixt cup and lips. A result must be implemented and this requires an assessment of what is feasible and what will occur in practice.

8.2 Enforcing Deals

In my study of committee assignments in the U.S. House of Representatives (Shepsle 1978), I encountered a practice among committee makers on the Committee on Committees (CC) known as *peeking*. In the CC each member was responsible for a geographic zone, and sought to get "good" committee assignments for legislators from his or her zone. This typically involved bargains and deals among CC members, viz., "I'll support your person for committee x if you support mine for committee y." But balloting in the CC for committee assignments was done secretly; the only public information was the total number of votes for each committee-assignment candidate, not which CC members voted for whom. Members therefore wondered whether "deals struck stayed stuck." There developed the practice of asking, at the time of a vote, "Did you vote for my person as you promised? Show me your ballot (let me peek at it)." It was surely possible in practice to obtain another CC member's support, so feasibility was not at issue. But his or her statement of intent, without an ability to monitor compliance, cast a shadow on such deals (alleviated at least occasionally by the glare of peeking).

As should be clear, ex post discretion is problematical for deal-making. In a complicated world it is nigh on impossible to eliminate such discretion, either because it is hopeless to nail down every margin (so deals are inevitably incomplete contracts at best) or because of difficulties in monitoring performance. For either reason, anticipation of exercises of discretion may cause deals to be stillborn.

Many models of deal-making avoid the problems of discretion by *assuming* compliance. Certainly, if preferences are aligned, then the assumption is a reasonable one.[1] If you and I share a private driveway to our respective homes (one full of curves and blind spots), and we promise one another ex ante to drive on the right-hand side from either direction, then, at the time action must be taken, each of us has an incentive to perform as promised (since this is a deal involving pure coordination and to do otherwise is to risk collision).

A more sophisticated version of motivational credibility is found in *reputational* models. Each agent in a particular deal-making situation is concerned not only about the outcome of a proposed deal, but also about a capital asset that will affect his or her ability to enter into deals in the future, namely, agent reputation. A reputation for honoring one's commitments enhances the prospects for gains from subsequent deals, even if the motivational force is weaker then. Indeed, honoring com-

---

[1]Elsewhere (Shepsle 1991) I refer to this as motivational credibility.

mitments precisely when motivational forces are weak expands the opportunity set because prospective partners are likely to be more trusting in the future. By driving on the right-hand side, as I promised, even when it is inconvenient or when I don't think anyone would notice if I did otherwise, I provide my neighbor with the basis for entering into other cooperative ventures with me, some of which may require even greater trust. Concern for reputation in an ongoing interaction, then, may constrain the temptation for opportunistic exercises of discretion.

As an alternative enforcement mechanism in our private-driveway problem, we could install gates that could only be operated in each direction from the right-hand side. Thus, whether or not, at the time either of us must act, we wanted to honor the ex ante agreement, we would have constrained one another to drive on the right-hand side by removing any discretionary degrees of freedom. Since discretion is effectively disabled in this case, the deal is said to possess *imperative credibility* (Shepsle 1991).

In each of these instances, the deal struck would stay stuck for endogenous reasons. Compliance mechanisms are part of the deal. Economic models of exchange in the neoclassical tradition, on the other hand, assume exogenous third-party enforcement of deals. Promises thus are taken to be (imperatively) credible because they will be enforced, costlessly and perfectly, by a specialized enforcement agent.

Whether the enforcement mechanism is endogenous or exogenous, it amounts to a *forecast* by an agent of what the other party to a deal will do: he or she may comply, fail to comply, comply in part, or comply (in part or in whole) under some contingencies but not others. Thus, while the deal-making technology transforms agent inputs into a deal, beliefs provide a forecast of the manner in which the deal will actually be implemented.

In most parliamentary democracies, for example, the occasion of the formation of a new multiparty government is often accompanied by a coalitional agreement or statement of the new government's program. The credibility of such a statement, however, depends in part on whether the various partners have incentives to carry out their respective parts of the bargain. A social democratic employment minister, for instance, will be loathe to implement policies that will throw party supporters out of work, and can be expected, announced government program to the contrary notwithstanding, to exercise whatever discretion he or she has to ameliorate such pain. Such discretion may have the effect of compromising the coalition agreement and, if the information environment is sufficiently rich, this effect can be anticipated ex ante. In particular, despite the words and sentiments uttered at the press conference introducing the coalition agreement, knowledgeable persons will anticipate the real policy effects of forming this government.

8.3 Implementation

Given the imperfections of enforcement and, consequently, a role for beliefs about the relationship between deals and outcomes, the set of feasible outcomes is not always what it seems. Let me illustrate this prospect with a simple unidimensional spatial model. Assume there are three political parties, no one of which possesses a majority of parliamentary seats, with spatial locations as follows:

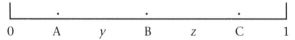

Suppose this is an environmental dimension, with party C most interventionist and party A least, and suppose further that each party is a unitary actor with policy preferences diminishing in distance from its ideal. Any two of the parties can form a government and determine environmental policy.

Most spatial analyses, depending upon additional assumptions, derive specific results about which parties will form the government and what the resulting policy of that government will be.[2] Illustrative of this kind of result is that parties A and B (or B and C) form the government and implement policy y in the interval [A,B] (z in the interval [B,C], respectively).

What tends to be suppressed in these analyses is exactly how the policy agreement arrived at between A and B (B and C, respectively) is actually implemented. Indeed, suppose, as is quite realistic, that only *one* of the parties actually gets the keys to the environment ministry and direct access to the machinery of policy implementation. In effect, there can be only one minister of environment. If that minister has any degrees of freedom when it comes to implementing the environmental policy deal, then y (or z) may not, as we saw in earlier discussion, be realizable. What if A became environment minister and actually implemented not y, but $y - \varepsilon$? $y - 2\varepsilon$? Indeed, what if party A's environment minister did his damnedest to push environment policy all the way to A? So long as a minister possesses some discretion – and surely most ministers possess some – will they not use that discretion to their own ends?

---

[2]The literature on coalitions is voluminous. An excellent recent survey is found in Laver and Schofield 1990.

By focusing on the implementation part of the deal-making technology, we discover that, with sufficient ministerial discretion (either because that is the nature of ministerial authority or because departures from the deal are unobservable), what looked, at the time of government formation, like a policy choice from the [0,1] interval is in fact a choice from the set {A,B,C} – one of the parties will run the ministry and, assuming sufficient discretion, will push policy to its ideal. I elaborate this example in a more general fashion in the next part of this essay.

In the remainder of this part, I want to focus on the abstract idea of *comparability* in social choice, since it has a bearing on implementation and the exercise of discretion. I do so by reminding the reader that the structure of the Arrow impossibility theorem, from which so much bad news about equilibrium in politics derives, entails five desiderata for social choice and three properties describing a social choice. The five normative criteria, which have been the subject of, perhaps, 2,000 journal articles in the forty years since Arrow's monograph first appeared, will not concern me here. Of the three definitional features of a social choice, however, one is germane to this discussion.

A social choice for Arrow is a *social ordering* describing how pairs of alternatives are evaluated socially. It satisfies (i) the identity relation (xRx for any alternative, x, where R means "at least as good as"), (ii) transitivity (xRy & $yRz \rightarrow xRz$, for any alternatives, x, y, and z), and (iii) completeness (either xRy or yRx, for any alternatives, x and y). The identity relation is uncontroversial. Transitivity has received an immense amount of attention, with various relaxations of it yielding alternative impossibility results (Brown 1975). Completeness, with few exceptions (Fishburn 1974), has been virtually ignored, and it is this property that draws my attention.

One of the features of institutional rules and practices, intended or otherwise, is to short-circuit comparisons. The institution of policy implementation via ministerial discretion, as in the example of the preceding few paragraphs, makes policy comparisons between x (or z) and other policies, quite beside the point, since x can never be implemented unless discretion is eliminated.[3] Once one moves beyond a model in which deals need merely be announced (with execution following automatically in some unspecified way), then one needs to take the extra step of explicitly incorporating the mapping from announced deal to

[3]There may, of course, be reasons why an agent would not wish to exercise available discretion, some of which were mentioned in the previous section. If any such reasons apply, then a policy like y may well be implementable. The point here, however, is that most spatial theories are silent on the issue of discretion and on what, if any, mechanisms are available to short-circuit it.

implemented deal. Announcements, per se, may be no more than mood music.

The concept of *structure-induced equilibrium* was formulated (Shepsle 1979) to capture the idea that nominally feasible alternatives may not be implementable for institutional reasons. Consequently, they will not figure in the calculations of rational agents, and therefore should not figure in equilibrium analysis. This generates three implications:

1. If a circumstance yields an equilibrium if implementation is *not* taken into account, and the equilibrium point is, in fact, implementable, then it will remain an equilibrium point.
2. If a circumstance yields an equilibrium if implementation is *not* taken into account, and the equilibrium point is *not* implementable, then equilibrium may be destroyed.
3. If a circumstance yields no equilibrium if implementation is *not* taken into account, then it may yield an equilibrium when implementation *is* taken into account.

The third implication is, perhaps, the most interesting, since most social choice situations in politics lack equilibrium (McKelvey 1976, 1979; Schofield 1985). The short-circuiting of comparisons owing to discretion and the institutional deal-making technology may create equilibrium where none otherwise would have existed. The reason for this prospect is *not* because some highly unlikely knife-edge distributional property of preferences is satisfied. Rather it is because the dense space of alternatives evidently available at the time of choice disguises the fact that only a finite set of these alternatives is actually implementable in light of incentives and available discretion. To the extent this is generally true, the Arrowian tradition in social choice and the chaos theorems in spatial modeling may be unduly pessimistic. It is this prospect that I illustrate in the next section.

8.4 Deal-Making, Implementation, and Government Formation

In this section I examine a spatial model of parliamentary government formation that places particular emphasis on the ministerial structure of government, on the one hand, and agent forecasts about what will really happen if a specific government is invested, on the other. I paint in broad strokes here since the details may be found elsewhere (Laver and Shepsle 1996).

I begin with a multidimensional policy space, each dimension of which is a salient policy issue. Parties are associated with particular positions on these issues from having just contested an election. The election results endow each party with a weight. Issue dimensions are partitioned into bundles, called jurisdictions; each jurisdiction is under the authority of a government ministry.

The government formation process has as its objective the allocation of ministerial authority among parties (which I take to be unitary actors). A government is a particular allocation of ministerial portfolios to parties. There are four possibilities. If all portfolios are given to a single party whose weight exceeds one-half, it is a single-party majority government; if its weight is less than one-half, it is a single-party minority government. If more than one party receives a portfolio, then the government is a coalition, with majority or minority status depending upon whether the sum of government party weights exceeds one-half or not. In what follows I will assume that no single party is of majority weight.

In a moment I will be explicit about the deal-making technology, laying out an extensive form game that describes the government formation process. At that point I will enumerate party endowments and opportunities. First, however, I want to review the more conventional spatial treatment, in which there is no concern for implementation, in order to display the disequilibrium that typifies this approach.

Figure 8.1 is a simple two-dimensional, three-party example. I assume here that parties A, B, and C have spatial locations/reputations (labeled AA, BB, and CC, respectively) and that, for any of a number of reasons, they seek to implement policies as close to their respective locations as possible. Since no party has majority weight, and since their locations are not radially symmetric about any point, we know that there is no majority rule equilibrium. Parties may seek to coalesce around policies – say, a point on the straight-line contract locus connecting a pair of party locations – but it is easily demonstrated that for any such point there is another that a majority of legislators prefers to it. Alternative government policies cycle endlessly as coalitions form and re-form to defeat proposed alternatives.

Though just an illustration, Figure 8.1 is quite typical. In any number of dimensions greater than one, with any number of parties greater than two, the circumstances in which some policy is a majority rule equilibrium is unusual.[4]

The conventional spatial approach is incomplete, however, as the argument of the previous section claims. Government policies do not just

---

[4]If parties were equally weighted, the circumstances would constitute, as the mathematicians say, a set of measure zero. The conditions for the existence of an equilibrium when parties are differentially weighted are given by McKelvey and Schofield 1987.

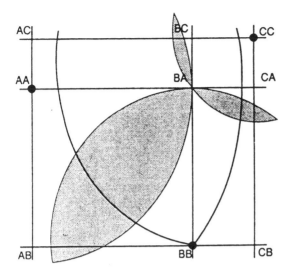

Figure 8.1. Credible points in a three-party, two-jurisdiction system.

happen; they must be implemented. Implementation, in turn, may be inferred from the institutional arrangements of a parliamentary regime. And once we take these features into account, a different set of considerations come into play.

The principal institutional arrangement of parliamentary regimes is *departmentalism* – issue dimensions are assigned to ministries. Ministers, in turn, are assumed to have some discretion. In particular, in the spirit of rational expectations, we assume that, in advance of government formation, politicians make common-knowledge forecasts of what government policy would be in each jurisdiction if particular parties in particular governments held particular portfolios. These forecasts factor in whatever discretion ministers have, on the one hand, and whatever constraints on its exercise (reputational, coalitional, constitutional, etc.) are in place, on the other. Subject to these constraints, however, it is assumed that each minister seeks to push the policies in his or her respective jurisdiction as close to his or her party's ideal as possible. Ministers, that is, are perfect agents of their parties.

The single most important analytical consequence of this perspective is that the number of alternatives available for social choice, for deal-making, is *finite*. With a finite number of parties and a finite number of ministerial portfolios, there is but a finite number of ways to allocate portfolios to parties; i.e., there is a finite number of governments. And associated with each, we assume, is a distinct policy forecast. Thus, despite an infinity of feasible governmental policies, our forecasting hypothesis implies that there is only a finite number of policy outcomes that are implementable. These are the social alternatives in play at the time of government formation among rational agents.

In Figure 8.1, for example, if each issue dimension is taken as a portfolio, there are nine possible governments. The three ideal points constitute single-party governments in which a party holds both portfolios. The six remaining points are coalition governments. In this figure, the nine policy possibilities are arrayed as a lattice, reflecting the forecast that a minister implements as government policy the relevant component of his or her party's ideal. (Thus the point AB reflects a government in which party A is given the horizontal jurisdiction and party B the vertical. BA is a government with the same coalition partners, but with portfolios swapped. In policy terms it is an entirely different government.)[5]

The government formation process is the extensive form game displayed in Figure 8.2. A random recognition device (a convenient and quite general way to model the head of state, who is assumed to be nonstrategic) selects one of the n parties, P_i. That party proposes an allocation of portfolios, x_i. The parties named in that proposal then have an opportunity to decline the invitation to be included in government; if any one named party does so, the proposal is vetoed and the process iterates. If no named party does so, then the proposal is taken to the full parliament for an investiture vote. If it passes, the new government is installed, but is immediately vulnerable to a no-confidence motion (i.e., a randomly recognized party can make a new proposal); if the proposal fails, the process iterates.

In this game parties are endowed with weights and spatial locations. Their preference, as mentioned earlier, is to install a government that will produce policies as close to their respective ideals as possible. Their respective opportunities are depicted in the game. When recognized, a party may propose a government. When included in a proposal, a party has the option to veto. When the process moves to an investiture vote, a party may cast its weighted vote.

I do not want to go into details here about the prospects for equilibrium in a game like this. Suffice it to say that, despite the conventional spatial preoccupation with generic disequilibrium, the restriction of al-

---

[5]Analytically, the various forecasts reflect a belief that ministers have considerable discretion. In our recent work (Laver and Shepsle 1996) we have made progress in analyzing this formulation. However, it is entirely possible to allow forecasts to be affected by the composition of government, for example, or any of a number of other factors. This will nonetheless produce one forecast per government, and hence a finite set of possibilities.

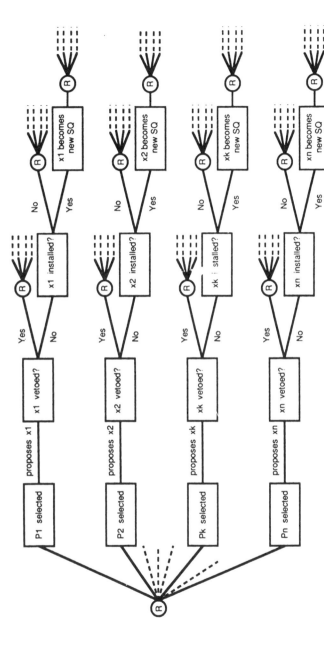

Figure 8.2. Repeat-play government formation game.

ternatives to a finite set often yields an equilibrium. In Figure 8.1, for example, government BA is an equilibrium. The indifference contours of each of the three parties through that point produce three "petals" that describe the policies that majorities prefer to BA. As the conventional spatial model forewarns, there are indeed such policies (shaded areas). *But*, none of them are implementable – the petals nowhere intersect the lattice of implementable policies. Thus, no policy that would be implemented by any of the eight alternative governments is preferred by any majority to BA; if BA forms it cannot be defeated.[6]

8.5 Conclusion

Deals are the mother's milk of politics. Politicians engage in deal-making all the time. Conventional wisdom, moreover, has it that deals struck stay stuck, either because there are exogenous enforcement mechanisms or there is honor among thieves (endogenous reputational mechanisms).

This faith in enforcement, however, sits uncomfortably with two commonly encountered features of most deal-making environments. First, deals are often complex and are shrouded in various kinds of uncertainty. Although many margins are affected by a deal, it may be neither feasible nor desirable to incorporate all of them explicitly into the agreement. This means that there will be margins on which discretion may be exercised unconstrained by the contents of the deal. And adaptation on unregulated margins may transform the nature of the deal.

Second, deals often involve neither simultaneous, reciprocal actions by the deal-makers nor contemporaneous benefit flows to them.[7] There may, as a consequence, be opportunities for reneging at least in part, either openly or surreptitiously, thereby victimizing one of the parties.

Enforcement mechanisms are being asked to carry an awful lot of water in these circumstances. Indeed, it is hard to imagine how one would operate in resolving, say, disputes arising on an excluded margin, or how one would deter hidden exercises of discretion. An alternative offered in the preceding remarks is to expand the notion of a deal to include agent forecasts about how discretion will be exercised. Hard-nosed and wily politicians, business executives, and university deans (!)

---

[6]In some circumstances, BB is also an equilibrium. This follows from the fact that, once this minority government is invested, the only governments preferred by a majority to it require party B's participation, something which B can veto. Whether B's veto threat is credible is a matter of deep strategy, a subject elaborated on in great detail in Laver and Shepsle 1996.

[7]Weingast and Marshall 1988 elaborate on the implications of a lack of simultaneity and contemporaneity in legislative deal-making.

know intuitively, once they have acquired sufficient experience, that they will be unable to squeeze all discretion out of a deal. In their dealings, therefore, they rely on enforcement mechanisms where they can, but they also acknowledge a willingness to live with anticipated exercises of discretion where they must.

References

Brown, Donald J. 1975. Aggregation of preferences. *Quarterly Journal of Economics*, 89: 456–69.

Fishburn, Peter C. 1974. Impossibility theorems without the social completeness axiom. *Econometrica*, 42: 695–704.

Laver, Michael, and Norman Schofield. 1990. *Multiparty Government.* Oxford: Oxford University Press.

Laver, Michael, and Kenneth A. Shepsle. 1996. *Making and Breaking Governments: Cabinet Formation in Parliamenary Democracies.* Cambridge: Cambridge University Press.

McKelvey, Richard D. 1976. Intransitivities in multidimensional voting models and some implications for agenda control. *Journal of Economic Theory*, 2: 472–82.

McKelvey, Richard D. 1979. General conditions for global intransitivities in formal voting models. *Econometrica*, 47: 1085–1111.

McKelvey, Richard D., and Norman Schofield. 1987. Generalized symmetry conditions at a core point. *Econometrica*, 55: 923–33.

Osborne, Martin J., and Ariel Rubinstein. 1990. *Bargaining and Markets.* New York: Academic Press.

Schofield, Norman J. 1985. *Social Choice and Democracy.* New York: Springer-Verlag.

Shepsle, Kenneth A. 1978. *The Giant Jigsaw Puzzle.* Chicago: University of Chicago Press.

Shepsle, Kenneth A. 1979. Institutional arrangements and equilibrium in multidimensional voting models. *American Journal of Political Science*, 23: 27–59.

Shepsle, Kenneth A. 1991. Discretion, institutions and the problem of government commitment. In Pierre Bordieu and James Coleman, eds, *Social Theory for a Changing Society.* New York: Russell Sage, pp. 245–63.

Weingast, Barry R., and William Marshall. 1988. The industrial organization of Congress. *Journal of Political Economy*, 91: 765–800.

9

Self-inventing Institutions: Institutional Design and the U.K. Welfare State

RUDOLF KLEIN

9.1 Introduction

THE ARGUMENT of this chapter is that in the 1980s Britain stumbled into a new approach to the design of the institutions of the welfare state: the creation of self-inventing institutions. This was not a deliberate strategy, born of some notion about postmodernist institutional architecture. Rather, it was the unintended result of the Thatcher administration's general stance to the delivery of public services: in particular, its introduction of mimic or quasi-markets into the public sector. The government's policies represented an experiment – in the sense that it was testing its theories about how these services should be organized – and the resulting institutions are inevitably vulnerable to the results of that experiment: that is, if the theories did not accurately predict the outcome (and what theories ever do?), the institutions will have to adapt accordingly. By accident, therefore, Britain may have designed welfare state institutions which, rather than setting policy goals in organizational concrete, will have to change in response to the environment which they themselves are creating: they represent, as it were, the shells of buildings which can be adapted for different uses. Built into their design are incentives to learn from what is an uncertain and turbulent environment.

To explore this theme, this chapter will examine the Thatcher administration's experiment in introducing mimic or quasi-markets in the National Health Service (NHS), the social services, and education (Le Grand 1991). These are the product of a compromise between ideological aspirations and political realities. If Mrs. Thatcher (as she then was) had followed the promptings of her ideological mentors at the Institute for Economic Affairs (Cockett 1994), she would have dismantled the

240

public services and replaced them by competitive markets. However, there was little political support – even within the cabinet – for such a radical step. From this flowed the invention of mimic markets: that is, the introduction of competition within the framework of services which continue to be publicly managed and financed.

Mimic markets, born of frustrated ideological ambitions, are therefore a peculiar hybrid. The idea of competition has been grafted onto hierarchical organizational structures. Instability is the inevitable by-product of the tensions between achieving national policy aims and leaving outcomes to be decided by competitive markets. The logic of leaving decision-making to the market is continually being confounded by the logic of ministers continuing to be accountable for the expenditure of public money: in the case of the NHS, for example, the introduction of mimic markets has led not to decentralization of decision-making but to greater intervention by central government to manage those markets. In short, the flux created by the introduction of mimic markets compels organizational learning and adaptation. This process of learning and adaptation causes, in turn, more flux – so creating a self-renewing cycle of change.

But although Britain's mimic markets were largely shaped by the circumstances of their birth, they also are members of a wider family. Interest in the notion of injecting competition into public services is international. This chapter will therefore also seek – more ambitiously but also more tentatively – to put the British policies in a wider context: to argue that the policy innovations in the United Kingdom during the 1980s reflect a response to linked political, social, and economic changes that affect all developed countries. In brief, the argument will be that the new approach to institutional design reflects a definition of policy rationality – viewing government essentially as a learning system and assessing institutions primarily by their capacity to seek out, and learn from, information – born of economic pessimism, uncertainty about the implications of technological change, and increasing skepticism about the legitimacy of expertise in determining the agenda and delivery of public services. To the extent that these are general phenomena, so the U.K. experiment of the 1980s may also have wider implications.

9.2 The End of History?

The history of institutional reform in Britain represents an attempt to impose order on a chaotic world on the basis of architectural rules about the principles of design. Once Bentham had challenged the view that it was dangerous folly to meddle with existing institutions, since these represented the accumulated experience and wisdom of our ancestors, the search was on for a "scientific" formula for designing institutions. Based on theories about the nature of efficient and effective organization (Self 1972; Dunsire 1973), this would allow governments to achieve their policy goals through the appropriate administrative mechanisms. Rational man would produce rational institutions for implementing rational policy goals.

The point can be briefly illustrated by looking at the influence of Edwin Chadwick (Finer 1970), an exponent of the "Benthamite deductive, geometric method" (Letwin 1965) in shaping the institutions of the welfare state. The 1834 Poor Law Report (Checkland 1974), of which he was one of the main authors, was notable for its translation of Benthamite ideas into practice. Its aim was to create an institutional expression for the set of principles which underlay its recommendations. If the principle of "lesser eligibility" was to be effectively translated into practice, it followed that the rules would have to be administered by impartial experts: in turn, this meant that the administration would have to be insulated from the corruption of parish pump politics. From this followed the emphasis on central control and the distrust of local government that have continued to shape the institutions of the welfare state to this day: while the principle of "lesser eligibility" was to be repudiated, the institutional philosophy to which it gave birth was to survive much longer.

It was a philosophy which defined the task of institutional design in terms of devising an organizational framework that would allow the experts the maximum possible scope for applying their skills. Its persistence is evident if, leaping more than one hundred years on from the Poor Law Report, we look at the creation of the National Health Service in 1948. Again, we find the same emphasis on creating scope for expertise: the NHS was designed, first and foremost, to allow the benefits of medical science to be diffused throughout the country (Fox 1986). Equity was, in effect, defined as technocratic rationality: the rationality of making efficient use of medical resources in what was, institutionally, a monument to the values of bureaucratic and professional paternalism. Hence the insistence on creating a national service, rather than one based on local government. Furthermore, implicit in all this, was optimism about the future – most obviously apparent in the Beveridge Report's assumption that spending on medical care would be self-liquidating because, self-evidently, the health of the population would be improved as a result.

The institutional shape of the NHS therefore reflected both certainty and optimism: certainty about what needed to be done and optimism that it could be done successfully. Only harness the resources of medical science, only ensure that its benefits were available to all, and everything would go well. It was a highly centralized system not only because of the British doctrine of parliamentary accountability (which meant that the minister of health would have to be answerable to Parliament for all the monies spent, since the NHS was funded by the taxpayer) but because there was no doubt about the appropriate geometry for the design of health services. The government was centralizing the service because it thought that it was thereby also centralizing credit for what would be an inevitably successful outcome.

The subsequent history of the NHS, particularly as we move toward the Conservative reforms of the 1980s, undermined both the certainty and the optimism. The NHS proved, in many ways, an outstandingly successful institution. The NHS provided a comprehensive, universal service, while yet controlling costs; moreover, it remained an outstandingly popular institution, as every public opinion survey confirmed. It also made massive strides toward the geographical rationalization of its services and the equitable delivery of its services. But the political price of successful cost control proved high. If there was no cost explosion, there were regular explosions of provider discontent: i.e., precisely because the NHS's budget was so tightly controlled, the producers (doctors, nurses, and others) had a self-interest in advertising the service's shortcomings in order to attract more resources for themselves. Instead of centralizing credit for the achievements of the NHS, governments discovered that they were centralizing blame for its inadequacies – symbolized by the waiting lists which proved stubbornly impervious over the decades to the attempts, by successive governments, to shorten them. And the Thatcher administration's reforms can, at least in part, be interpreted as an exercise in blame diffusion.

The changes in the NHS introduced in the government's 1989 White Paper, *Working for Patients* (U.K. Secretary of State for Health 1989), can perhaps best be interpreted as a pragmatic response to an acute political dilemma by frustrated ideologists. The political dilemma was clear: how best to satisfy demands for improved and more responsive services while containing public expenditure. The ideological frustration was also clear: although the Thatcher government had a strong commitment to market models and was being urged to adopt an insurance-based system of health care by many of its own supporters, it was apparent that any such solution would be politically disastrous – quite apart from any other objections there might be to such a move. The result was the creation of a mimic market within the NHS: the financial basis and administrative structure of the NHS were retained, most notably its universality and the principle of free treatment, but the institutional dynamics were radically changed (Day and Klein 1991).

In brief, a market system was injected into the shell of a hierarchic paternalistic institution, in which the providers – particularly the medical profession – had been able to exercise veto power over change: an example of what might be called corporate stalemate (Klein 1995). Previously, the health authorities – each of whom were set a budget by central government – were responsible for the production of health care for the populations in their areas. Under the post-1989 system, they have become exclusively purchasers of health care – contracting to buy whatever is deemed necessary from providers (who may be hospitals previously in their charge, now transformed into independent trusts, or in other parts of the country or private providers). This is the notion of the internal market, introduced to Britain by the American economist Alain Enthoven in a highly influential paper published in the mid-1980s (Enthoven 1985). It is a market of a peculiar sort, where the purchasers are health managers acting as proxy consumers, and taking decisions on their behalf about what health care is appropriate: money follows patients, but it is not the patients who decide where to go.

Complicating the picture further is that the government introduced a rather different sort of market in primary care. Here financial incentives were introduced designed to encourage general practitioners to compete to attract patients: i.e., implicit was a notion of direct consumer choice. Furthermore, general practitioners were given the option of becoming "fundholders," i.e., miniature health maintenance organizations (HMOs) buying health care on behalf of their patients. In this model it is the general practitioners who are the proxy consumers. It is therefore a very different model from that introduced in the rest of the NHS and, it may be argued, ultimately incompatible with it. Fundholders and purchasing authorities draw on the same pool of funds, and to the extent that fundholding becomes generalized, so the capacity of the purchasing authorities to plan the health care needs of their populations diminishes.

The new NHS is therefore very much a hybrid institution. On the one hand, it relies (in theory at least: it is too early to come to a judgment about the practice) on market signals to determine which providers shall produce health care. If a hospital is inefficient or unresponsive to demand for the production of good-quality medical care then, so the logic of the new system runs, it will lose custom and will have to close down unless it can mend its ways – much like any other firm operating in the market. Blame for closing down hospitals, always a politically sensitive issue, will be diffused. Similarly, the new system is based on the principle that it is the responsibility of individual health authorities to determine their own priorities for the purchase of health care: i.e., to make the rationing decisions. So, again, this can be seen as an exercise in diffusion of blame.

However, because the NHS remains a centrally funded service, it is far from clear that the logic of the internal market will be allowed to work its way through. The tradition of central direction, and the central determination of priorities by paternalistic experts, remains strong. Since the reforms, the government has, if anything, been more directive than before. It has increasingly moved toward setting health authorities' specific targets – for the lengths of waiting times and for the number of specific operations to be carried out – and strengthened the machinery for calling them to account for their performance in moving toward these targets. Indeed the introduction of the reforms was accompanied by a large injection of extra funds into the NHS (encouraged no doubt also by the approach of a general election) on the calculation, presumably, that this would allow some centralization of credit as well – or at least diminish the amount of blame.

The result of these policy innovations has thus been to create an institution which has yet to achieve a steady state. On one interpretation, it is unstable precisely because it is a hybrid with in-built tensions (the view taken by critics of the reforms, some of whom smell a conspiracy to privatize the NHS and see the changes as a halfway house toward the achievement of this aim). On another interpretation, it is an institution which has incentives to be inventively adaptive and to experiment with new organizational forms (the view taken by those who, like myself, believe that the pre-1989 NHS was a sclerotic institution dominated by provider interests). Hence the case for presenting the NHS as an example of a self-inventing institution, forced to deal with the unforeseen consequences of change.

Already the result has been to create a new agenda of health care policy-making. The process of contracting for care has focused attention on the definition of quality (a topic totally neglected in the previous forty years, when quality was taken on trust); the process of making purchasing plans has concentrated minds on the problem of defining priorities and needs; the introduction of fundholding has tilted the balance of power from hospital consultants toward general practitioners. And so on. Similarly, the organization itself has been forced to adapt: health authorities have started to amalgamate in order to become more effective purchasers and there is every likelihood that the administrative separation of the authorities responsible for primary and hospital care will soon end. Finally, it is already becoming apparent that the mimic market will also be a managed market: that the State will have to intervene both to deal with the forces inhibiting competition – notably the medical profession (Miller 1992) – and to deal with the consequences of competition, such as the wholesale closure of expensive teaching hospitals in central London (James 1994).

It is difficult to predict the outcome of this process. And that, of course is the central point. The creation of the NHS in 1948 marked – as argued – the optimism of an era which believed that the future could be molded by appropriate institutions. The introduction of the 1989 NHS, in sharp contrast, marked the uncertainty of an era which believes that institutions are likely to be molded by events. For this, clearly, is the logic of introducing a mimic market into the public sector. There may be some (Mrs. Thatcher among them, possibly) who believe that markets are efficient because they are driven by the profit motive: i.e., that the case for markets rests on the case for the private ownership of the means for production. But, equally, it may be argued that the case for markets rests on their ability to generate information, to respond quickly to signals about changing preferences or circumstances, and to overcome institutionalized resistance to change by providers who have a self-interest in perpetuating the practices in which they have invested their intellectual capital. Taking the latter view, it may be possible to argue for a market approach which deliberately seeks to eliminate the profit motive: a market of co-operatives, for example (Miller 1989).

Taking the latter view, the problem of institutional design becomes one of trying to create an organizational framework which combines the advantages of market competition while yet maintaining the principle of assigning merit goods like health care on nonmarket criteria, and avoiding the possibility that the production of such goods may be corrupted by the profit motive (since it is well recognized that in health care, consumer demand is to a large extent shaped by provider preferences). And it was precisely this problem that the architects of the 1989 NHS reform were trying to address, although it is unlikely that they saw it in such explicit terms.

At this point in the argument the skeptic may, however, object that too much is being made of a British eccentricity. The invention of the new NHS was, as argued earlier, the outcome of a combination of frustrated ideology and political pragmatism. From this flows, of course, its hybrid nature and the need to keep on inventing itself as time reveals incoherences in its design: most notably, the tension between the 1948 model of rational, central planning and the 1989 model of diffusing decision-making in a market. Why make a big deal about this, and try to build theories of emerging welfare state institutions on the basis of this peculiar oddity? What evidence is there that this is part of a larger and more general change in the institutions of the welfare state – the transformation of the Welfare State into the Regulatory State (Day and Klein 1987) – and why should this be happening?

The first point can be answered relatively easily by invoking the case of Sweden. The Swedish case is particularly interesting for a number of reasons. Like Britain, Sweden has a universal, publicly funded health care system. Unlike Britain, however, the Swedish system delegates responsibility for running (and funding) services to local government. Unlike Britain, too, Sweden has always been among the relatively high spenders on health care (OECD 1990). Yet the 1990s have seen increasing interest in the notion of an internal market in Sweden: an interest that predates the loss of office by the Social Democrats and which cannot be explained by the features specific to Britain's NHS in the 1980s – such as excessive centralization, "underfunding," or the ideological predilictions of Mrs. Thatcher. A number of variations on the theme of the internal market have been experimentally tried out by various local authorities (Garpenby 1992). Moreover, in some cases, these appear to be more radical than the British version of the internal market in that they allow for consumer-driven demand. Again, the aim is to design planned markets which, however, allow for competition for the custom of consumers between public providers (Saltman and von Otter 1992).

The changes in Sweden are still local and experimental: a Parliamentary Commission has been set up, in true Swedish style, to work out the long-term institutional design of health services. So it is not clear, as yet, how the inherent tension between top-down planning and diffused decision-making by consumers is to be resolved – if, indeed, it can be resolved. As in Britain, there may be a long period of creative instability as the institutions of health care adapt to the new demands on them.

The Swedish case disposes of the argument that the changes in Britain's NHS can be explained in exclusively national terms. Moreover, it would be possible to point to other countries (with rather different health care systems) which appear to be moving in the same direction – Holland, for one. But, before trying to explain the new model of institutional design in terms of underlying social or economic factors, another argument needs to be addressed. This is that there is something peculiar or unique about health care which drives change in a particular direction. So, for example, it might be said that health care is distinguished by its complexity, by the pace of technological change, or by the dominance of the medical profession. To deal with this contention, the next section briefly discusses some of the other changes in the institutions of the British welfare state that took place in the 1980s.

However, before doing so, it is worth noting that the adoption of a Regulatory State model is not a peculiar British or Swedish idiosyncrasy, any more than it is limited to the field of health care. Indeed it could be argued that, in an international context, these two countries are exceptional only in identifying the Welfare State with the Provider State in the first place: i.e., in developing systems where public finance went hand in hand with public provision. A more representative case is probably provided by the Bismarkian model in Germany if only because it was so widely followed by other nations. In this model the role of the state is primarily regulatory: i.e., it determines the framework of laws and rules which determine the finance, provision, and delivery of services rather than engaging in the production of welfare. So, by experimenting with more diverse and pluralistic systems, Britain and Sweden are moving toward what has always been the norm outside the countries of the former Communist bloc.

9.3 Moving toward the Market

Perhaps the most radical changes introduced by the Thatcher administration took place in the field of education. These not only preceded the reform of the NHS but also provided some of the ideas that shaped the 1989 White Paper. The underlying ideological drive was the same: to switch the balance of power from providers to consumers and to introduce competition among the latter for the custom of parents. But the institutional setting was very different. Responsibility for providing and funding school education in Britain has always been the responsibility of local authorities (rather like health care in Sweden), though with a strong element of central government planning of expenditure levels and resource allocation. The government's policies cannot therefore be explained in terms of a blame-diffusion strategy. On the contrary, the Thatcher administration's strategy in the case of education was marked by an emphatic assertion of central power.

This strategy had two strands, both driven by distrust of local authorities and of the teaching profession (jointly seen as responsible for a deterioration in educational standards as a result of pursuing trendy pedagogic theories). First, the government introduced a national curriculum and a national system for testing the attainment of pupils. Second, it introduced local management of schools (Glennerster 1991): schools were given extensive powers of self-government as well as the choice of opting out of local authority control altogether and becoming independent (rather like hospital trusts). In addition, and most crucially, their income was to depend on their ability to attract children. Parent choice, so the theory of the reforms ran, would be the driving force in the new system: the producers (i.e., the teachers) would have to accommodate their practices to what the consumers wanted (Brain and Klein 1994). The resulting system thus is intended to achieve most of the aims of the earlier advocates of educational vouchers, but within the institutional framework of a publicly provided service.

The result is, as in the case of the NHS, to create institutional instability – designedly so, since the aim of policy has been to build incentives for change into the system. Indeed, ministers have been quite explicit in stating that their aim is to achieve a diversity of provision which mirrors the choices of parents. But, as in the case of the NHS once again, some of the resulting tensions may not have been anticipated by the architects. Choice is to be contained within the constraints of the national curriculum, and the assumption has been that parental empowerment will reinforce the government's desire to curb what are seen as the excesses of educational theory. But what if the new mimic market produces politically embarrassing results such as a progressive deterioration of standards in those schools – notably in the inner cities – where the most assertive and articulate parents have decided on the exit option? This may require direct intervention to improve standards, as the Prime Minister has already warned. And what role, if any, is left for local education authorities, caught between parental power and central government direction?

Policy has also moved in a similar direction in the case of the social services delivered by local authorities. Here the changes are less radical than in the case of education and nearer the more cautious model implicit in the NHS model, since they offer no scope for direct consumer choice. Here, too, an internal market is to be introduced (U.K. Secretary of State for Health and Social Services 1989). Here, too, there is to be a separation of the purchaser and the provider roles – with local authorities buying care rather than being in the business of producing it through their own services. Their prime function, it is envisaged, will be the assessment of need for their populations, the case management of care for individuals and the regulation of services produced by both not-for-profit and for-profit providers. Again, there are large uncertainties about how this new institutional design will evolve: specifically, about the role of the purchasing authorities in shaping the market – since no automatic congruence between their plans and the response of the market can be assumed.

So it would appear that the new institutional model of Britain's NHS is neither country- nor service-specific. We are clearly tapping some more general phenomenon. The next section therefore examines – speculatively and tentatively – possible explanations for the rise of self-inventing institutions across services and across countries: explanations which might be anchored in changes in both the ideology and technology of public management or in wider social and economic movements.

9.4 The Case for Indeterminacy

One possible line of explanation for the trends in institution design, analyzed in the preceding sections, might be to start with the changes in the global economy prompted by the oil price shock and the subsequent stagflation of the mid-1970s. This marked the end of the post-1945 age of economic optimism which, in turn, had prompted the belief that the expansion of the Welfare State could be painlessly financed out of the dividends of the Growth State (Klein 1975). From this perspective, the challenge in designing the institutions of the welfare state was to devise organizations which could rationally plan the distribution of rising resources in order to achieve predetermined ends: the apogee, as it were, of Benthamite geometry.

The end of economic optimism marked an emphatic shift in perspective: certainty about the future was one of the casualties of the 1970s. Extrapolating the public expenditure trends of the previous decades, it was only too easy to devise a doom scenario, with welfare state spending absorbing the entire national income of at least some countries (Rose and Peters 1978). The dominant concern, across countries and documented in a succession of reports from the Organisation for Economic Cooperation and Development (OECD) (1978, 1985), thus became how best to curb growth and increase efficiency. From this flowed, in turn, a growing interest in managerial techniques designed to strengthen control over spending and to enhance efficiency. No longer was the production of services by welfare professionals – whether doctors or teachers – seen as self-evidently beneficial. No longer was the presumption that the more such services were produced, the better would it be for society. Instead, increasingly, the demand was for measures of effectiveness as attention switched from the inputs of the welfare state to the outcomes. Hence the emergence of what has been called the "new public management" (Hood 1990), although in many ways this simply reflected the resurrection of ideas that had first emerged in the 1960s.

It is this background which helps to explain the growing appeal over the past fifteen years of the New Right analysis of institutional behavior. On this interpretation institutions were not neutral instruments for achieving the aims of public policies but rather self-serving organizations driven by the interests of the providers and bureaucrats. Instead of being seen as the solution to the problem of achieving the aims of public policy, institutions were perceived as part of the problem itself. For the purposes of this chapter, it does not matter whether this is a complete or adequate model of institutional behavior. What does matter, in trying to make sense of the changes described in the first section, is that it became an increasingly popular model in the 1980s: a point that would, I think, be confirmed by a citation count of references to the works of Niskanen (1971) and others using the same intellectual framework.

Moreover, the New Right diagnosis was echoed by the Left. The welfare state had not only failed in many of its distributional aims (Goodin and Le Grand 1987), it was argued, but had also institutionalized the interests of middle-class providers at the expense of working-class (and other) consumers. The result was bureaucratized services unresponsive to the needs of consumers. In short, there emerged during the 1980s a widening consensus about institutional failure in the welfare state and acceptance of the fact that, given economic prospects, there was little chance of remedying the situation by pouring more resources into the same institutional bottle. Again, the point is not whether this analysis was right or wrong (my own view is that it was substantially right), but that it provides the key both to what has been happening and what is likely to happen in future.

The growing appeal of markets is the mirror-image, as it were, of the growing disillusion with state institutions. Moreover, reinforcing this intellectual transformation, there was the collapse of the Soviet regime to point to the same moral: the ultimate model of centralized, bureaucratized planning – which had so impressed heirs of the Benthamite tradition like the Webbs – had patently failed. The notion of markets in the context of welfare state is, as previously noted, ambiguous. On the one hand, it may mean leaving both the provision and finance of welfare to market forces: privatization in the full sense. On the other hand, it may mean introducing market mechanisms into a state system of welfare provision. The difference is, of course, crucial and we shall return to it. But at this stage in the argument, the crucial point is the widespread acceptance of the desirability of markets on one or the other of these two definitions.

It is one thing, however, to note a change in the intellectual climate. It is a very different matter to draw prescriptive conclusions for the design of institutions from such a change. After all, it may well be that "Thatcherism" – in all its various international forms – will turn out to have been a temporary phenomenon: a dead-end on the unrolling map of intellectual evolution. But this view becomes less persuasive if Thatcherism is seen as the product of a changing economic and social environment: as a symptom, rather than a cause. Hence the importance of the argument, put forward by a group of British intellectuals associated with the recently defunct *Marxism Today*, that the changes in Britain in the 1980s should be seen as part of the "post-Fordist" revolution – an unlovely phrase for an important phenomenon.

This analysis has a number of strands. It argues that the "mass-production of standardized products in manufacturing plants" is becoming a thing of the past as large firms break themselves down into smaller units and rely increasingly on subcontracting or franchising (Urry 1988) and that communications technology is revolutionizing techniques of control, thereby allowing a far greater devolution of power and responsibility (Mulgen 1988). Moreover, the argument continues, "social life, culture and politics are no longer predominantly organised in terms of social class" (Urry 1988), thus leading to a fragmentation both in terms of patterns of consumption and the expression of social demands. The emphasis, therefore, is increasingly on the ability of organizations to adapt and react flexibly: hence the challenge to the institutions of the welfare state to develop the same kind of capacity that is already being demonstrated by firms in the marketplace. The argument is perhaps particularly strong in countries which, like Britain or Sweden, have traditionally had a highly prescriptive, top-down approach; it appears to have less resonance in countries which, like Germany, have had a more fragmented welfare system administered through a variety of quasi-non-governmental agencies.

This line of analysis suggests that the case for the kind of institutional experiments that characterized Britain in the 1980s rests, to return to a distinction made earlier, not so much on the superiority of capitalism (seen as a system driven by the profit motive) as on the advantages of competitive markets (seen as a system for generating information and diffusing the ability to shape decisions). Such reasoning builds not only on the arguments of Hayek (1944) about the superiority of markets for generating information but also on the views of those like Schon (1971) who have argued that public organizations should be seen as learning systems, developing their capacity to adapt and respond to changes in a fast-changing environment. Given the increasing turbulence in the environment, and in the rate of technological change, it is not surprising that such arguments have become ever more persuasive over the past decade.

Implicit in this approach is, of course, the assumption that political institutions are themselves inadequate as learning systems: that the political marketplace either does not provide adequate signals or, indeed, distorts them. Without necessarily embracing this line of reasoning, it is still possible to argue that political institutions, i.e., governments, may become captive of the institutions created to carry out their purposes: that the latter may in practice frustrate public purposes because they institutionalize the self-interest of providers (precisely the kind of argument used, as noted earlier, in the case of the British NHS reforms). Hence the case for introducing some form of market mechanisms – mimic or managed market – into welfare state institutions does not necessarily rest on sharing the distrust of politics that characterizes so much of the New Right analysis.

However, the welfare state does pose some special problems for the application of this kind of institutional theory. The reason why mimic markets are also managed markets is that they embody a tension be-

tween the continued commitment of states to pursue certain public ends and the acceptance of indeterminacy in policy goals implicit in the introduction of markets of any kind. Institutions like health
care or education delivery systems are created precisely in order to
carry out certain aims and to embody certain values, such as equity in
the distribution of resources, which cannot be left to the market.
But it cannot automatically be assumed that the signals from the
market – even of the mimic or managed sort – will necessarily be consistent with these aims and values. Indeed the whole point of introducing market mechanisms is to provide information about whether
the preferences of consumers (or proxy consumers, in the case of Britain's NHS) match those of providers. If there is dissonance between the
two, whose preferences will prevail? The easy answer to this question
is that market signals will shape the way in which policy aims are delivered – that they will make services more responsive – but that they
will not affect the goals themselves. But that answer may take too
much for granted: a conclusion reinforced by the British experience
of the 1980s which suggests that greater reliance on "market forces"
may actually mean a greater state role, particularly in the field of regulation.

Hence the proposition with which this chapter began: that the 1980s
saw the creation of self-inventing institutions, reflecting not just the
eccentricities of a particular government or the victory of a particular
ideology but wider societal changes. The loss of faith in hierarchic organizations embodying certainty not only about policy goals about also
about policy means is leading to the creation of institutions where instability is the price paid for flexibility – and which almost certainly will
evolve in ways not anticipated by their designers. Where once institutions were created in order to impose order on turbulence, in future
they may themselves be in a constant process of adaptation to uncertainty.

References

Brain, J., and Rudolf Klein. 1994. *Parental Choice: Myth or Reality.* Bath, England: Centre for the Analysis of Social Policy, University of Bath.

Checkland, S. G., and E. O. A., eds. 1974. *The Poor Law Report of 1834.* Harmondsworth, England: Penguin.

Cockett, Richard. 1994. *Thinking the Unthinkable: Think Tanks and the Economic Counter-revolution, 1931–1983.* London: Harper Collins,

Day, Patricia, and Rudolf Klein. 1991. Britain's health care experiment.
Health Affairs, 10 (3), 39–59.

Day, Patricia, and Rudolf Klein. 1987. The business of welfare. *New Society,*
19 June, pp. 11–3.

Dunsire, Andrew. 1973. *Administration: The Word and the Science.* London: Martin Robertson.

Enthoven, Alain C. 1985. *Reflections on the Management of the National Health Service.* London: Nuffield Provincial Hospitals Trust.

Finer, S. E. 1970. *The Life and Times of Sir Edwin Chadwick.* London: Methuen.

Fox, Daniel M. 1986. *Health Policies, Health Politics.* Princeton, N.J.: Princeton University Press.

Garpenby, Peter. 1992. The transformation of the Swedish health care system. *Journal of European Social Policy,* 2, 17-31.

Glennerster, Howard. 1991. Quasi-markets for education. *Economic Journal,* 101, 1268–76

Goodin, Robert E., Julian Le Grand, et al. 1987. *Not Only the Poor.* London: Allen & Unwin.

Hayek, F. A. 1944. *The Road to Serfdom.* London: Routledge.

Hood, Christopher. 1990. Beyond the public bureaucracy state? Mimeo., London School of Economics.

James, John H. 1994. *Transforming the NHS: The View from the Inside.* Bath, England: Centre for the Analysis of Social Policy, University of Bath.

Klein, Rudolf. 1975. *Inflation and Priorities.* London: Centre for Studies in Social Policy.

Klein, Rudolf. 1995. *The New Politics of the NHS.* London: Longmans.

Le Grand, Julian. 1991 . Quasi-markets and social policy. *Economic Journal,* 101, 1256–67.

Letwin, Shirley. 1965. *The Pursuit of Certainty.* Cambridge: Cambridge University Press.

Miller, David. 1989. *Market, State and Community.* Oxford: Clarendon Press.

Miller, Frances. 1992. Competition law and anticompetitive professional behaviour affecting health care. *Modern Law Review,* 55, 453–81.

Mulgen, Geoff. 1988. The power of the weak. *Marxism Today,* December, 24–31.

Niskanen, William A. 1971. *Bureaucracy and Representative Government.* Chicago: Aldine Atherton.

Organisation for Economic Co-operation and Development (OECD). 1978. *Public Expenditure Trends.* Paris: OECD.

Organisation for Economic Co-operation and Development (OECD). 1985. *Social Expenditure, 1960–1990.* Paris: OECD.

Organisation for Economic Co-operation and Development (OECD). 1990. *Health Care Systems in Transition: The Search for Efficiency.* Paris: OECD.

Rose, Richard, and B. Guy Peters. 1978. *Can Government Go Bankrupt?* London: Macmillan.

Saltman, Richard B., and Casten von Otter. 1992. *Planned Markets and Public Competition.* Buckingham: Open University Press.

Schon, Donald A. 1971. *Beyond the Stable State.* Harmondsworth, England: Penguin.

Self, Peter. 1972. *Administrative Theories and Politics*. London: Allen & Unwin.

U.K. Secretary of State for Health and Social Services. 1989. *Caring for People*. London: HMSO.

U. K. Secretary of State for Health. 1989. *Working for Patients*. Command 555. London: HMSO.

Urry, John 1988. Disorganised capitalism. *Marxism Today*, October, 30–33.

10

Selection and the Currency of Reward

GEOFFREY BRENNAN

The best security for the fidelity of mankind is that interest be made co-incident with duty.

–James Madison, *Federalist Paper* No. 72

10.1 Incentives and the Economic Theory of Institutions

Within the economic theory of institutional design (within which I somewhat gratuitously include the writings of the American founding fathers – hence the epigraph), the central features of any institutional arrangement are captured by the structure of incentives that that arrangement embodies. The central property of the idealized free market, for example, is seen to be the fact that producers are encouraged to operate in the interests of their customers by virtue of the incentive effects created by market prices. Equally, market "failure" is identified when market incentives fail to reflect adequately the interests of relevant others, as is the case with monopoly or externalities or in the provision of public goods. Somewhat analogously, within the economic theory of politics, the success or otherwise of democratic political processes is seen to depend on the extent to which electoral competition constrains candidates to offer policy platforms that are in the interests of their constituents (assumed under the democratic rubric to include all the relevant citizenry). And the normative analysis of alternative political institutions – such as bicameralism, or representation or political parties or the separation of powers – mainly focuses on the extent to which those institutions support or deflect electoral competition in encouraging would-be political agents to act in constituent interests.

Because the incentive structure of institutions is the focus of analysis, it is common practice in the economics of institutions to assign uniformly self-interested motivations to all agents. As I have argued elsewhere (e.g. Brennan and Buchanan 1985, chap. 4) this practice reflects analytic purpose rather than any appeal to empirical reality. The extent to which under various institutional arrangements it is in an individual actor's *interest* to behave in a manner that promotes the collective interest is a matter for investigation: to assume at the outset that the actor is motivated directly by a desire to promote the collective interest simply subverts the analytical exercise. Accordingly, the analysis of monopoly proceeds on the basis that monopoly firms will exploit their monopoly power to the maximum long-run advantage of the firm's decision-makers (standardly taken to be the profit-recipient owners); those decision-makers *may* be concerned about their consumers' interests in a way that cannot be explained by profit-maximization, but this fact does not seem to bear in any way on the extent to which monopoly markets support any such concern. In the same way, the analysis of Pigou's famous smokey factor (Pigou 1932) assumes that that factory is totally unconcerned about the nearby laundry as such, and remains unconcerned because relations between the factory and laundry are not mediated by any price incentives. But if the appropriate Coasian bargain (Coase 1960) between the two can be struck, or if the two firms were owned by the same set of shareholders or profit-recipients, then the factory would have a market-based incentive to take into account the effect of its activities on the laundry's operations. The existence of a generalized environmental concern on the part of the factory's managers could in principle be incorporated into the discussion, but it is not clear that doing so would in any way illuminate the analysis of market failure.

In other words, the assumption of universal self-interest is an analytic device designed to test out the incentive properties of alternative institutional arrangements. The method is one encapsulated in an often-quoted remark by Hume (1741): "In constraining any system of government and fixing the several checks and controls of the constitution, every man ought to be supposed a knave and to have no other end in all his actions than private interest." And what goes for the "constitution" narrowly conceived goes equally for the whole range of institutional devices designed to support the public interest. For this method not to be inappropriate, two assumptions only seem to be required: first, that agents do not invariably pursue the public interest (properly identified) for its own sake (call this the "virtue realism" assumption – VR); and second, that the institutional devices so designed do not undermine any public-interested motivations that may be in place (call this the "ceteris paribus" assumption – CP).

The first of these assumptions seems unexceptionable. The second is more contentious, though the mechanisms by which public-interested motivations are secured (*other* than via generalized incentive effects) are not, it seems to me, well-understood. Arguments, for example, that commercial society undermines the moral fabric on which commercial society relies for its good functioning are by no means unfamiliar – but such arguments have not been uncontested, and it seems to me that these are matters on which the jury is still out.[1]

In any event, for the purposes of the present exercise, I wish to accept these two assumptions (VR and CP) without further debate. I want nevertheless to argue that this "Humean" method is narrowing in its scope, and encourages institutional economists to overlook potentially important aspects of institutional design – those which depend on the operation of selection devices or "screens" rather than incentive devices or "sanctions." In this chapter, I wish to focus attention on these selection devices – both on selection as a relevant and potentially significant dimension of institutional analysis, and on a specific mechanism by which such selection may be made more effective. The argument will be developed in terms of a particular example, namely the case of selection (and incentives) within academia. This example is taken both because it will be familiar to most of the readership of this volume and because it is of some interest in its own right. But the moral to be drawn is a general one – that selection is a potentially significant dimension of any institution's operation and that the methods of economic analysis tend to suppress that dimension.

10.2   Selection within Institutions

The Humean methods tend to suppress analysis of selection devices by virtue of its assumption of motivational homogeneity. It is clear that one can retain the assumption of "virtue realism," as here understood, without assuming everyone to be a knave: all may be knavish to some extent, but some may be less knavish than others – and this fact gives the institutional designer/reformer some scope for normative progress. If one can identify the less knavish from the more knavish, one can locate the less knavish in those employments in which knavishness is most destructive. Put another way, unless incentive structures can be found which will induce agents to operate in the

[1]See A. O. Hirschman (1982) for a discussion of relevant possibilities.

public interest all the time (unless invisible-hand mechanisms are ubiquitous), then such virtue as exists in a society will be a positive resource for that society, and should be located in its highest valued use just like any other resource.[2]

It is somewhat surprising that economists seem to have largely overlooked this possibility. It is of the essence in economics that individuals differ – in tastes *and* in capacities – because it is in such differences that the prospects for trade and specialization are seen to lie.[3] Friday and Crusoe on their island can do better with trade than without, because trade enables each to specialize in that activity in which he has a comparative advantage. If Crusoe and Friday specialize in that activity in which each has a comparative *dis*advantage, both will be worse off in general than if they had not specialized at all. The allocation of specific persons to tasks is a critical piece of the normative enterprise, and the competitive market is efficient because, inter alia, it secures that desirable allocation simply on the basis of the agents' own self-interests. In short, the idealized market operates a selection mechanism, and the proper functioning of that mechanism is, and is widely recognized to be, a critical piece of the market's normative performance.

It is of course a standard piece of welfare economics that the market works less well in the provision of some kinds of commodities than others – and that the case for reliance on institutional forms other than the market is correspondingly stronger in relation to those commodities. It is also recognized (though perhaps less commonly) that the good functioning of markets depends on an institutional superstructure (mechanisms for the enforcement of property rights, for the registering and enforcement of contracts, and so on) most of which cannot necessarily be adequately provided by the market itself. Within those non-market institutions – the courts and political process most notably – the invisible-hand properties of markets are less operative (or at least less well established) and one may be rather more reliant on the "virtue" of politicians and bureaucrats and judges than of market actors. If so, virtue is a resource that commands a higher social value in these nonmarket institutions, and the good functioning of society will depend on the

---

[2]I understand "virtue" here in the "civic humanist" sense to be the dual attribute of a capacity to discern the true public interest and a motivation to act as the public interest, so discerned, requires.

[3]Such specialization may itself develop differences, as individuals learn particularized skills. On one reading, Smith's account of the division of labor depends on "economics of specialization" among a community of otherwise identical persons, so that the essence of Smith's account of the market is the existence of "increasing returns" rather than intrinsic comparative advantages. See Buchanan and Yong Yoon (1994).

extent to which the relatively virtuous are selected for nonmarket offices.

Of course, even within the well-functioning market, monitoring costs and transactions costs will differ across commodities: the need for "trust" in contractual relations is not uniform across all contracts. Trustworthiness will be differentially prized across alternative employments, and the market will work better to the extent that it can allocate relatively trustworthy persons to those arenas where trust returns the highest social value.

To state the problem is not, however, to solve it. Those employments in which trust or virtue are most prized are precisely the employments in which there is a greatest scope for private-interested agents to exploit opportunities for gain at the expense of others. Actor discretion implies vulnerability to exploitation. Accordingly, any signals on the basis of which virtue may be identified are also signals which self-interested agents will have an incentive to emulate plausibly. What is required is a set of tolerably reliable selection devices – devices that will enable virtue to be detected on a better-than-average basis, and which will be relatively impervious to the antics of the rational dissembler. I wish to offer one such device in this paper.

Before doing so, however, I want to make one small point and then move to a more general example. The small point is this: even if there were no possibility of selecting for virtue, the presence of some relatively virtuous persons in the community may render some institutional arrangements viable that would be unworkable in a world composed totally of Humean knaves. If so, the Humean method will distort the analysis of institutions even though no effective selection mechanisms exist to distinguish virtue where it exists. I am fond of quoting in this connection a remark of Alexander Hamilton's to the effect that: "the assumption of universal venality in human nature is little less an error in political reasoning than the assumption of universal rectitude" (Madison, Hamilton, and Jay 1788, no. 76). I conjecture that Hamilton's claim may be true even if one cannot select for relative rectitude, though I shall not argue further here in support of that claim.

To point up the distinction between the incentive and selection aspects of institutional arrangement, it may be useful to appeal to a particular example. The one I offer here is that of representative democracy. The distinction at issue is represented by two possible descriptions of the way in which electoral processes work. Both descriptions are somewhat idealized pictures, but it is the difference between them rather than the idealization that is relevant here. According to one picture (a conventional public choice picture) the role of electoral competition is essentially to constrain potential candidates to offer policies that are in the voters' interests. Rival candidates are like rival tenderers for a contract or rival bidders at an auction; given that the contract will be assigned to the tender that offers at the lowest price (or obversely the bidder that makes the highest bid), the candidates will have an incentive to discover what it is that voters want, and offer a policy platform that an appropriate majority of those voters prefers. Furthermore, candidates will have an incentive to fulfill any policy promises because failure to do so will virtually ensure electoral defeat on the next occasion. The "discipline of continuous tradings" will operate to encourage compliance (though of course deviations which the voters perceive to be in their interests will not be punished). To the extent that continuous trading is undermined by the candidate's being in her last term of office, there will be a role for (longer-lived) parties in monitoring the conduct of individual candidates. (See Brennan and Kliemt 1994.) On this account, then, candidates are ideally ciphers for the policy platforms they represent: the role of electoral competition is, as the epigraph has it, to bend the candidate's interests to the service of duty.

In fact, however, the *Federalist Papers* themselves offer a rather different picture of representative democracy. The picture is this. Ordinary voters have relatively little skill in understanding the intricacies of policy – nothing in ordinary life prepares them for evaluating the effects of alternative policies (except by experience ex post).[4] Voters do, however, have skills in assessing the qualities of persons: they deal with each other and develop well-honed capacities to discern reliability, good sense, trustworthiness, public-spiritedness, benevolence, and so on. Voters will, therefore, have the capacity and the incentive to select as their representatives persons who are better in these respects than they themselves are on average. And that *selection* process is what democratic elections are to perform. On this account, the policy platforms that candidates present are more to be seen as indicators of personal quality than as contractual obligations, and perform much the same function as accounts of the candidate's past or personal endorsements from other figures in public life whose judgments are held in high regard. Popular elections are to be seen as a mechanism for the laundering of the electorate, and the institution of *representation* as such is essential to that laundering process. It should perhaps be added here that, notwithstanding the alleged laundering effects of democratic representation, the *Federalist Papers* remained deeply skeptical about the operations of the legislature: it is not entirely clear how confident the authors were in their own argument.

Nevertheless, it seems clear that the *Federalist's* argument about the

---

[4]A rationalist reconstruction might refer here to Downsian "rational ignorance" (Downs 1957) or Brennan-Lomasky "non-decisiveness" (Brennan and Lomasky 1993).

role of democratic elections involves quite a different picture from the public choice one. Indeed, on the public choice argument, there is no persuasive argument for representation as such at all – which explains perhaps why many public choice scholars are strong proponents of direct democracy. Equally, the public choice picture presents the *ad hominem* personal dimension of electoral competition as just so much irrelevant and unfortunate noise, distracting attention from the real issues. Why should one care whether one's president was a draft-dodger, or is maritally unfaithful, any more than one cares about such things in one's plumber? Public choice orthodoxy makes much play of the idea that politicians and public agents are, after all, no better than the rest of us: that idea is a critical piece both of the "politics without romance" (Buchanan 1979) that public choice theory represents and of the general antipathy to "benevolent despot" conceptions of government that characterizes the public choice approach. The *Federalist Papers* account, while retaining a healthy dose of political skepticism, nevertheless suggests why we *might* reasonably expect that our political representatives will be better than we are – and why, if they are not, that that fact constitutes a failure in our electoral processes.

Now, although the "incentive"-focused and the "selection"-focused pictures of electoral processes offered here are interestingly different, it should be clear that, at least over a broad range, they are not mutually exclusive. It is true that the better one's incentive devices the less one need rely on selection devices and vice versa, but since all such devices are bound to be imperfect to some extent and since selection can only yield us the *most* virtuous persons and not totally virtuous ones, there will always be a role for mechanisms of both types. Moreover, on at least some occasions, the same institutional device will perform both incentive and selection functions. But there is, in my view, a clear case for focusing some analytic attention on how selection processes work and how they could be made to work better – if only because such processes have, at least in economistic circles, been very largely ignored.

10.3 Selection in Academia

I turn now to an example that I wish to develop at somewhat greater length and that represents in one sense the core of this chapter. This example deals with selection devices (and in passing, incentive devices) in academia. Several background facts are relevant to this example and I begin by setting those facts out. I shall then offer a highly simplified model of behavior within academia, and focus attention on the particular device that I shall argue can support selection processes – namely, the currency of reward. I shall attempt to say something about the optimal pattern of reward, and about the stability of that optimal pattern under competitive forces. This will lead me finally to a few conjectures about the variations in institutional practice in universities in different countries, and to an attempt to connect the more specific conclusions about universities back to the general issue of selection mechanisms.

10.3.1 Background Facts

There are three background facts that I take as given. First, there is considerable institutional variation among university systems in different countries, particularly in the extent to which they reward differential performance and in what ways. That variation may be tending to erode somewhat over time – a fact which demands explanation in itself – but it still exists to a significant extent. In general, the pattern of rewards across scholars according to academic performance is larger in the United States than in the United Kingdom and a fortiori in Australia. Certainly, the variation in rewards across alternative fields has always been much greater in the U.S. than in the U.K. or Australia. In Australia, until very recently, virtually every full professor was paid the same salary irrespective of field or institution or perceived quality. More recently, market loadings for appointments in fields of perceived priority and scarcity have been introduced, but basic salaries have been set by bargains struck between national unions and a national system. "Merit" loadings based on outstanding performance, where they exist, are uncommon and small: salary is regulated by seniority within the standard professional ranges (up to the top of the senior lecturer grade), and although there has been a nominal barrier at the top of the lecturer grade, promotion over that barrier has always been more or less automatic for all except perhaps the bottom 10% of performers. This system was modeled on the U.K. system, although over the recent past that system has introduced rather greater variation in salary at the professorial level. In both the U.K. and Australia, salaries were (again until recently) putatively indexed for inflation, in such a way that relativities between persons within the same grade (and pretty much between grades) were maintained. In some work I did some years ago on research performance among Australian academic economists over the decade 1974 to 1983, I was struck by the extent of the variation in the apparent quality and quantity of research output across persons at identical levels in the academic hierarchy for that decade. Certainly, the difference between actual rewards and anything faintly resembling a piece rate system turned out to be very large indeed. My own experience in the U.S. (at a state university incidentally) was that the annual increments policy was extremely aggressive: one person received raises of 25% and 33% in successive years; several others had received no increment at all for a considerable number of years.

The second notable fact about academic life is that strictly pecuniary motives do not seem to be the only or even the most significant motives in play. To be sure, in the U.S., academics seemed to care very deeply about the size of their annual increments, but it appears to be the increment *relative* to that received by one's colleagues rather than the absolute increment that matters; indeed in my experience quite tiny differences can be the source, variously, of considerable angst or elation, depending on how large were the increments earned by one's fellows. The increment seems to be valued essentially because it is taken as a symbol of perceived level of performance:[5] in other words, academics care much more about the good regard of (respected) peers than about salary level per se. Many academics seem to be prepared to sacrifice very much higher salaries in order to belong to a more prestigious department or university. In another paper, Philip Pettit and I discuss the motivations of academics in some detail (Brennan and Pettit 1991). Our claim there is that many academics are motivated more by a quest for regard than for income, and this is an assumption I shall continue to make here.

The third observation is that, even in the U.S. where increments policy is such as to tie salary rather more closely to academic performance than in the U.K. or Australia, nothing remotely like a piece rate system prevails. There is a great deal of attention paid to *selection*; but rather less to monitoring performance once selected. Certainly, in all cases with which I am familiar, selection involves quite lengthy and elaborate procedures, and these procedures are regarded as the primary mechanism by which the university seeks to improve and/or sustain its performance and academic reputation.

In what follows, I shall take it that monitoring costs in academia are such that any piece rate system of reward would be extremely expensive to operate, and that a primary role of selection procedures is to assess not merely the past performance of any scholar but also the likely future performance. I accept that past performance *in itself* may be of value to a university choosing among alternative candidates, since reputation and name recognition are objects that a university may be seeking in filling particular jobs. However, I am taking it that past performance is also valued, perhaps predominantly, *because* it is the best available index of *future performance*. There is, of course, a question as to *why* selection

---

[5]A conjecture that is decidedly Smithian in spirit.

panels should want to select the candidate with the best expected future academic performance. But if that *is* so, selection panels will want to select candidates who will also, like them, select for future academic performance when the successful candidate comes to occupy selection status herself.

10.3.2 A Simple Model

On the basis of this impressionistic background, consider the following simple model. The assumptions are

  (i) that candidates for an academic job are to be selected, in an environment in which scope for future reward or punishment in the light of performance is limited;
 (ii) that candidates are of two types: the true scholars, denoted S, who place a high value on academic pursuits (either for their own sake or the sake of the prestige in the eyes of peers academic excellence brings); and the expedients, E, who are motivated mainly by the full income (including leisure) that the academic life affords.

It may be useful, in spelling out the distinction between E's and S's, to depict their preferences diagrammatically. In Figure 10.1 we show in standard indifference curve form the allocation of time between academic activities, denoted A, and other activities, denoted L, given that the agent is essentially free to allocate her time at will between those pursuits. The scholars choose an allocation at S on this basis; the expedients choose an allocation E. The s_1, e_1 are the respective indifference curves for the two types.

Several comments about this simplified formulation are called for. First there is no reason to postulate that expedients in this model have *no* interest in academic activities. Indeed, it seems likely that they would have *some* such interest, because otherwise they would not have entered the academic market in the first place. Scholars and expedients are classified by reference to their *relative* positions. Second, the assumption that "scholars" and "expedients" form two mutually exclusive classes is simply for ease of analysis. It would be possible to model a continuum of agents according to their scholarly proclivities, and attempt to select for the most scholarly. To do so would complicate the analysis without adding significantly to the central points at issue.

Third, given that there are rents to be enjoyed from success in this contest, the E's will have an incentive to appear like the S's. If this contest is, for example, the race for a chair at Oxford, expedients will have found it desirable in the past to act like scholars in *order* to enjoy the

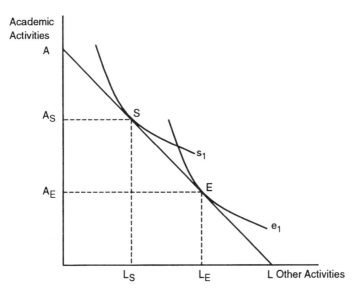

Figure 10.1. Scholars and expedients: the basic case.

satisfactions that an Oxford chair entails. In other words, the positions occupied by the S's and E's are the positions they will occupy *in the future* and cannot readily be read off past performance. Indeed, since what is at stake in academic activity is academic effort, including expenditure of creative imagination and mental energies, the difference between S's and E's may be difficult to capture even ex post, and certainly not capturable on the basis of time spent. The distinction between the academic, who genuinely *is* working desperately to complete the definitive study of y, and the one who is merely spinning his wheels may not be easy to detect at any point.

I shall, however, assume that the differences between S's and E's *can* be detected at the selection stage, with probability less than 1, but greater than the proportion S/(S+E) in the population of candidates. This assumption is necessary because we have to allow for selection processes being used at all (hence, the selection process must be better than random), and also for the need to bolster selection processes by institution supports (hence, the selection process must be imperfect). To simplify the discussion let us suppose that the population of candidates, in the absence of any institutional intervention, consists of half S's and half E's – and that selection procedures achieve a 60% success

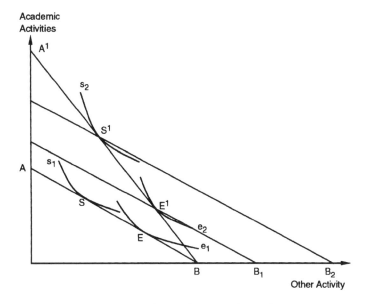

Figure 10.2. Scholars and expedients with academic piece-rates.

rate, in the sense that six of every ten appointments will on average turn out to have been S's.

10.4 The Currency of Reward

On this basis, a question arises as to how we might help those selection processes work better – how we might raise the proportion of S's in the successful cohort. It is important to note that *one* possible mechanism would be to tie rewards more closely to academic activities. Such a mechanism alters the relative price between academic and other activities, as shown in Figure 10.2. The postmechanism possibilities frontier shifts from, say AB to A^1B. As a result, both E's and S's shift toward the more attractive "academic activities" via a "substitution" effect, and it is this substitution effect that is the center of analytic attention within the incentive-oriented tradition of institutional design. But note here a different fact – that the S's and E's benefit *differentially* from the change in relative prices. Using the initial set of relative prices, AB, to evaluate the benefit for S and E, we see that E is made better off by an amount equivalent to BB_2, which is greater than BB_1. Obviously, if relative prices are changed by making other activities *less* attractive, then the E's lose more than the S's. That is, any relative price change that makes academic activities relatively more attractive (and other activities relatively less) will make academic employments relatively more attractive to the S's and less to the E's, via the pattern of differential income effects. If academic appointments are made relatively more attractive to the S's than the E's, this will in general shift the sample of applicants in favor of the S's. The simplest case to see is that of a change that makes "other activities" less attractive; the E's are more encouraged to take employment elsewhere than the S's are, and it can be presumed that more of them will respond.

Here, then, and in general, policies argued for under incentive effects will also tend to have selection effects – that is, there will be differential income effects that redistribute relatively in favor of those persons who more highly value the activity that we seek to encourage. However, this is not invariably the case: sometimes, the differential income effects and the substitution effects work in opposite directions. But in any event, "incentive-effect" analysis will often proceed under the assumption of homogeneous agents and the possibility of differential income effects (and of selection possibilities more generally) is ruled out. More to the point for the current example, we have explicitly ruled out any such *direct* change in relative prices between academic and other activities. Is there nevertheless a way in which we might secure the relative differential income effects *indirectly*? I believe that there *is*, and it is this possibility that represents the core "institutional design" feature that I wish to promote here.

Given that scholars to some extent (and expedients to a much lesser extent) value academic pursuit for its own sake, and given that academic activity requires certain inputs (research equipment, good library access, secretarial and research assistant support, capacity to allocate postdoctoral positions or PhD scholarships to areas of one's own research interests, discretion over the identity of colleagues etc. etc.), the provision of those inputs represents a form of income to the successful candidate. That is, we can translate Figure 10.1 into an associated diagram (Figure 10.3), which shows the various type's preferences between such academic inputs and cash. Since cash is totally fungible, this diagram can be thought of as showing the combination of "academic input" and "cash" that the various types would choose if they had total discretion over the relevant expenditure.

(There are two complicating factors that I wish to abstract from here. One is the fact that tax is normally payable only on the cash component, so that there are in practice incentives to take a larger share than would otherwise be the case in the form of academic inputs. The second

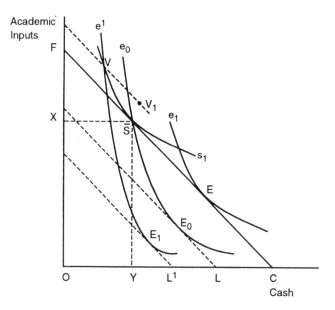

Figure 10.3. Scholars and expedients with academic-specific payment.

is the fact that academic inputs are often joint, in the sense that they are simultaneously valued by a number of scholars; for example, the quality of the library collection in philosophy is a "public good" to all scholars with strong interests in philosophy. These "economies of scale" would give each academic, choosing unilaterally, a tendency to choose too few academic inputs: standard "free rider" problems arise. Accordingly, over a significant range, the academic input/cash mix must be chosen for groups as a whole. To some extent, the tax and economies-of-scale effects operate in different directions. Here I merely note them as important complications, and move on.)

It is important to the argument here that although cash is fully fungible, all academic inputs are not. Those academic inputs represent cash forgone, but they cannot be sold to other academics in return for cash. The *currency* in which total "income" is received, whether as ordinary cash salary or as access to academic inputs of value to scholars, does matter. And it matters *differentially* to "scholars" and "expedients."

Consider specifically, on Figure 10.3, the income package represented by the point $\bar{S}$. This package is represented by a cash income of OY and academic inputs of OX, which at prices represented by the slope of FC are equivalent to a further amount YC in cash-equivalents. Here, by definition, scholars enjoy a total income-equivalent package of OC (measured in cash-equivalents). But by offering this package, we reduce the cash-equivalent income available to expedients to OL. That is, E's indifference curve through $\bar{S}$, e_o, is the level of indifference E would have achieved with a total income-equivalent of OL if E could have had that income in E's preferred cash-equivalent academic input mix. By offering the package represent by $\bar{S}$, S is offered a total income-equivalent of OC; E is offered a total income-equivalent of OL. That is, by altering the currency mix we are able to increase the relative attractiveness of the job to the S group, and thereby *reduce* the proportion of E's in the applicant sample assuming that other labor markets are working more or less independently. The currency of reward operates, in other words, to increase the likelihood of selecting "scholars": it supports existing selection processes by *pre*selecting the sample of applicants.

There is another argument, familiar from incentive-based literature, which may yield similar results, but which is quite distinct. This other argument is a variant of the "optimal tax" argument and one of a class of applications of the so-called theory of the second best. In its tax guise, the line of reasoning is that where leisure is tax exempt (as it invariably is under income taxes based on annual income levels), it will be desirable to tax leisure complements at higher rates, and leisure substitutes at lower rates, than other goods. Doing so will discourage individuals from substituting away from income-producing activities toward leisure activities in response to taxes, and hence allow given revenue requirements to be met with lower rates of tax overall. The argument depends on the assumption that leisure consumption cannot be observed (and taxed) directly; the "second-best" arrangement is to tax leisure consumption *indirectly* by taxing leisure complements more heavily. The analogue to the argument in the case at hand is that since academic effort cannot be observed and rewarded directly, we may be able to encourage academic effort *indirectly* by more extensive access to things that are complementary with academic effort. But this argument, though it *looks* rather like the argument I have made here – partly because it involves similar-looking policy recommendations – is a different argument, for it does not depend at all on selection of persons of different types, but rather on indirect incentives. The optimal tax argument, and its academic-effort-monitoring counterpart, can proceed perfectly coherently with a cohort of identical persons: the selection argument cannot. The selection argument works by making the employment relatively more attractive to persons of the relevant type – namely, those who more highly value academic activity for its own sake.

There is a further question to be pursued here – that is, whether the currency of reward will be "efficient" in the sense, at least, that all S's will prefer the prevailing reward mix to any other involving more cash. This will, of course, be so provided the reward mix involves a share of at least OY/OC in cash. So the question we have posed is equivalent to asking whether it will ever be in the institutional designer's interests to choose a mix that involves a *smaller* share of cash than at point $\bar{S}$. In fact, we do not have enough structure in the model to answer that question decisively: to do so, we would have to provide more information about alternative competitive employments. However, it is worth emphasizing that there is nothing unique about the point $\bar{S}$, and that it seems very likely that a reward mix involving less cash than at $\bar{S}$ will be desirable on selection grounds. What is critical in choosing the reward mix is the effect on the *relative* attractiveness of academic employment to E's and S's: at $\bar{S}$, the total income-equivalent value is OC to the S-group and OL to the E-group and the ratio is OC/OL. We can in general increase that relative attractiveness by reducing the cash component below that at $\bar{S}$. For example, if we move to a point on s_1 above and to the left of $\bar{S}$, we leave the S-group at an income-equivalent level of OC, by definition; but we further reduce the income-equivalent level of the E's. For example, at point V on s_1, the income-equivalent for the E-group is reduced to OL^1 (as E's level of indifference is reduced from e_0 to e^1). Of course, the mix at point V *costs* more in total than the mix at point $\bar{S}$ and leaves S-type persons no better off. Put another way, the reward mix at point V could be altered at no extra cost into another mix, say at V_1, which all S-types would individually prefer. However, the mix at V_1 would involve a great proportion of E's in any cohort of applicants, and would not induce selection effects as favorable to the academic enterprise as would the mix at V (involving more academic inputs and less cash than at V_1). In other words, selection considerations may involve a mix in the currency of reward that involves, in itself and selection effects aside, too little cash from the point of view of the existing cohort of academics *even if they were all "scholars"* in the sense here defined.

It is worth noting, however, that any such "excessively" academic reward mix could only survive in a monopoly system. To see this, suppose that there is a variety of independent universities all competing for the best staff, and suppose further that they are all offering a reward mix like that at point V in Figure 10.3. Then clearly any one university could allow all other universities to offer the mix represented by V, thereby securing the benefits of selection support, and bid those preselected staff away by offering a reward mix of the type represented by V_1 (involving more cash and less academic input). In short, reward mixes that are more academic-input oriented than S can never survive competitive pressures, even though they may be desirable from a selection viewpoint.

10.5 Summary, Synthesis, and Generalizations

It may be useful at this point to summarize the argument. I shall do so in the form of four simple propositions:

1. Institutional arrangements can affect the pattern of social outcomes by selecting among agents of different types as well as by altering incentives for agents.
2. An institutional arrangement will support a particular selection process to the extent that the arrangement rewards some types of agents more than others.
3. Rewards can be appropriately differentiated by means of the "currency of reward," understood as the mix of forms which rewards take – and can be so differentiated even when agents of different types cannot be identified.
4. In the academic case specifically, individuals with a relatively high taste for scholarly activities can be differentially rewarded (and hence selected for) by a currency of reward that takes the form of a high proportion of academic support and a correspondingly low proportion of cash.

By way of conclusion, I should like to suggest three extensions of the line of reasoning developed here. These extensions are at differing levels of generality, and are somewhat speculative. I offer them as means of indicating how the foregoing argument might be of more general interest.

The first set of speculations is firmly focused on the academic case. One question that arises in that context is why it is that in the U.S. there is greater variation in academic salaries according to performance than exists (or at least existed until quite recently) in the U.K. and Australian systems. I want here to conjecture that an important difference between the U.S. and U.K./Australian systems lies not so much in the differential *variance* in rewards offered, but in the different currencies of reward. That is, U.K. and Australian institutions offer, I want to suggest, a higher proportion of the salary package in terms of research assistant and secretarial support, more generous sabbatical leave arrangements, better superannuation entitlements and (relatively) greater access to research equipment. (This is, I concede, a conjectural fact since I have nothing more than casual observation to support it.) It is also worth noting that the U.S. system has a rather more competitive labor market than the

U.K/Australian system. In the latter settings, there has been a much more monopsonistic market in the purchasing of academic services: academic salaries have been largely determined and regulated by a single systemwide employer. If, as I have suggested earlier, the currency mix that best selects for scholarly inclinations is only viable in the absence of competitive pressures, then this fact would provide one possible explanation for a currency of reward in the U.S. case that is more cash oriented. More generally, there is at stake here a conjectural account of institutional variation. This account is, incidentally, consistent with the tendency of such institutional variation to disappear as academic labor markets become more internationally competitive which is what seems to have happened over recent decades.

The second area of generalization moves beyond the academic example to other employments. It is clear that wherever monitoring of output levels and quality is costly, employers will have an interest in selecting for "conscientious" and habitually motivated workers – for compulsive workaholics. And the reasoning concerning the currency of reward as a selection device seems to be no less applicable in such cases. Providing an attractive workplace, perhaps more expensive uniforms for relevant employees, and the right kind of on-the-job consumption, are plausible alternatives to high salaries and serve to attract the "right kind of employees." In general, on-the-job consumption has had a poor press in mainstream economics: on-the-job consumption has been seen largely as an inefficiency that owes its existence to some form of regulation which prevents monopoly rents being taken in the form of cash. The standard claim is that on-the-job consumption (thicker carpets, larger offices, more attractive support staff, etc.) is more likely to be characteristic of monopoly than competition, and more common in public monopolies, where the scope for managers to appropriate monopoly rents in noncash forms is taken to be greater. The argument offered in this chapter does not refute the more familiar line – but it does suggest that on-the-job consumption *can* serve an important selection role (and indeed an incentive role as well) and that, if monopoly arrangements tend to generate more on-the-job consumption than other arrangements do, this is not necessarily a wholly lamentable fact.

The third level of generalization involves application to nonmarket institutions, where difficulties of monitoring and the scope for exploitation tend to be most marked. I have already made mention of the *Federalist*'s argument for representative institutions, which is clearly a selection argument of a kind. But the relevant question for my argument here is whether the currency of reward can be used as an instrument to bolster such selection effects in these more general contexts. There clearly is a strong prejudice against paying huge salaries to public officers: that prejudice goes with the judgment that public officers "shouldn't do it for the money" – and a corresponding desire to select *out* the especially venal. But there is no necessary implication involved in such desires as to how the nonvenal might be *differentially* rewarded, or more generally as to how the nonvenal can be selected *in*. The payment of low salaries to judges may, for example, increase the likelihood that they will accept bribes, and certainly does not in itself imply that venal judges are less likely to be selected than if salaries were higher. In short, unless some currency particularly valued by conscientious judges can be found, then selecting those who are *not* "doing it for the money" (and who are in that sense relatively impervious to bribes) remains an intractable problem. Ordinary persons may have the capacity to discern the characteristics of potential judges to some extent, but it would be reassuring to have in place institutional arrangements to bolster that capacity. In this chapter, I have indicated one such institutional arrangement. And I have suggested how it might work in the academic context where we have some sense of what a currency of reward associated with conscientious scholarship might be. But that academic example does not serve to indicate what the relevant currency of reward might be in other cases of more general interest. All the analysis here can do is to suggest that a relevant currency is something to look for.

References

Brennan, Geoffrey, and James Buchanan. 1985. *The Reason of Rules*. Cambridge: Cambridge University Press.

Brennan, Geoffrey, and Hartmut Kliemt. 1994. Finite lives and social institutions. *Kyklos*, 47, 551–72.

Brennan, Geoffrey, and Loren Lomasky. 1993. *Democracy and Decision*. Cambridge: Cambridge University Press.

Brennan, Geoffrey, and Philip Pettit. 1991. Modelling and motivating academic performance. *The Australian Universities' Review*, 34 (1), 4–9.

Buchanan, James. 1979. Politics without romance. *IHS Journal-Zeitschrift des Instituts für Höhere Studien*, 3 (Wien), B1–B11.

Buchanan, James, and Yong J. Yoon, eds. 1994. *The Return to Increasing Returns*. Ann Arbor: University of Michigan Press.

Coase, Ronald. 1960. The problem of social cost. *Journal of Law & Economics*, 3, 1–44.

Downs, Antony. 1957. *An Economic Theory of Democracy*. New York: Harper & Row.

Hirschman, Albert O. 1982. Rival interpretations of market society. *Journal of Economic Literature*, 20(4), 1463–84.

Hume, David. 1741. On the independency of Parliament. In Knud Haakonssen, ed., *Hume's Political Science*. Cambridge: Cambridge University Press, 1994.

Madison, James, Alexander Hamilton, and John Jay. 1788. *The Federalist Papers*. Harmondsworth, England: Penguin, 1987.

Pigou, A. C. 1932. *The Economics of Welfare*. London: Macmillan.

Name Index

Subject Index